MASTERING NEGOTIATING STRATEGIES AND TECHNIQUES

SETTLING
FOR MORE

MASTERING NEGOTIATING
STRATEGIES AND TECHNIQUES

ALVIN L. GOLDMAN

BNA
BOOKS

The Bureau of National Affairs, Inc., Washington, DC 20037

Copyright © 1991
The Bureau of National Affairs, Inc.

Second Printing June 1991

Illustrations appearing throughout this book
were prepared by BNA's Graphics Unit.

Library of Congress Cataloging-in-Publication Data

Goldman, Alvin L.
  Settling for more: mastering negotiating strategies and techniques/Alvin
L. Goldman.
    p.   cm.
  Includes bibliographical references and index.
  ISBN 0-87179-651-1
  1. Negotiation. I. Title.
BF637.N4G64 1991   90-19282
302.3—dc20   CIP

Published by BNA Books, 1250 23rd St., N.W.
Washington, D.C. 20037–1165

Printed in the United States of America
International Standard Book Number 0-87179-651-1

This book is dedicated to Ellie, Polly, and Doug
"More than you'll ever know."

Introduction

Settlement is the way people adjust disputes, alter ownership, and rearrange their relationships. Because we reach settlements by negotiating, bargaining pervades personal, commercial, social, and political life. Thus, everyone has a need to master negotiating strategies and techniques. This need is especially compelling for those who are paid to represent the interests of others in negotiations such as business people, government officials, lawyers, and sales, claims, and purchasing agents.

Skillful bargaining is an art. Like any art, mastery requires aptitude, experience, and a thorough understanding of the tools and methods. An assumption underlying *Settling for More* is that a book about negotiating cannot substitute for experience. However, a book, this book, can help you avoid some of experience's more bitter lessons while undergoing the trial-by-fire method of learning. In addition, this book can enhance bargaining performance at all levels of experience by providing a framework for analyzing bargaining behavior, by offering expanded knowledge concerning alternative negotiating techniques, and by presenting guidelines for making sound strategic and tactical decisions.

Negotiation—A Method of Conflict Resolution

Negotiation is not the only means by which conflicts are settled. As we learn more about negotiating we discover that mastery of the process requires an understanding of which characteristics distinguish it from the other methods of dispute resolution. Therefore, we need to take a moment to examine what we mean by the term negotiating.

Although some writers try to distinguish negotiating from bargaining, in popular usage the terms are interchangeable. Moreover, efforts to distinguish the two words do not enhance our understanding of the process. Therefore, the terms are used interchangeably in this book and, as defined here, negotiating, or bargaining, means the method by which two or more parties communicate in an effort to agree to change or refrain from changing:

a. their relationship with each other,
b. their relationship with others, or
c. their relationship with respect to an object or objects.

Thus, if Adam and Betty discuss entering into a sales distribution arrangement, they are negotiating (change of relationship with respect to each other). They are bargaining as well if they discuss whether Adam will terminate Betty's employment or whether Betty will leave Adam's employment (change or refrain from change in relationship with each other). Similarly, they are bargaining if they discuss Betty's request that Adam provide nursing home services for Betty's parents (change in their relationship with others). In like regard, they are bargaining if they discuss the terms under which Adam might become the owner of Betty's house (change in their relationship with respect to an object).

Negotiation can result from implicit as well as from explicit communications. Conduct or restraint often speaks as loudly as words. For example, in late September of 1986 Shiite and Christian forces in southern Lebanon began skirmishing. After several days of escalating fire fights between the two opposing forces, Israeli tanks and troops, in well-publicized movements, started massing near the border. The Lebanese combatants disengaged and the massed Israeli forces returned to their bases. As far as we know, there were no verbal exchanges among the interested parties. Nevertheless, the message implicit in the troop movements had the same result as a truce worked out through the written and oral exchanges of diplomatic emissaries.

All of us experience implicit bargaining in a variety of ways. For example, suppose you are in your office with your radio tuned to music and someone in an adjacent office whose radio is tuned to a different station suddenly increases the volume. If it occurs to you that a message is being conveyed in your neighbor's volume change, you may decide to try turning down your radio. If your effort is reciprocated by a drop in the neighbor's volume, an implicit deal has been completed.

The guidance offered in this book is designed to be useful in all bargaining contexts, implicit as well as explicit.

The Special Attributes of Negotiated Settlements

In Chapter 1 we will examine alternative methods of resolving differences. It is important to recognize the availability of such alternatives because the negotiator who settles for more sometimes concludes that bargaining is not the best method for achieving his goals. Therefore, in order to decide whether to use an alternative method for accomplishing a desired change, it is necessary to appreciate the positive and negative characteristics of negotiated settlements.

One special attribute of negotiation as a method of resolving differences is flexibility, both with regard to the manner in which the parties proceed and with respect to the ultimate accommodations reached. A related attribute is that it allows the parties to adjust differences in a way that either maximizes mutual gains or meets at least some of the needs of all parties to the settlement. A third attribute is that it implicitly recognizes the dignity and worth of all participants since a negotiated resolution requires the parties' assent. Finally, unlike some other methods of resolving differences, negotiation takes into account unofficial as well as official values—that is, it can reflect values that are important to the parties even though these values may not have legal status.

On the other hand, negotiation is a relatively inefficient method of conflict resolution. During the course of bargaining the parties have no assurance they will reach a settlement. Nevertheless, the process requires an investment of time, effort and, often, other expenses. In addition, the soundness of the resolution may be impaired if the parties misrepresent their goals or background information. Finally, negotiated settlements do not necessarily satisfy community mores and thus may be unenforceable or illegal.

Distinguishing Bargaining Strategy From Bargaining Tactics

Our examination of the negotiation process separates the analysis of bargaining into two parts: strategy and tactics. The distinction between these two terms is, perhaps, most familiar to military planners. In the analysis of warfare, strategy is the overall plan of battle including choosing goals and priorities, selecting what resources will be available, deciding where efforts will be concentrated, and establishing what general coordination will take place.

Tactics, on the other hand, are the means for carrying out each segment of the plan—the techniques of implementation. Thus, in a typical military operation, the result of strategic planning may be to gain the advantage of the high ground by taking Hill 566 through devoting two infantry companies and an artillery brigade to accomplish that task. The tactical planning for the operation may select an assault on a moonless night involving a diversionary frontal bombardment while sappers crawl their way around the left flank to blow up fortifications, followed by an infantry charge through that opening.

In this book we similarly separate the activities of a negotiator into the categories of strategy and tactics. For purposes of discussing bargaining, strategy involves selecting and reevaluating goals and priorities, deciding what information is needed, determining and allocating the resources to devote to the negotiating effort, deciding whether to continue negotiating, and choosing which variables of bargaining power will be the targets of attempted alteration. Bargaining tactics, on the other hand, are the techniques used in gathering, assembling, evaluating, keeping track of and retrieving information, and attempting to alter the variables of bargaining power. The nature of this distinction becomes clearer later in the book.

This division between strategy and tactics is not intended to suggest that negotiating is a form of warfare. Although bargaining can have similarities to the battlefield, it need not be conducted with that level of intensity nor need it be pursued in an adversarial fashion. Indeed, as we will see, doing combat with the other side is often the least effective approach at the bargaining table.

The purpose in posing the division between strategy and tactics is to give clearer direction to efforts devoted to information gathering, analysis, and decision making. This protects against oversights and offers a more efficient method of organizing the negotiator's many tasks. If more than one person represents a party, the strategy-tactics distinction also provides a basis for dividing responsibilities and efforts.

Contents

Part II. Bargaining Tactics

Part I

Bargaining Power and Strategy

Chapter 1

The Elements of Bargaining Strength

A. The Model—A Framework for Analysis

Childhood memories often are very clear and enduring. Frequently, elderly people who have difficulty remembering what they ate earlier in the day can offer vivid accounts of childhood experiences. Yet, most of us, young or old, have little or no memory of events dating back to when we were two or three or four. Even the cleverest of children soon forget the details of those early experiences. Why is that? We have ample evidence that the brains of young children are functioning adequately since they quickly learn the rudiments of language and arithmetic—no small achievements when we consider the extent of illiteracy. Perhaps an explanation is that the very young mind is bombarded with so many new experiences and that much of it is too chaotic to be sorted out. Tasks such as remembering language and numbers and learning to read provide structured systems that enable the child to find a path through the chaos. Thus, the difference between the lack of very early memories and the strength of later childhood memories may be that in time experiences fall into patterns that the child can begin to sort through, identify and classify, and thereby have a basis for remembering particular events.

Our everyday experiences offer much evidence that we function more effectively when we have such a framework for understanding information, assessing alternatives, and making decisions. When we look out the window at the beginning of an August day and see a clear sky and little or no wind rustling the leaves, we know it is almost certain to be very hot and make our clothing selections accordingly. That decision is based upon our understanding of the general relationship among the various elements that

3

affect air temperature, the characteristics of the summer season, and body comfort—an understanding that constitutes the framework for deciding what weight of clothing to wear.

The advancement of knowledge, technology, and civilization has largely been a search for ways to transform seemingly chaotic sequences of events into ordered systems that allow for analysis and prediction. Social, physical, and biological scientists have found that it is easier to understand a process if its general "model" or "paradigm" is identified. A model or paradigm describes the elements of a process and their relationships with each other. A model serves as a metaphor of reality; it identifies the constants and variables in a process and portrays how they influence one another. In addition, a model generalizes and simplifies to a degree that allows observance of the impact made by changes in the variables.

For example, the game Blackjack, like all casino games, is designed to favor the house; over the long haul, even the best players will lose money. Some years ago, however, a few mathematically adroit players statistically analyzed the game's structure and devised simple "card counting" procedures for determining when in the course of a game the probabilities favor the bettor. By betting large amounts of money at those times, and minimum amounts at other times, these players found a way to "beat the dealer." Thus, by learning the model or paradigm, the card counters were no longer gamblers. Given a legitimately operated game, their investment of time and a modest stake became a means of earning a reliable livelihood—at least until the casinos discovered what was happening and took steps both to alter the way the game was played and to keep these experts away from the tables.

A more formal example of a model or paradigm, one that is more easily stated than is the one used by Blackjack experts, is Newton's familiar Second Law of Motion. That law is summarized in the formula:

$$\text{Force} = \text{Mass} \times \text{Acceleration}$$

$$\text{or}$$

$$F = ma$$

By applying the mathematics of calculus to this paradigm, together with the use of standardized measurements of weight, distance, and time, engineers and scientists have accomplished extraordinary feats in predicting and controlling the movement of all sorts of vehicles and projectiles. Thus, it is no exaggeration to say that the development of the paradigm, or model, known as Newton's Second Law of Motion, revolutionized the world in which we live.

As we have seen with the Blackjack example, people engaged in technical, scientific, and quasi-scientific endeavors are not the only ones who use models to analyze problems and reach decisions. Although less likely to use terms such as model or paradigm, those involved in other sorts of activities similarly find it helpful to use this type of framework to guide judgments. For example, one goal of our legal system is to maintain an ordered society by holding people to normative rules of conduct. A model the law frequently uses as a reference point for defining those rules is the model of the "reasonable person." Normally we do not call the "reasonable person" concept a model or paradigm, but essentially that is what it is. There is no one person in society who constitutes the reasonable person. Yet that concept serves as a guideline; it aids us in identifying variables and relationships to be weighed in reaching a satisfactory result when we must establish and apply legal norms of conduct. For example, suppose that on a foggy day a car driving on a country lane collides with a prize bull that has wandered from its field and that the farmer sues for the bull's value. In order to determine whether there was negligence on the part of the car's driver, we ask the jury whether a reasonable person would have been driving that fast under the circumstances.

Another illustration of the use of models by people pursuing the practical arts is the business community's concept of market value. Although for a small number of commodities there is a method of determining a defined market value at any time during a normal business day, for most transactions market value is but an abstract notion of what variables would influence a price if all potential buyers and sellers were solely profit motivated, had the same information, and were competing at the same time in the same transaction.

In recent years several authors have offered models describing the process of negotiation. Some provide useful guidance in increasing understanding and mastery of the process. The discussion that follows presents a new model, one that builds and expands upon earlier work. This model identifies the elements that constitute bargaining power and describes their interrelationships with each other. In the pages that follow, our new model is explained in the text and is illustrated graphically.[1]

---

[1]Although the text uses graphic descriptions of the model, the Appendix states it using algebraic formulas, a presentation that some will find too abstract but that others may find to be a more convenient tool for analyzing bargaining decisions.

Learning the bargaining power model enhances negotiating skill by providing an improved method for making bargaining strategy decisions. However, before examining this model, it is necessary to become familiar with its component elements. In at least two respects, understanding the elements of the bargaining power model is as important as the model itself. First, thorough familiarity with the elements makes it much easier to remember the diagrams provided and formulas offered for guiding bargaining strategy. Second, a thorough understanding of the component elements improves the negotiator's ability to settle for more.

B. Elements of the Bargaining Power Model

1. Perception (P)

Every skilled negotiator understands that what counts in bargaining is not reality; what counts is the parties' *perception* of reality. To illustrate, if one is selling a house beneath the flight path of an international airport, the negotiated price will be affected if the buyer views the house on a foggy day when the airport is closed. Thus, much of negotiating skill involves:

   a. bringing your own perceptions in line with reality,
   b. ascertaining the other side's perceptions of the proposed transaction and the available alternatives, and
   c. finding ways to favorably alter the other side's perceptions.

Perception, therefore, is an element that has a direct impact upon all other elements of bargaining power. For that reason, the bargaining power paradigms described later in this chapter reflect the impact perception has upon the other elements in the negotiating process.

Our perceptions are shaped by the information we receive as filtered by our personalities, assessment of the sources of information, emotional status, values, and analytic ability. These in turn are influenced by the manner in which information is received, the modes of analysis we use, and the environment in which we analyze the information. For example, if a stranger approaches you in mid-Manhattan and whispers that he will sell you an 18-jewel gold watch for $100, your perception of what is being offered is not likely to be the same as it would be if the identical information were conveyed to you by a high school classmate in a jewelry store in your home town. If your assessment is the same, most would conclude that you are very naive or might question whether you are sober or sane.

Negotiating is largely a sequence of transactions through which the parties attempt to alter each other's perceptions. Skilled negotiators do this by attempting to control the information received by the other side; by managing the environment in which the transactions are conducted; by posing arguments; and by offering proposals and weighing the impact of the manner in which arguments, information and proposals are formed, selected, and communicated. The proposals that are transmitted in the course of negotiations, as well as the information presented and arguments posed, have the potential of altering perceptions not only because they convey information and suggest ways to analyze the available information, but also because such communications sometimes affect emotional status.

Due to the pervasive influence perception has upon bargaining power, the negotiator who settles for more must understand how to influence it. Accordingly, in later chapters we examine models, concepts, and techniques that show how to successfully modify perception and how to insulate ourselves from the manipulation of our own perception.

2. Offer to Meet the Other's Needs (OMON)

Several books about bargaining pay particular attention to the importance of recognizing and meeting the needs of a bargaining adversary. Once stated, the significance of this element seems obvious enough. (Indeed, the surprising thing is that much that is published about the subject says little or nothing about the importance of this factor.) However obvious it may seem, this element warrants close scrutiny because thorough examination provides considerable insight into available choices among negotiating strategies and tactics.

There are many dimensions to the role played by a party's Offer to Meet the Other's Needs. (For convenience, in our discussion we sometimes abbreviate this term as "OMON"). A first proposition is that if negotiation is to succeed in bringing about a resolution, each side must be willing to make some effort to meet its opponent's needs. Thus, much of the negotiator's effort involves ascertaining what is needed by the other side.

The significance of the other side's needs, however, is not based on an objective appraisal; rather, it is the opponent's subjective assessment of its needs—its *perception* of its needs—that constitutes the fuel that drives the bargaining mechanism. For example, even though Adam's business in fact has all the computer capacity it can use efficiently, if Adam thinks his company needs a bigger unit and Betty sells such units, Betty has a chance of negotiating a sales agreement with Adam.

Additionally, when examining another's perceptions of his needs we must attempt to understand those needs from the other side's perspective. We are given a reminder of this in the anecdote, recounted in Woody Allen's *Annie Hall*, about the guest at a resort complaining to a friend, "The food in this place is awful." "I know," the friend commiserated, "and they serve such small portions!"

a. Relationship Between Each Side's Needs

Each party to a negotiated transaction has perceived needs. If there is to be a settlement, each must also have the perceived ability to meet at least some needs of the other side. As will soon be seen, the respective perceptions of the negotiating parties' *relative needs* play a significant role in determining the potential effectiveness of particular bargaining strategies.

The perceived needs of negotiating parties are related to each other in one of four ways. They may be perceived to be:

1. common,
2. compatible,
3. conflicting, or
4. incompatible.

Common needs are present when opposing parties stand to mutually benefit from a particular resolution or facet of the resolution of the conflict. To illustrate, suppose Adam supplies parts to Betty and that Betty generally maintains an inventory of one week's supply of the parts. Suppose further that both plants annually close for three weeks of vacation. Both parties have a need to time their vacation shutdowns to minimize special costs. If Adam's vacation period came at the beginning of July and Betty's at the beginning of August, in advance of his shutdown Adam would have to produce and Betty would have to build up a special inventory of the parts to ensure supplies for Betty during the Adam shutdown. During Betty's shutdown, it would also be necessary for Adam to stockpile the normal shipments to Betty or reduce or eliminate the production of those parts. Unless the need respecting the timing of the vacation shutdown is perceived as common, the parties are likely to bargain over the warehousing and timing of delivery of parts needed during July. However, if either side perceives that they have a common need with regard to the timing of the vacation shutdown, a suggestion might be offered that they coordinate their vacations. For example, if they shut down at the same time or if Adam's shutdown begins a week ahead of Betty's, it should not be necessary to build up a special inventory. While the parties will still have to decide how to divide the cost savings, recognizing the existence of this potential mutual gain should aid in their reaching an agreement.

Compatible needs exist when one side, though not gaining any particular benefit for itself, can accommodate the other party's special need without sacrificing anything that it needs. For example, if Adam's parts must be packaged in rectangular cartons to protect them from breakage, and if Betty's warehouse shelves require stacking the boxes on the long ends with the short ends facing in the direction of the freight handlers, Betty likely will want the parts information labels to be stenciled on the short end of the boxes. If, without any added cost, Adam can accommodate this request, Adam's need to stencil the boxes is compatible with Betty's need to have the information facing the freight handlers.

Conflicting needs arise when one side's gain is the other side's loss with respect to a particular need. For example, the price of parts sold by Adam to Betty involves resolving conflicting needs. Betty's need is to obtain the parts at the lowest available cost; Adam's is to sell them at the highest price he can get. Thus, a negotiated resolution will represent only a partial accommodation of this aspect of each side's needs.

Incompatible needs are involved in a transaction if one side's needs can be met only at the expense of not meeting some need of the other side. For example, if Adam's packing machines are designed to package parts in sets of 10 but Betty's inventory control system is designed to balance stock ratios in sets of 12, the contractual terms respecting the packaging of shipments involves incompatible needs. Of course, incompatibility of needs does not eliminate the possibility of a negotiated resolution. Both sides also have monetary needs. Therefore, given an adequate monetary incentive, either side might be induced to modify its systems design or resort to custom packing or repacking of the items.

b. Integrative, Exchange, and Mixed Transactions

When a negotiation involves only common or compatible needs, it can be called an *integrative* or *problem solving* transaction. Both sides stand to gain their maximum benefit if a resolution is achieved that fully or substantially meets the needs of all participants. If both sides recognize the integrative nature of their transaction, the only issue they must decide is how to best meet their respective mutual or compatible needs. Since both sides stand to gain by finding the optimal solution, ideally the negotiation of a transaction with purely integrative needs should be a cooperative, and not an adversarial, effort.

One problem, of course, is that the parties may fail to recognize the integrative nature of their transaction. Another problem is that upon realizing that their needs are common or compatible, the participants may have different opinions regarding how the maximum benefit can best be achieved. A danger under those circumstances is that a negotiator's personal ego needs may cause him to place excessive weight upon the wisdom of his own suggestion and thereby interfere with his search for the optimal solution. Thus, the negotiator whose goal is to settle for more seeks to identify the relationships among the parties' different needs and, when dealing with integrative needs, accepts the fact that the other side's proposals may offer a superior solution.

In many negotiating situations the parties' needs are wholly conflicting or incompatible. If this is the case, the nature of the transaction is an *exchange.* In a pure exchange transaction, sometimes called distributive bargaining, each side has the ability to accommodate some or all of the other side's needs but only by failing to meet part or all of its own needs. Thus, for each side the question is whether the degree of sacrifice necessary to meet the other's perceived needs is outweighed by the extent to which its own perceived needs are met by the other side.

Often negotiations involve a *mixed* integrative and exchange transaction. That is, the parties share a combination of common or compatible with conflicting or incompatible needs. To the extent that both sides recognize which needs are common or compatible, that portion of the bargaining transaction can be conducted as a problem-solving exercise. However, if only one party recognizes the common or compatible nature of particular needs, it may decide to maintain silence respecting that realization and use this knowledge to obtain the other side's concessions as part of the exchange transactions. For example, if Betty's warehouse shelves require stacking the boxes on the long ends with the short ends facing in the direction of the freight handlers, Adam may pretend that accommodating Betty's need to have the boxes stenciled on the short end will require extra costs but offer to meet this requirement if Betty will accept the goods packaged in a lighter weight, less expensive box.

Later we will see how the character of the transaction—integrative, exchange, or mixed—alters the skilled negotiator's choice of strategy and tactics.

Negotiations sometimes are facilitated by the intervention of mediators. A mediator, or conciliator (the terms are used interchangably in the United States), is an impartial party who attempts to aid the negotiators in reaching a settlement. (The term should not be confused with arbitrator— a neutral third party who imposes a decision upon the parties.) Two of the principal roles of a mediator are reflected in the previous discussion. One way in which a mediator serves the parties is by attempting to bring their perceptions of the bargaining elements either closer to reality, or at least closer to each other's perceptions. A related way in which mediators aid settlement is by helping the parties recognize the extent to which the issues under discussion have integrative rather than exchange characteristics and, therefore, require an effort at discovering the mutually most beneficial solution.

c. *Offer to Meet, Not Ability to Meet, Needs*

Just as it is perception, not reality, that fuels negotiations, so, too, it is the offer to meet needs, not the ability to meet needs, that provides bargaining power. That is, settlement is shaped by what a party is currently willing to do, not by what it has the capacity to do for the other side. Therefore, while the ability to meet an opponent's needs affects *potential* bargaining power, the opponent's perceived willingness to meet needs is what affects actual bargaining power. For example, if the richest person in town is interested in purchasing my home but is unwilling to offer more than $200,000, and another local bidder is prepared to offer $210,000, the second bidder has more actual bargaining power with respect to meeting my needs. Of course, the prospect of meeting the other's needs is not the only element of bargaining power. Shortly, we will see how other aspects of the power equation might enhance the wealthy bidder's actual negotiating power despite the lower offer to meet my monetary needs.

d. Whose Needs? Principal's or Agent's?

Still another dimension of assessing a party's Offer to Meet the Other's Needs is the identification of whose needs are to be met. In today's complex economy, ownership and management often are separate. Even when owners manage their own business, the responsibility for bargaining often is assigned to an agent. The needs of the manager or the agent generally are not quite the same as the owner's. For example, if a corporation purchases a new subsidiary it will have liquid assets available for distributing dividends to the owners. On the other hand, having responsibility for an enlarged enterprise might justify a higher level of compensation for the corporate officers. Therefore, the corporate officers may be motivated to support an expansionary move that enhances their positions despite the fact that it reduces the owners' rate of return. Accordingly, mastering negotiating techniques requires assessing not only the perceived needs of the opposing entity, but also the perceived personal needs of the individuals who represent or control the representation of the other side.

Because the agent's needs may intrude upon maximum servicing of the principal's needs, one problem for the party being represented in a negotiated transaction is to ensure that its representative's personal needs have the least possible impact upon the outcome. A method of doing this is to give the representative a stake in the outcome that is compatible with the owner's interests. Such a stake may be provided in the form of a commission, bonus, or profit sharing. Another method is to ensure accountability by establishing goals and evaluating performance for salary, promotion, or continued employment based upon success in achieving such goals. An alternative method of achieving accountability is to audit and evaluate the results in order to compare them with the performance of others. More favorable outcomes can then be rewarded and less favorable ones penalized.

The law limits the extent to which a bargaining representative may put personal needs above those of the party being represented. One method of doing this is to hold the representative to the legal standards of fiduciary responsibility. A fiduciary who places his own interests above those of the party being represented stands not only to be liable for any resulting losses but also to forfeit all personal gain, including the representative's normal fee or salary, in favor of the represented party whose expectation of fidelity was disappointed.

Inducing a representative to breach his duty of loyalty to his principal can also result in liability for tortious interference with a beneficial contractual relationship. In addition to having to pay compensatory damages, the party guilty of such a tort may be subject to the added, and often very substantial, burden of punitive damages.

The law also places some constraints in the form of criminal penalties upon bargaining representatives. Thus, laws against commercial bribes impose penalties both upon those who solicit and those who offer a personal benefit as an inducement to do less than one's best as a bargaining representative.

e. Are Needs Functional, Emotional, Conscious, Subconscious?

Assessment of needs must also be made with awareness that there are different forms of needs; some are consciously perceived while others are perceived subconsciously. The skilled negotiator additionally realizes that needs can be functional (physical or fiscal) or emotional.

Because emotional needs often exist subconsciously, they are, in effect, the hidden needs of the negotiated transaction. As such, a negotiator cannot readily insulate his decisions from the influence of these needs. Accordingly, the negotiator who settles for more attempts to raise his own emotional needs to a conscious level and recognizes that meeting the other side's emotional needs is a powerful bargaining tool. Chapter 4 explains how the Transactional Analysis model of psychotherapy provides a useful method for discerning the presence of such needs and understanding how to respond to them. For now, it is useful to identify the five basic categories of emotional needs. These can be summarized using the acronym SLAPS to abbreviate the emotional dimensions as follows:

S ecurity
L ove
A musement
P ersonal Achievement
S ocial Status

3. Best Alternative to the Proposed Agreement (BAPA)

Sound guidance for effective negotiating of integrative (problem solving) transactions is presented in the best-selling book on negotiations by Roger Fisher and William Ury[2] who urge that, among other techniques, a skilled negotiator should not begin bargaining without first determining what his best alternative is to reaching a negotiated settlement. They refer to this as the Best Alternative To a Negotiated Agreement (BATNA).

Instead of borrowing the Fisher and Ury term BATNA, we have modified it to the Best Alternative to the Proposed Agreement (BAPA). We do this not to be different, but to provide a descriptively more precise term. The term BATNA is misleading to the extent that it indicates that the negotiator's bargaining power depends only on available alternative forms of conflict resolution (that is, something other than a negotiated settlement). Often, however, the best alternative for a negotiator is to reach a negotiated agreement with some other party—for example, one who has a perception of greater needs than does the current opponent or one whose perceived needs are more compatible with those of the moving party. As a result, the phrase Best Alternative to the Proposed Agreement (BAPA) more accurately describes what it is that the negotiator must weigh in making bargaining decisions.

Fisher and Ury emphasize that it is important for a negotiator to be innovative as well as rigorous in exploring what is the best alternative to a proposed agreement. This, too, is an aspect of negotiating in which a mediator can contribute to the parties' ability to find a suitable resolution. Often the mediator, by taking a fresh look at the parties' needs, sees an alternative solution that has been overlooked by the parties. Similarly, the mediator's special knowledge or experiences may generate ideas that have not occurred to the negotiators. Thus, the best alternative may be a different settlement package for meeting the needs of the currently negotiating parties.

As with the OMON, it is the perception of one's BAPA, not its actuality, that determines negotiating strength. Moreover, while the importance of the Best Alternative to the Proposed Agreement (BAPA) deserves great emphasis, its function cannot be fully appreciated in isolation from the other basic elements of bargaining power.

---

[2]*Getting to Yes: Negotiating Agreement Without Giving In* (Houghton-Mifflin, 1981).

However, before examining the remaining bargaining power elements, it is necessary to complete our exploration of the concept of the Best Alternative to the Proposed Agreement. As previously noted, that alternative may take the form of bargaining with someone else, or it may involve resorting to an alternative method of conflict resolution.

a. Alternative Methods of Conflict Resolution

There are six basic methods by which people resolve conflicts: negotiation, adjudication, acquiescence, governmental fiat, political discipline, and voting. Each has its own special characteristics. The Introduction discussed the special attributes of negotiation. Let us now look at the special attributes of these other conflict resolution mechanisms.

Acquiescence. We commonly encounter acquiescence when we go into a shop and conduct our business on the basis of the posted price. If the label on the jar says $1.25, either we buy the jar for that price or move on to the next item on our shopping list. Acquiescence is a very efficient method of conflict resolution. There is no energy or time expended on seeking adjustments. The result, moreover, can be tailored to meet the needs of the situation, but that tailoring is unilaterally determined by the party whose position dominates the transaction. Thus, if the other side is dissatisfied with the proposed result, either it will go elsewhere (no deal) or it will reluctantly submit and, as a result, have a strong motivation for later attempting to evade or subvert the resolution or to gain retribution. In addition, because there has not been an exchange of information or mutual exploration of alternative resolutions, to the extent that the transaction may involve common or compatible needs, there is a reduced prospect that the result imposed on the acquiescing party is the most advantageous settlement for either side. Finally, because the result is dictated by an interested party, it need not be responsive to interests of the broader community. Therefore, in a variety of ways the law often intervenes and prohibits resolutions by acquiescence in situations in which it is judged that the compliant party is excessively dominated. Examples include minimum wage laws, food and drug laws, some aspects of securities law and antitrust law, labor law, and many aspects of family law and criminal law.

Adjudication. In adjudication a neutral third party imposes a resolution upon the parties' conflict. Adjudication can be by a publicly appointed or elected tribunal (a court or administrative agency), or by an arbitrator privately selected by the parties.

Adjudicative processes follow varying degrees of formal procedure and rely on the convenience and judgment of the intervening party to reach a resolution. Such procedures often require considerable expenditure of the parties' time, energy, and resources to educate the decision maker concerning the facts, the issues and the competing considerations. The parties may also be required to expend much time, energy, and resources satisfying formalities that may not contribute to the merits of the result in the particular situation. In addition, judgments reached through adjudication tend to be formally structured, thus limiting the ability to tailor the resolution to the parties' special needs. Moreover, the guiding principles for decision generally are officially recognized norms that may not be responsive to the shared values of the affected parties. On the other hand, the adjudicatory method is designed to maximize the likelihood that the resolution will be based on wisdom and fairness, and not on raw power. Also, where the decision maker is publicly appointed or elected, it is likely that the resolution will be responsive to community standards of propriety and virtue.

Political Discipline. The term political discipline is chosen here to represent the method by which conflicts often are resolved by the hierarchy of an alliance shared by the parties to the conflict. The alliance might be a political party or it might be a fraternal order, a group of business or professional associates, members of the same family, and the like. Accordingly, the bounds of the alliance can be ideological, emotional, economic, or opportunistic.

Settlement of differences through political discipline can be efficient and can be expected to be responsive to the shared norms that mold the alliance. On the other hand, the results also can be expected to be more responsive to the alliance's collective interests, or those of a dominating faction, than to the interests of the particular people or entities whose differences are at issue. In addition, the shared norms of the alliance may not be compatible with the general community's ethical standards. As a result, the law may refuse to enforce or may prohibit some resolutions attained through the process we have described as political discipline. Antitrust law, the law of private associations and partnerships, corporate law, and the like contain many such restraints.

Voting. Voting provides an efficient method for collective self-determination in selecting from among specified alternatives. Once those alternatives have been selected, however, voting usually provides no flexibility. Moreover, while the result reflects a defined level of consensus (e.g., majority, plurality, two-thirds), it does not necessarily represent the wisest solution, offer an accommodation of a competing party's interests, or reflect standards of fairness or justice beyond those of the participating voters.

Governmental Fiat. Governments are formed to provide a means of enforcing and altering society's norms. If differences have an impact upon the interests entrusted to governmental supervision and if that conflict is perceived by those in power as not being adequately regulated by existing norms, governmental fiat can be exercised to impose the desired adjustment. Assuming the efficient, honest operation of government (often a rash assumption), resolution of conflicts through governmental fiat should be a rational solution that is responsive to the collective values and interests of the social order. On the other hand, at its best, resort to governmental fiat generally is a cumbersome, expensive, inefficient process that often is incapable of adjusting the results to special or momentary needs. In addition, it disregards and sacrifices the interests of the disputing parties in favor of the perceived interests of the larger community.

Use of Alternative Conflict Resolution Methods. There is no hierarchy of conflict resolution methods. No one approach stands out as the preferred method for all situations. Nor is each method available in all situations. Moreover, sometimes different methods are used sequentially; other times they are used simultaneously in settling the same or related differences.

To provide an example of the range and interaction of conflict resolution methods, consider a situation in which a gas pipeline explodes in the middle of town injuring many people and destroying an extensive amount of property. In such a situation one conflict that arises is determining the source and extent of compensation, if any, that will be provided for those who suffered losses. Some claimants may be satisfied with and accept whatever settlement is offered to them (Acquiescence). Others may not be satisfied with any offered settlement and elect to bargain with the potentially liable parties to seek what the claimant considers to be a more suitable resolution (Negotiation). Either during the course of negotiations or upon reaching an impasse, the claimant may file suit (Adjudication). Some claimants may join forces and poll their number to decide upon their common course of action (Voting). Another possibility is for the state legislature to intervene. For example, it might decide to establish a special fund to assist the victims and assess the costs as a tax on future gas consumption or as a payroll tax or net income tax on energy companies (Governmental Fiat). If the parties who appear to be liable for the explosion do not offer reasonable settlements, the town officials might suggest that they will transfer to competitors the license to supply this form of energy. Similarly, business leaders, who can influence such things as the type of energy source used in future construction in the town and who are the social peers of the gas company officials, may announce what sort of conduct they expect from a responsible business (Political Discipline).

As can be seen in the above hypothetical situation, a variety of methods of conflict resolution are available to those pressing their interests. Some or all of the methods for seeking relief may be pursued simultaneously or sequentially and the claimants' success or failure in following any particular avenue is likely to influence what other methods will be used and the effectiveness of that utilization. Thus, whether pursuing or resisting a claim, the skilled representative must constantly evaluate and reevaluate the available alternative methods for resolving the conflict.

b. Illustration of BAPA's Impact upon Bargaining Results

To illustrate the significance of the Best Alternative to the Proposed Agreement, let us examine a negotiating situation in which the perception of one side or the other's BAPA will have an obvious impact upon the bargaining outcome. Assume, for example, Betty has been injured while riding as a passenger in Adam's automobile due to Adam's failure to stop for a red light. Betty is approached by an agent of Adam's insurance company who offers to settle any claims by paying Betty $2,200 in medical expenses. Betty was out of work for five weeks and continues to suffer pain. She does not think that the offer to pay medical expenses is adequate but is not sure that she would be allowed to sue Adam inasmuch as Adam was doing Betty a favor in driving her home from work. Betty has not consulted with a lawyer because she has very little money left and has heard that lawyers are expensive.

Betty, of course, does have a right to sue Adam. That right is her BAPA. If she learns this, her bargaining position is strengthened to the extent that she perceives that her net recovery from adjudication will be greater than the $2,200 offered by the insurer.

It is further strengthened if the insurance company's agent perceives both that it will cost well in excess of the offered $2,200 to go to court and that Betty recognizes that adjudication will be much more generous to her. In this illustration, the insurance company's perception of its costs of an adjudicated resolution is its BAPA. As we can see, a change in the insurance company's perception of its BAPA alters its bargaining position. If it perceives adjudication as being much more costly than the offered $2,200 it likely will be prepared to increase its offer. Similarly, although the insurer's perception of Betty's understanding of her BAPA does not alter its bargaining power, it is likely to affect the insurance company's bargaining conduct. Thus, even though it realizes that Betty can do much better than $2,200 in court, the insurance company is less likely to increase its offer if it thinks that Betty is unaware of her ability to resort to an adjudicated resolution.

In our hypothetical situation, Betty's first recourse is to obtain legal counsel. Lawyers, of course, generally accept such cases on a contingency fee basis with the result that she can get not only advice but also professional representation without having to advance any fees. Indeed, Betty may find a lawyer who will agree to exclude the amount of the present offer in calculating the amount of the contingency fee with the result that she has nothing to lose by turning her affairs over to the attorney. But until Betty discovers the true nature of her legal rights and her ability to get professional representation, her negotiating power is weakened by her failure to perceive that she has an attractive BAPA.

One way Betty may discover her BAPA is by more thoroughly preparing to bargain with the insurance company's agent. For example, she might consult friends and acquaintances who have had similar problems, or she might question her physician, or she might attempt to do some of her own legal research in the local library. In the course of such efforts she is likely to discover the legal profession's practice of taking such cases on a contingency fee basis or she might get a clearer idea of the extent of her legal recourse. Either way, her increased knowledge of the norms surrounding the transaction (her changed perception of her BAPA) increases her relative bargaining power. Assuming that in fact it would be much more costly for the insurance company to go to court, Betty's mere suggestion that she will retain counsel if a more generous offer is not forthcoming is likely to produce a more favorable result—though not necessarily the most favorable potential result.

Another way Betty may discover her BAPA, and thereby gain increased bargaining strength, is through either the inadvertent comment of an otherwise callous insurance company representative, or through the information provided by an ethically sensitive representative of the insurance industry. That is, in the first instance the insurance company's agent may, in an effort to increase the seeming attractiveness of the settlement offer, make a remark such as "and of course if you accept our offer you won't have some lawyer taking a third of it for a contingency fee." As an alert claimant, Betty will realize, at that point, that she ought to find out more about lawyer contingency fees before going any further. In the second instance the agent, recognizing an ethical responsibility, or complying with a government regulation, may simply explain the steps a well-informed claimant would take before accepting a settlement offer. Taking those steps should lead Betty to an awareness of her real BAPA and alter her bargaining position to the extent that the BAPA is or is not more attractive than was her initial perception of it.

4. Accrued Costs (AC)

Whether successful or not, bargaining has its costs. These costs always include time and effort. Often additional expenditures are incurred. The more one invests in carrying on a transaction, the greater will be the desire to resolve the conflict through that transaction rather than to incur a whole new set of transaction costs that might not produce a more favorable result. Thus, while hindsight might inform the negotiator that he would have been better off pursuing a different course of action from the start, the investment in the current negotiation often persuades a bargainer that it is better to accept the proposed terms, or something close to them, than to begin afresh in exploring an alternative with someone else.

For example, assume that Adam wants to purchase a house and Betty has a house for sale that Adam finds suitable. Further, assume that Adam and Betty have exchanged six offers and counteroffers, Adam has had an architectual survey and engineering inspection done on the house, and has made two special trips from out-of-town to pursue negotiations with Betty. If they are 1 percent apart in their respective positions, is it not likely that Adam will be more willing to close the gap than he would be if he had made a series of offers and counteroffers through an agent without incurring any of the other costs—that is, without incurring a high AC (Accrued Cost)?

5. Costs of Impending Negotiations (COIN)

The greater the cost a negotiator expects will be required to continue to carry on a transaction, the greater will be the bargainer's motivation to abandon that transaction and seek the best alternative to the proposed agreement (BAPA). Thus, the perceived Costs Of Impending Negotiations (COIN) adds to the attractiveness of the BAPA and detracts from the other side's perceived bargaining power.

The impact of the perceived costs of impending negotiations varies depending on the ultimate stakes involved—that is, the perceived size of the offer to meet the other's needs (OMON), the extent to which the BAPA and OMON are perceived to be comparable or very different in value, and the quantity of those costs. Thus, where bargaining costs are negligible and the stakes are high, the perceived COIN is unlikely to affect bargaining. On the other hand, the perceived impending costs of bargaining is likely to be significant where that perceived cost is high and the value of the OMON and BAPA are perceived to be comparable. For example, if Alpha is a U.S. corporation negotiating for the sale of used mining equipment to Beta, an Argentinian company, and additional bargaining requires travel by a three-member team to Buenos Aires and hiring interpreters and international lawyers, that Cost of Impending Negotiations (COIN) might be critical if a strong prospective U.S. or Canadian buyer—the BAPA—is available. The importance of the Cost of Impending Negotiations (COIN), as a factor influencing the American company's willingness to persevere or abandon its bargaining with the Argentinian entity, is diminished if the expected profit from the transaction will be counted in hundreds of thousands of dollars as contrasted with being counted in tens of thousands of dollars. That is, if the potential profits are very high, the importance of the COIN element in shaping bargaining strength will be greatly overshadowed by the strength of the offer to meet the American company's needs (the OMON). Similarly, reaching agreement will be facilitated if it can be agreed that the final terms will be worked out by long distance conference telephone calls (thereby reducing the COIN). Thus, the negotiator who has mastered the skills of the task weighs the perceived impending costs of bargaining and, when appropriate, seeks to alter the other's perceptions of those costs.

6. Probability of Performance (POP)

Another element affecting negotiating power is each side's perception of the likelihood that the opponent will in fact do what it promises to do. That is, each side's perception of the other side's offer to meet its needs is discounted by the extent to which it anticipates that the other may fail to meet them. Another way to put this is that the perceived Probability of the Other's Performance (POP) alters the net value that one places in the other side's offer to meet one's needs (OMON).

An illustration of the importance of POP as an element of bargaining power is to consider what happens when companies such as General Motors Corporation and Blowhard Corp., a new manufacturer of auto horns, approach the same bank asking to borrow a million dollars. If the bank offers to lend GM the money at 9.25 percent interest, it almost certainly is going to insist that Blowhard pay a higher rate of interest. The reason is no mystery. Because of GM's strong financial position, the bank anticipates no risk of nonpayment. The interest rate reflects what the bank must earn to pay its interest and administrative costs and to earn what it believes to be a suitable margin of profit. However, the probability that Blowhard will repay the borrowed amount with interest is much less certain. Therefore, Blowhard is in a weaker bargaining position than GM and, consequently, will be offered a less desirable settlement. To improve its bargaining position, Blowhard must assure the bank of a higher Probability of Performance (POP). One way it can do this is to pledge some sort of security for payment of the loan. For example, if it is prepared to mortgage its land as security for the loan, it may be able to negotiate an interest rate as favorable or almost as favorable as the one that is available to GM on an unsecured loan.

The potential negotiating power of the Probability of Performance is more dramatically illustrated in international affairs. Because there is no enforceable rule of law establishing accepted principles of behavior in international relations, achieving settlements often is hampered by the high degree of suspicion and skepticism respecting the bargaining table motives and intentions of national adversaries. All sides may readily see the benefits of an accord, but each side may be wary of altering the status quo out of fear that only it will abide by the agreement and that it will thereby weaken its security or lose economic advantages.

For example, proposals for dramatic reductions in nuclear armaments made at the 1986 Iceland Summit between the United States and the Soviet Union failed because of President Reagan's refusal to contain the Strategic Defense Initiative (Star Wars) within the research laboratories. Of course, we do not know the extent to which either side's stated positions at the bargaining table accurately reflected its true intentions. However, we can analyze what took place at the overt level of communication.

The United States took the position at the Iceland Summit that the only real assurance of Soviet compliance with disarmament is a shield against nuclear attack. The Strategic Defense Initiative is supposed to provide that shield and thereby serve as the basis for the United States' high assessment of the Soviets' Probability of Performance. The Soviet Union, on the other hand, held the position that the Strategic Defense Initiative is not, and cannot be, confined to serving defensive purposes only. From the Soviet point of view, the system has significant offensive potential and, therefore, U.S. tests of the system will serve to shift the balance of terror further in the direction of the United States. Moreover, if the SDI is perceived by American leaders to be effective, the United States could then safely launch against the Soviet Union whatever nuclear weapons remained after the reduction of arms and still cripple the Soviets. Thus, at least so far as the expressed positions of the parties was concerned, the talks broke down because the United States failed to convince the Soviet Union that the Strategic Defense Initiative is truly intended to have, and will have, defensive capability only and thereby serve to enhance the Probability of Performance (POP) rather than alter the extent of the Offer to Meet the Other's Needs (OMON).

An agreement for a modest reduction of nuclear weapons was achieved in late 1987. What happened between the 1986 and 1987 summit meetings? Several things changed and at least one such change affected U.S. perceptions of the Soviet Union's Probability of Performance. The key change was that in the 1987 negotiations the Soviets dropped their previous resistance to on-site inspection of weapons facilities. This gave the U.S. greater assurance that it could verify Soviet compliance with agreed weapons reductions. At the same time, Congress' resistance to the SDI program, plus the Soviet Union's reported revision of its assessment of its ability to destroy SDI weapons, apparently altered the Soviet perception of its need for a clear pledge to abandon development of this new technology. In addition, there are indications that despite Reagan administration assertions to the contrary, there was an understanding that the United States would informally accept the Soviet interpretation of those parts of the treaty language that arguably place a restriction upon developing SDI beyond the laboratory stage.

The stakes in the Soviet–U.S. confrontation are too high for either the AC or COIN to materially alter the weight of any bargaining position. On the other hand, the POP, the Probability of Performance, is of critical importance in this particular bargaining transaction. Thus, a persistent stumbling block at U.S.–Soviet peace talks is over ways to ensure that the other side is in fact performing its end of the bargain. The effect of an increased POP is to increase the strength of each side's OMON—each side's perceived offer to meet the other side's needs. As a result, a negotiated resolution is far more attractive to both sides because each side's OMON is then greater than the costs and risks of maintaining a balance of terror— the Best Alternative to the Proposed Agreement.

Let us consider one final example of the impact of Probability of Performance as an element of bargaining strength. Earlier in this chapter it was noted that bargaining strength is influenced by a party's *offer* to meet the other's needs, not the party's *ability* to meet the other's needs. As a hypothetical to illustrate this point we examined the situation in which the richest person in town offers $200,000 for my home while another person offers $210,000 and observed that although the richest person may have the greater potential bargaining power, that person in fact had exercised less actual bargaining leverage than the other by offering a lower bid. However, the reduced bargaining strength provided by the richest person's lower bid might well be offset by my perception of the bidders' respective Probability of Performance. Since I know that the richest person in town can raise the funds to pay the offered price, my need to be certain that the house will be sold by a particular date may persuade me to accept the lower bid if I have doubts respecting the higher bidder's ability to get a needed mortgage. Thus, my doubts respecting the Probability of Performance (POP) of the party with the higher Offer to Meet the Other's (my) Needs (OMON) may cause me to accept the lower OMON.

7. Predictive Accuracy (PA)

One who has mastered the process of bargaining recognizes that one can rarely assess with 100 percent reliability the value of the Best Alternative to the Proposed Agreement (BAPA) or the Costs of Impending Negotiations (COIN). Unforeseeable events, judgment errors, and gaps and mistakes in information, all detract from the Predictive Accuracy (PA) of the BAPA or COIN. Therefore, in weighing whether to turn to an alternative to the proposed agreement, one who has mastered the skills of negotiating discounts the attractiveness of that alternative to the extent that he has a high or a low level of confidence in the accuracy of his assessments.

For example, in the posturing of national military rivalry, nations do not share accurate information about the capability of their military armament, level of supplies, size and distribution of their forces, or state of readiness. To the contrary, efforts are normally made to indicate that there are secret resources and that whatever information the other has is inaccurate and inadequate. Espionage efforts may be undertaken in an effort to improve the accuracy of information about the rival, and counterespionage efforts may be undertaken to further confuse such information. The goal of these efforts is to prevent the other side from perceiving that it has attained a high degree of reliability in its assessment of armed engagement with the rival. The lack of that reliability forces each side to factor in the uncertainties of its Predictive Accuracy (PA) in weighing whether it dare resort to warfare as its BAPA—its alternative to agreement. And, often that perception of predictive accuracy is sufficiently low to keep highly antagonistic parties engaged in international diplomacy rather than resort to the alternative of armed conflict.

8. Data Accurancy (DA)

Most often, a party should be able to accurately measure the bargaining strength element Accrued Costs (AC) because the investment of time, effort, or expenses has already been incurred. However, in some instances there may be uncertainties regarding the precise amount of those costs. For example, bills may not have been received for such things as lawyers' services or long distance telephone calls. Additionally, collaborators may not yet have provided reports indicating the time and effort they have devoted in carrying out their assignments. To the extent that at any stage of bargaining there is such uncertainty regarding the Accrued Costs, the role of AC in measuring bargaining strength is diminished. That certainty or uncertainty respecting a party's knowledge concerning its accrued costs can be identified as its Data Accuracy— abbreviated as DA.

9. A Further Note on the Role of Perception

The preceding explanation of the various elements of bargaining power provides illustrations of how alteration of the perception with respect to each of these elements, as separate variables in the bargaining power equation, alter a negotiator's bargaining strength. It is important to realize, too, that efforts to modify perceptions of one element of bargaining strength can indirectly alter perceptions of other bargaining elements. In other words, if the selected method for modifying a party's perceptions respecting a particular bargaining power element affects the other side's emotional status, the bargaining environment, or information, it will thereby alter that party's overall perceptions. To use a simple illustration, if in an effort to persuade the other side that it has a very weak or non-existent BAPA (Best Alternative to the Proposed Agreement), a negotiator resorts to threats of dire consequences resulting from nonagreement, the other side might conclude that the threatening party is more intent on getting its way than on living by the rules. This in turn may diminish the other side's perception of the threatening party's POP (Probability of Performance) and thereby offset any impact it had upon the threatened party's perception of its BAPA. Thus, perception as an element of bargaining power links together all of the other variables in the bargaining power equation. Accordingly, the negotiator who settles for more does not assess a strategy or tactic with respect to any element without considering its potential indirect impact on the rest of the bargaining power equation.

Chapter 2

Models of Bargaining Power and Process

A. Paradigms of Bargaining Power

Having identified the elements of bargaining power, let us examine them in the form of diagrams representing the relationships among these elements. Before doing so, however, it should be understood that the purpose of these paradigms is not to describe how negotiators in fact analyze what they are doing or how negotiators in fact make bargaining decisions. Most negotiators probably do not engage in a structured analysis of what transpires in the bargaining process. Nevertheless, that does not mean that there is no structural relationship among the elements of bargaining power. After all, people used mechanical devices long before Newton provided the model for understanding the precise relationships involved in such activity. Similarly, it is possible to fly an airplane, drive a car, or fire a rifle without understanding the Second Law of Motion. However, understanding the elements of the process and their relationships makes it possible to design and use such devices with greater efficiency and predictability. Hence, using descriptive models to examine the negotiating process assures more precise examination and weighing of bargaining decisions by providing a better understanding of the available choices and the likely consequences of alternative courses of action.

In our previous discussion, we saw how each element of bargaining strength is directly related to another element; that is, the strength or weakness of one element directly affects the impact of the interrelated element upon bargaining strength. One of those sets consists of the Offer to Meet the Other's Needs (OMON) and the Probability of Performance (POP). For example, if Betty's perception of Adam's Probability of Performance is increased (e.g., Adam provides a letter of credit from a bank ensuring his ability to pay what is offered), that also increases the significance of what Adam has offered—his OMON. This interrelationship is particularly important if the other side perceives one of the interrelated elements to have a zero value. Therefore, if Adam offers Betty the highest price she can expect to get for a car she has for sale but Betty's understanding is that Adam is broke, has no assets, and is about to be sent to prison for ten years, her perception that his Probability of Performance is zero renders his offer irrelevant. No matter how high his offer, she assumes that she is just wasting time (and possibly alternative opportunities) even talking to him.

We can diagram the interrelationship of linked bargaining strength elements as the two dimensions that determine the volume of a cylinder shaped weight. One element is represented by the base of the cylinder, the other by its height. By recalling the principles of plane geometry, we know that the resulting volume is determined by multiplying these two dimensions. Thus, if we assign the bargaining strength element OMON (Offer to Meet the Other's Needs) as the dimension of the height of the cylindrical weight and assign the bargaining strength element POP (Probability of Performance) as the base of the same weight, we can diagram the relationship between these elements as follows:

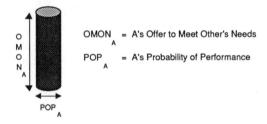

As we can see, an increase or decrease in either element will cause a corresponding increase or decrease in the total weight of the linked elements.

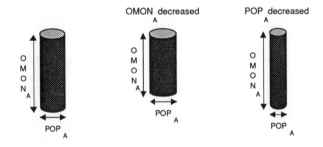

In addition, this representation shows us that if the value of either element is reduced to zero, there is no longer any weight giving volume to the cylinder no matter how large a value is attributed to the linked element. Hence, our diagram of the weight created by combining the linked elements would have the following appearance if one element has a value of zero:

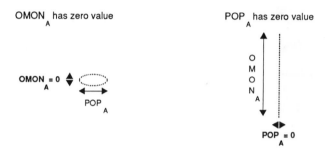

The diagram of the linked impact of the bargaining strength elements additionally demonstrates that though the other side may perceive one bargaining strength element as having increased or decreased weight, the forces of the paired elements continue to work in the same direction. To illustrate, suppose Adam is offering to sell Betty a mare that he identifies as a fine breeder of race horses. Betty's perception of the elements of this offer influences how much bargaining strength Adam possesses. If Betty is interested in acquiring a thoroughbred brood mare to breed race horses, Adam's offer, if credible, carries significant weight in meeting her need. Of course, Betty's interest is based, also, on the assumption that Adam has the ability to deliver the horse—that is, he owns it or is the agent for an owner who is willing to sell. The following diagram shows the relationship of these two paired elements of Adam's bargaining strength—the weight of the diagrammed cylinder is the combination of Adam's offer to meet Betty's need and his probability of performance.

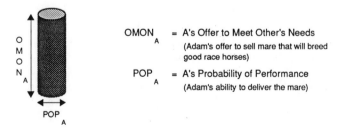

Undoubtedly, if in the course of discussing the horse, Adam informs Betty that five seasons earlier the mare had an offspring that won the Kentucky Derby, and if Betty perceives that for this reason the mare's next foal should also race well, Adam's bargaining strength will be greatly enhanced. This is graphically illustrated in the next diagram.

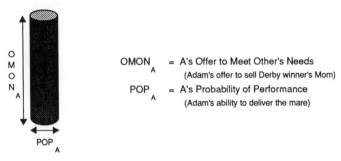

$OMON_A$ = A's Offer to Meet Other's Needs
(Adam's offer to sell Derby winner's Mom)

POP_A = A's Probability of Performance
(Adam's ability to deliver the mare)

Of course, Betty's perception that the mare Adam offers for sale will meet her needs is dependent, too, upon the assumption that the mare is healthy and fertile. Conversely, the significance of Betty's expectations regarding the potential value of the mare's offspring is reduced to the extent Betty has questions regarding the mare's ability to produce another foal. Thus, if she learns that the mare is infirm or miscarried two of the last four times she was with foal, Adam's bargaining strength is diminished.

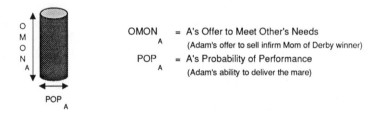

$OMON_A$ = A's Offer to Meet Other's Needs
(Adam's offer to sell infirm Mom of Derby winner)

POP_A = A's Probability of Performance
(Adam's ability to deliver the mare)

Finally, in the next diagram we can see that, as previously noted, if the value of one element is reduced to zero, the interrelated element will no longer exert any weight in the scale representing bargaining strength. Accordingly, in our horse sale example, if Betty were to learn that Adam is Smith's agent and that Smith himself sold the mare three days earlier, her perception of the quality foal the mare might produce becomes irrelevant. Inasmuch as she knows that Adam cannot deliver, that he lacks the ability to sell the mare, its value no longer has any importance to Betty. Thus, even if Betty is convinced that the mare is healthy and that her offspring will have great racing potential, Adam has lost his bargaining strength. In our diagram we can see that when one of the paired elements, here the Probability of Performance, loses all value, thus shrinking the diameter of the paired-element cylinder to zero, the weight of the cylinder (now a one-dimensional line) becomes zero, regardless of the value of the other paired element (here, the Offer to Meet the Other's Needs).

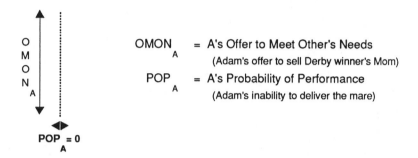

The other paired bargaining strength elements are Data Accuracy (DA) linked with Accrued Costs (AC), Predictive Accuracy (PA) linked with Best Alternative to the Proposed Agreement (BAPA), and Predictive Accuracy (PA) linked with the Cost of Impending Negotiations (COIN). In the case of the element we call Predictive Accuracy (PA) it should be noted that although its nature is the same, whether linked to the best alternative to the proposed agreement or to the costs of impending negotiations, its strength may differ depending on whether what is being forecast are the Best Alternatives to the Proposed Agreement (BAPA) or the Costs of Impending Negotiations (COIN). For example, Betty may know that the horse auction begins the next day and that she will bid on a mare at the auction unless she closes a deal with Adam today. Hence, she can predict rather accurately the costs of her impending bargaining with Adam. On the other hand, her predictions respecting what the high bid will be for a comparable mare at the auction involves considerable speculation. Therefore, the weight to be given her Predictive Accuracy (PA) as linked to the Costs of Impending Negotiations (COIN) is very different from the weight assignable to her Predictive Accuracy (PA) as linked to her Best Alternative to the Proposed Agreement (BAPA).

Paradigm 1

Let us now examine a diagram that portrays all of the elements of bargaining strength in a single paradigm. In the diagram that follows, we again visualize the paired elements of bargaining strength as weights balancing in favor or against accepting party A's bargaining proposal. The bargaining strength paradigm places the weights in their respective positions on a balance scale. On the left side of the balance scale are the elements of bargaining strength that weigh in favor of B accepting A's proposal. Therefore, these elements are identified as the plus (+) factors. Greater force on the plus side of the scale—that is, greater weight of the elements on that side—represents A's increased bargaining strength; reduced force on that side represents decreased bargaining strength for A.

The weights on the right side of the balance scale represent the elements that weigh against the other side (B) accepting A's proposal. Accordingly, this side of the scale is labeled as the minus (−) side. Therefore, greater weight on the minus side of the scale represents A's decreased bargaining strength and reduced force on that side represents increased bargaining strength for A.

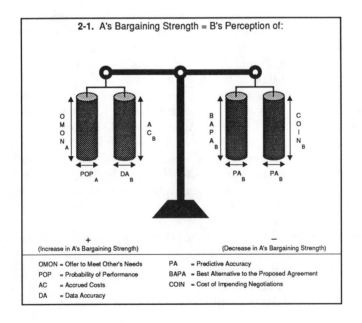

2-1. A's Bargaining Strength = B's Perception of:

+
(Increase in A's Bargaining Strength)

−
(Decrease in A's Bargaining Strength)

OMON = Offer to Meet Other's Needs	PA = Predictive Accuracy
POP = Probability of Performance	BAPA = Best Alternative to the Proposed Agreement
AC = Accrued Costs	COIN = Cost of Impending Negotiations
DA = Data Accuracy	

Paradigm 2

Of course, as we see in the diagram below, the same approach can be used in Paradigm 2 to represent the measure of B's bargaining strength.

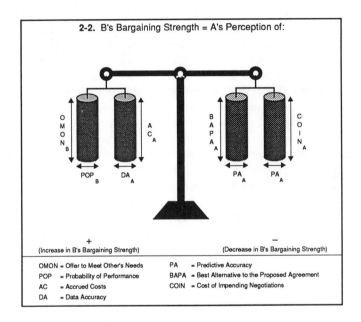

2-2. B's Bargaining Strength = A's Perception of:

+	**–**
(Increase in B's Bargaining Strength)	(Decrease in B's Bargaining Strength)

OMON	= Offer to Meet Other's Needs	PA	= Predictive Accuracy
POP	= Probability of Performance	BAPA	= Best Alternative to the Proposed Agreement
AC	= Accrued Costs	COIN	= Cost of Impending Negotiations
DA	= Data Accuracy		

It may take a while to become sufficiently familiar with the abbreviations so that the relationships can be identified quickly from the diagram. However, in the text that follows, these elements and abbreviations are repeated and explained with sufficient frequency so that this shorthand soon will become quite familiar— just give it a try. In any event, mastering the shorthand and diagrams is not essential to understanding the overall discussion of bargaining strength and strategy.

Paradigms 1 and 2, above, show the respective sources of bargaining strength for negotiators A and B. Reviewing Paradigm 1, we see that all elements of A's bargaining strength are a function of B's perception of those elements. We find, of course, that the converse is true when we review B's bargaining strength—that is, with respect to B's bargaining strength (Paradigm 2), all elements of bargaining power are a function of A's perception of them.

As shown in Paradigms 1 and 2, the weight of the elements of bargaining strength are presumed to be balanced. Since our model presents these weights on a balance scale, we can see that changes in the elements' weights will tilt the balance in one direction or the other or to a greater degree in one direction or the other. For example, in Paradigm 1 we see that B's increased perception of the degree of weight to be placed on any of the elements on the left side of the scale, the plus side of A's bargaining strength, results in an enhancement of A's bargaining strength. If B perceives that several elements on the left side of the scale (e.g., POP, OMON, and DA) have greater weight than he previously thought, A's bargaining strength is enhanced that much more.

Let us look at an illustration of what we have just observed. Assume that B wants to build a house and A is a house carpenter. The two are meeting at B's office where A has examined the architectural plans. A's offer to meet B's needs (OMON) is A's ability to do the carpentry work, and his Probability of Performance (POP) is A's reputation for getting work done as scheduled. B's Accrued Costs (AC) is the time B spent contacting A and checking A's background and reputation and B's Data Accuracy (DA) respecting that amount of time depends upon whether he kept careful track

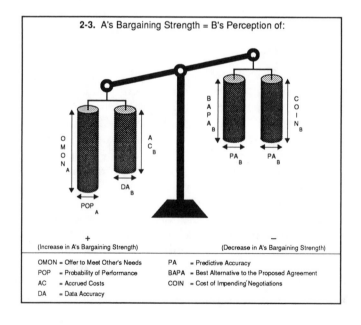

2-3. A's Bargaining Strength = B's Perception of:

+ (Increase in A's Bargaining Strength)   − (Decrease in A's Bargaining Strength)

OMON = Offer to Meet Other's Needs	PA = Predictive Accuracy
POP = Probability of Performance	BAPA = Best Alternative to the Proposed Agreement
AC = Accrued Costs	COIN = Cost of Impending Negotiations
DA = Data Accuracy	

of that time and noted it before A arrived at B's office. B's Best Alternative to the Proposed Agreement (BAPA) is his ability to find another carpenter to hire for the work and his Predictive Accuracy (PA) regarding that ability reflects the degree of accurate knowledge he has respecting the number of new jobs coming on the market and the number of carpenters looking for work. Finally, B's cost of impending bargaining (COIN) will depend upon the ease or difficulty in coming to terms with A, and B's Predictive Accuracy (PA) respecting that factor reflects his familiarity in dealing with A.

In illustration 2-3, we can see that A's bargaining strength is enhanced to the extent that B perceives of A as being a skilled, experienced carpenter. (That is, A's OMON, his offer to meet B's needs, is heightened in B's perceptions.) Moreover, if B is persuaded that A is the most skilled and most experienced carpenter in town, B's perception of A's offer to meet B's needs ($OMON_A$) is likely to attribute larger significance to that bargaining strength element. As we can see in illustration 2-4, this moves the bargaining strength balance in the direction of further enhancing A's bargaining strength.

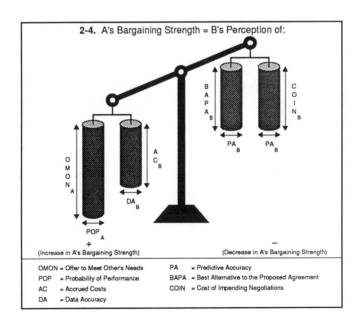

2-4. A's Bargaining Strength = B's Perception of:

OMON = Offer to Meet Other's Needs	PA = Predictive Accuracy
POP = Probability of Performance	BAPA = Best Alternative to the Proposed Agreement
AC = Accrued Costs	COIN = Cost of Impending Negotiations
DA = Data Accuracy	

However, what if B has heard rumors that indicate that A is an alcoholic who cannot be relied on to show up regularly? This, impression will, of course, reduce A's bargaining strength because B's perception is that A has a small POP—Probability of Performance. In illustration 2-5, we can see the impact of that change.

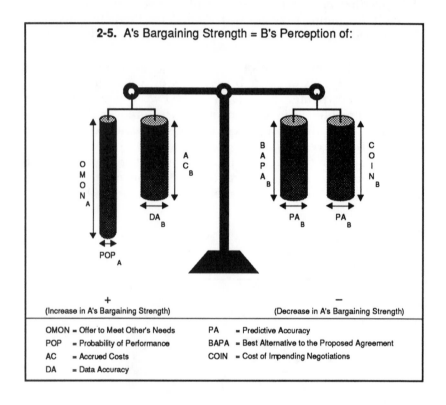

2-5. A's Bargaining Strength = B's Perception of:

OMON	= Offer to Meet Other's Needs	PA	= Predictive Accuracy
POP	= Probability of Performance	BAPA	= Best Alternative to the Proposed Agreement
AC	= Accrued Costs	COIN	= Cost of Impending Negotiations
DA	= Data Accuracy		

The bargaining strength of A can be rehabilitated if he discovers B's reservations respecting A's POP and if A improves B's perception of the value to be given to A's POP by, for example, providing B with references who will attest that A is a recovering alcoholic who has performed reliably on recent jobs. In that situation, we can see that the balance again swings toward increased bargaining strength for A. (B's perception of its own Accrued Costs of bargaining (AC) also has the potential of adding to A's bargaining power.)

Of course, the paradigm of B's bargaining strength (Paradigm 2 in the initial presentation of the bargaining strength model) is the mirror image of A's bargaining strength. Accordingly, as shown in illustration 2-6, if A, for example, perceives that getting the job working for B will restore A's good reputation in the community, A will have an increased perception of the value of B's offer to meet his needs (normally what B proposes to pay for the job) with the result that B's bargaining strength is increased.

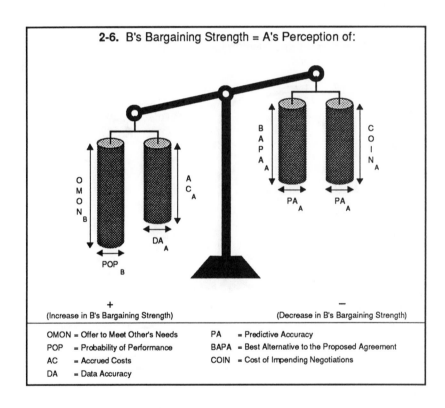

2-6. B's Bargaining Strength = A's Perception of:

+
(Increase in B's Bargaining Strength)

−
(Decrease in B's Bargaining Strength)

OMON = Offer to Meet Other's Needs	PA	= Predictive Accuracy
POP	= Probability of Performance	BAPA	= Best Alternative to the Proposed Agreement
AC	= Accrued Costs	COIN	= Cost of Impending Negotiations
DA	= Data Accuracy		

The bargaining strength paradigms also demonstrate that bargaining power is diminished to the extent that the other side places a high value on its Best Alternative to the Proposed Agreement (BAPA). For example, in the illustration of B's need for a carpenter, if B perceives the job as simple and not requiring much trade skill, B may find a number of reliable, efficient, moderately skilled workers in town who could competently do the job. Thus, as shown below, the balance swings in the direction of reducing A's bargaining strength.

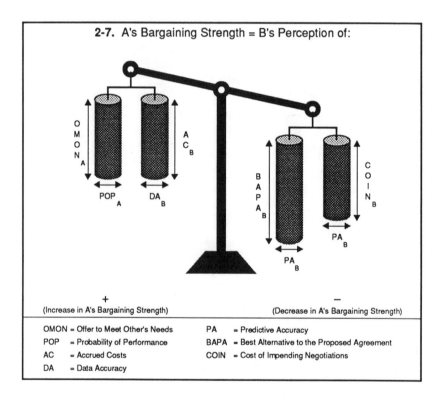

2-7. A's Bargaining Strength = B's Perception of:

OMON = Offer to Meet Other's Needs	PA = Predictive Accuracy
POP = Probability of Performance	BAPA = Best Alternative to the Proposed Agreement
AC = Accrued Costs	COIN = Cost of Impending Negotiations
DA = Data Accuracy	

Similarly, the paradigms show how the impact of the elements on the minus side, the right side of the balance scale, increase or decrease depending on whether the other party has considerable confidence or little confidence in the reliability of its assessment of those alternatives (PA—Predictive Ability). Accordingly, A can increase his bargaining strength if he can alter B's perception by explaining to B that an unskilled wood worker is liable to waste a high percentage of the building materials. That is, as shown below, A's efforts, if successful in altering B's perceptions, decrease B's assurance that he has accurately predicted the value of the alternative of hiring a moderately skilled worker to do the job.

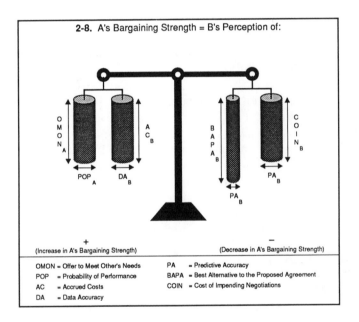

2-8. A's Bargaining Strength = B's Perception of:

+
(Increase in A's Bargaining Strength)

—
(Decrease in A's Bargaining Strength)

OMON = Offer to Meet Other's Needs	PA = Predictive Accuracy
POP = Probability of Performance	BAPA = Best Alternative to the Proposed Agreement
AC = Accrued Costs	COIN = Cost of Impending Negotiations
DA = Data Accuracy	

The above paradigm of A's bargaining strength also reveals that it is diminished to the extent that B thinks it will be costly to engage in protracted negotiations (COIN—Cost of Impending Negotiations) in order to settle on terms more favorable than those presently being offered to A. That is, B's perception of the element representing B's Cost of Impending Negotiations (COIN$_B$) is expanded and this results in the balance shifting toward the direction of a reduction in A's bargaining strength.

Finally, it is important to remember that bargaining strength does not remain static during the course of negotiations. It is dynamic and is likely to change with each alteration of available relevant information, each material modification of the negotiating environment, and each proposal or other tactic that effectively alters a party's perceptions. The greater the negotiator's mastery of bargaining skills, the greater is that negotiator's ability to detect and manage such changes so as to increase bargaining strength. The negotiator must accomplish this while maintaining the momentum of the transaction either until a decision is made to abandon the process as not offering a favorable result or until a favorable settlement has been concluded.

Paradigm 3

Each side to a negotiation must weigh its own bargaining strength and that of the other side. Thus, whether a bargaining transaction between party A and party B should turn out favorably to party A depends not on A's bargaining strength alone, but on A's bargaining strength relative to the bargaining strength of B.

Diagram 2-9 illustrates how the balance scale model can be used to visualize the relationship among the bargaining strength elements of both sides to determine one party's relative bargaining strength. Because the paradigm shows A's relative bargaining strength, the identification of the plus elements (those whose greater paired weight increase bargaining strength) and the minus elements (those whose greater paired weight reduce bargaining strength) reflects their impact upon A's relative negotiating leverage. Accordingly, in the bottom balance scale that shows the elements in terms of A's perceptions (the measure of B's bargaining strength—see Paradigm 2, at page 33), the sequence of the elements is reversed—instead of the OMON, BAPA, AC, and DA elements being on the plus side, the plus elements are A's Predictive Ability, A's Best Alternative to the Proposed Agreement, and A's Cost of Impending Negotiations. Thus, as the weight of these elements increases, B's bargaining strength is reduced and, therefore, A's relative bargaining strength increases. We can see from this diagram that A's relative bargaining strength is altered to the extent that there is a modification of either A's or B's perceptions of the basic elements of bargaining power. Of course, changes in both parties' perceptions may also alter A's relative bargaining strength.

2-9. A's Relative Bargaining Strength = B's Perception of:

+
(Increase in A's Relative Bargaining Strength)

−
(Decrease in A's Relative Bargaining Strength)

PLUS
A's Perception of:

+
(Increase in A's Relative Bargaining Strength)

−
(Decrease in A's Relative Bargaining Strength)

OMON	= Offer to Meet Other's Needs	PA	= Predictive Accuracy
POP	= Probability of Performance	BAPA	= Best Alternative to the Proposed Agreement
AC	= Accrued Costs	COIN	= Cost of Impending Negotiations
DA	= Data Accuracy		

For example, suppose the parties are negotiating a long-term lease under which A will become a tenant at B's shopping center. If B has the only highly attractive retailing location in town, A has less bargaining power than it would if there were several attractive locations available. One way A can increase its bargaining strength, therefore, is to discover alternative locations (increase its BAPA). Another way to increase its bargaining strength is for A to develop marketing devices that will diminish the importance of location in its retailing activities (reduce the value to A of B's OMON). Still another approach for A to enhance its bargaining strength is to persuade B that alternatives are soon to become available.

A's discovery of alternative locations, or marketing devices that substitute for strategically valuable locations, increases A's Best Alternative to the Proposed Agreement because it informs A that another rental location might be available at favorable terms. But note that this information will not modify B's bargaining position unless B is made aware of the change in A's BAPA. That is, obtaining new alternatives increases A's *potential bargaining strength* but does not alter A's actual bargaining strength until it has had the effect of altering B's perceptions. Persuading B that such an alternative location exists further helps A because it reduces B's BAPA. This is achieved by making B think it will have greater difficulty renting to some other tenant who might also have an interest in the alternative location. It also may have the psychological impact of reducing B's perception of its Predictive Accuracy, thus further increasing A's bargaining strength (see diagram 2-10).

Assuming that A is a carpenter negotiating for a contract to build B's house, the list that follows examines the possible ways A's relative bargaining strength may be increased or diminished. Each can be seen by observing the change in relative bargaining strength that would occur if the appropriate dimension was altered in Paradigm 3, above. Despite its length, the list is not complete. We will see in Part B of Chapter 3 that there are three types of strategic approaches to altering perceptions. The list that follows covers possible bargaining strength changes achieved using two of those strategic approaches. Additional possibilities are available by resorting to what is described in Chapter 3 as the Type III strategic approach.

A's Relative Bargaining Strength Is Enhanced If:

- B's perception of the value of A's Offer to Meet B's Needs is increased. (B is persuaded that a carpenter of A's skill is essential for the job.)

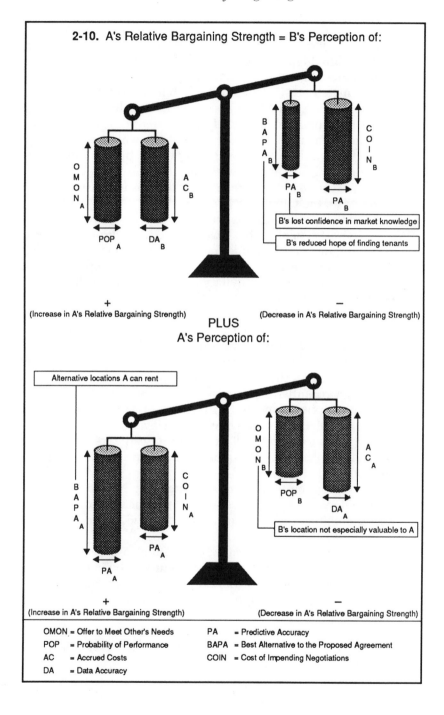

2-10. A's Relative Bargaining Strength = B's Perception of:

B's lost confidence in market knowledge

B's reduced hope of finding tenants

+
(Increase in A's Relative Bargaining Strength)

−
(Decrease in A's Relative Bargaining Strength)

PLUS
A's Perception of:

Alternative locations A can rent

B's location not especially valuable to A

+
(Increase in A's Relative Bargaining Strength)

−
(Decrease in A's Relative Bargaining Strength)

OMON	= Offer to Meet Other's Needs	PA = Predictive Accuracy
POP	= Probability of Performance	BAPA = Best Alternative to the Proposed Agreement
AC	= Accrued Costs	COIN = Cost of Impending Negotiations
DA	= Data Accuracy	

- B's perception of the value of A's Probability of Performance is increased. (B is persuaded that A has no competing commitment and is very reliable.)
- B's perception of his own Accrued Costs of bargaining with A is increased. (B looks at his watch and suddenly realizes that he has spent three hours discussing the job with A.)
- B's perception of his own Data Accuracy is increased. (B's secretary notifies him that the patient who was waiting to see him while he was talking to A just left the office announcing he was finding a new physician.)
- A's perception of his Predictive Ability is increased. (While B was on the telephone, A checked a local trade publication listing all bid invitations for large construction contracts.)
- A's perception of his Best Alternative to B's Proposed Agreement is increased. (While B was on the telephone, A opened an envelope he had picked up as he left his shop and found that it contained an invitation to bid on three large new jobs.)
- A's perception of his Cost of Impending Negotiations with B is increased. (During negotiations, B reveals that he is still waiting for final plans from his architect.)
- B's perception of his Predictive Ability is decreased. (B learns from A that two other carpenters he intended to contact recently took factory jobs.)
- B's perception of his Best Alternative to A's Proposed Agreement is decreased. (While discussing the job with A, B receives a telephone call from another carpenter who examined the plans and who quotes a higher price than A's initial proposal.)
- B's perception of his Cost of Impending Negotiations with A is decreased. (A offers to examine the final drawings at the architect's office and drop a detailed, signed proposal off at B's house that evening.)
- A's perception of the value of B's Offer to Meet A's Needs is decreased. (B tells A that payment will be in four installments over a one-year period after work is completed.)
- A's perception of B's Probability of Performance is decreased. (A learns that B's wife has just filed for divorce.)
- A's perception of his Accrued Costs of negotiating with B is decreased. (The negotiations take place over lunch and B picks up the bill.)
- A's perception of his Data Accuracy is decreased. (A obtained a copy of the building plan from B's architect and A doesn't know if the architect will bill him for the copy.)

A's Relative Bargaining Strength Is Diminished If:

- A's perception of the value of B's Offer to Meet A's Needs is increased. (A learns that the local newspaper will do a story about the building project with photos of the principal contractors.)
- A's perception of the value of B's Probability of Performance is increased. (B informs A that the funds from the construction loan are in a bank escrow fund and will be paid as the architect certifies the completion of each phase of the work.)
- A's perception of his Accrued Costs of bargaining with B is increased. (Negotiating takes place over lunch and A gets stuck with the bill because B had to rush to the hospital in response to an emergency call.)
- B's perception of his Predictive Ability is increased. (In the midst of negotiations, B opens his mail and finds a memo from his architect with detailed construction cost estimates.)
- B's perception of his Best Alternative to A's Proposed Agreement is increased. (While discussing the job with A, B receives a telephone call from another carpenter who examined the plans and who quotes a lower price than A's initial proposal.)
- B's perception of his Cost of Impending Negotiations with A is increased. (B's architect insists that B require contractors to execute a standard form agreement and A says that before he signs an agreement he will have to show it to his niece who is a law student.)
- A's perception of his Predictive Ability is decreased. (B informs A that he has received a bid from a carpentry contractor that A had assumed would not be interested in a job as small this one.)
- A's perception of his Best Alternative to B's Proposed Agreement is decreased. (While B is answering a telephone call, A opens a letter he picked up as he was leaving his office and learns that a job he was preparing to bid on has been cancelled.)
- A's perception of his Cost of Impending Negotiations with B is decreased. (B tells A he will be happy to come to A's office or home for further discussions and that he will be available to do so in the evening so as to not interfere with A's work on a construction project he has underway.)
- B's perception of the value of A's Offer to Meet B's Needs is decreased. (A tells B that he cannot begin work on the project until at least a month later than B's planned starting date.)

- B's perception of A's Probability of Performance is decreased. (At lunch A washes his meal down with three beers.)
- B's perception of his Accrued Costs of negotiating with A is decreased. (In the course of discussions, B learns that A did the carpentry work on a building B is considering buying and A reveals that the builder insisted on using substandard materials for that project.)
- B's perception of his Data Accuracy is decreased. (B checks his watch to see how long they have been negotiating and discovers that it is not working.)

Paradigm 4

Paradigm 4, presented in diagram 2-11, shows the conditions under which reasonable negotiators should be able to reach a settlement. The balance scales in Paradigm 4 illustrate that a settlement should be attainable as long as each side perceives that its current investment in negotiating with the other side (plus what it expects the other side to do to meet its needs) outweighs its perception of what it will cost to bargain to the point of settlement (plus what it thinks it probably could gain by pursuing an alternative to settling with the other side).

One lesson demonstrated by Paradigm 4 is that, contrary to the assertion made by some people, not every situation is negotiable. If there is to be a negotiated settlement, each side must perceive that a bargained resolution is more beneficial to it than would be no deal. If we look at the possible combinations—a proposed settlement is acceptable to side A, but not to side B; a proposed settlement is acceptable to side B but not to side A, etc.—we see that of the four possibilities (A-yes, B-no; A-no, B-no; A-no, B-yes; A-yes, B-yes), only the last one is conducive to a settlement. Thus, a skilled negotiator recognizes that reaching a settlement often is a complex and tedious process of finding the right circumstances and combination of accommodations. Therefore, sometimes it is necessary to reassure the other side (and oneself) that a proposed settlement is of mutual (though not necessarily equal) benefit and that if the proposals on the table are unsatisfactory, a bit more exploration should produce the acceptable solution.

Paradigm 4 also offers guidance respecting the difference between integrative (i.e., involving common or compatible needs) and exchange negotiations (i.e., involving competing or incompat-

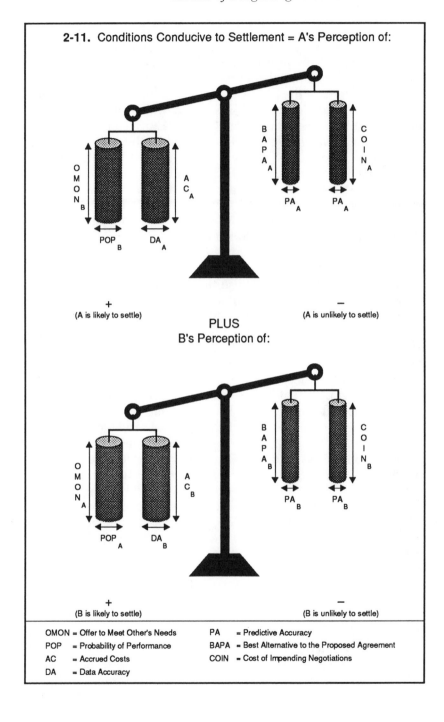

2-11. Conditions Conducive to Settlement = A's Perception of:

+
(A is likely to settle)

−
(A is unlikely to settle)

PLUS
B's Perception of:

+
(B is likely to settle)

−
(B is unlikely to settle)

OMON = Offer to Meet Other's Needs	PA = Predictive Accuracy
POP = Probability of Performance	BAPA = Best Alternative to the Proposed Agreement
AC = Accrued Costs	COIN = Cost of Impending Negotiations
DA = Data Accuracy	

ible needs). In pure exchange bargaining, an increase in one side's OMON should be accompanied by a decrease in the other side's OMON. That is, because the respective needs of the parties are competing or incompatible, a proposal that better serves one side's needs will decrease the prospect of meeting the other side's needs. Thus, if Adam, a physician, wants Betty, who also is a physician, to cover his practice while Adam is on a European vacation, the more Adam must agree to pay Betty, the less the proposed settlement meets Adam's needs. As a result, if the transaction is perceived by both sides strictly in fiscal terms, the increase in Adam's OMON ($OMON_A$—what Adam will have to pay Betty) is accompanied by a decrease in Betty's OMON ($OMON_B$—Adam's perception of the net value of what he will gain from purchasing Betty's services). By referring back to Paradigm 4, we can (in diagram 2-12) see that increasing Adam's payment to Betty reduces the likelihood that Adam will be willing to accept a settlement on the proposed terms. That is, because the net value to Adam (A in the diagram) of Betty's offer—$OMON_B$—is reduced, in the balance scale A's perception has less weight on the plus side than it would have had had Betty asked for a lower amount of remuneration.

Of course, in the above illustration, Adam might still be willing to retain Betty's services even though he may have to pay more than he initially expected. In terms of Paradigm 4, there still will be a good prospect that Adam will accept if the remaining factors result in the left hand side of his perception of the balance outweighs the right hand side of the scale. For example, Betty may be seeking no more or only a little more remuneration than other available physicians (Adam's Best Alternative to the Proposed Agreement—$BAPA_A$) and this may be more than offset on the balance scale by Adam's desire to quickly resolve the matter of who will cover for him and, thereby, reduce his perceived Cost of Impending Negotiations ($COIN_A$). In the latter situation, we can see from Paradigm 4, below, that despite Betty's demand exceeding Adam's expectations, the conditions may still remain conducive to settlement. Thus, the balance scale for Betty's perceptions is tipped further in the direction of increased likelihood of reaching agreement because the more Adam pays Betty the greater is her perception of the value of Adam's offer to meet her needs ($OMON_A$). At the same time, Adam's perception of the reduced size of his cost of impending negotiations ($COIN_A$) offsets, or more than offsets, the reduction in his perception of the value to be given to Betty's offer to meet his needs ($OMON_B$). Therefore, despite the

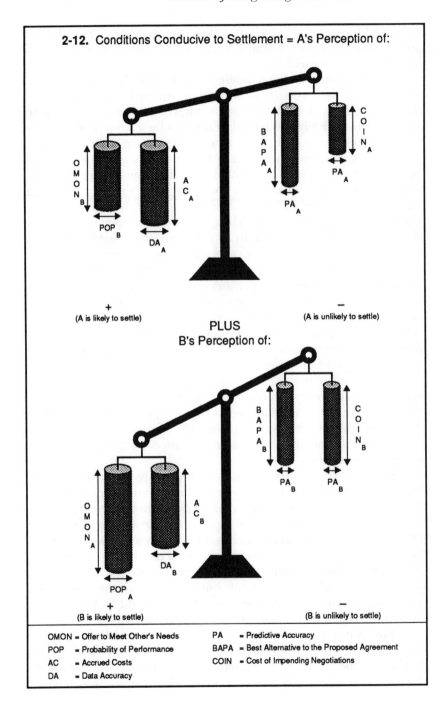

2-12. Conditions Conducive to Settlement = A's Perception of:

+
(A is likely to settle)

PLUS
B's Perception of:

−
(A is unlikely to settle)

+
(B is likely to settle)

−
(B is unlikely to settle)

OMON = Offer to Meet Other's Needs	PA = Predictive Accuracy
POP = Probability of Performance	BAPA = Best Alternative to the Proposed Agreement
AC = Accrued Costs	COIN = Cost of Impending Negotiations
DA = Data Accuracy	

increased fee to be paid to Betty, the balance representing Adam's perceptions may also continue to tilt in the direction of increased likelihood of settlement.

Accordingly, Paradigm 4 demonstrates that the negotiator who has mastered the structure of bargaining strength should recognize that in dealing with exchange items, efforts to obtain a more favorable settlement increase the risk of not reaching agreement. Therefore, the negotiator who seeks to settle for more must attempt to offset that danger by finding ways to alter the opponent's perceptions so as to maintain a balance favoring settlement. For example, in our hypothetical case, Betty might attempt to persuade Adam that her potential of meeting Adam's needs involves greater value than Adam thought it would. Thus, Betty might point out to Adam that since she likes to get off to an early morning start in attending to her professional activities, she can phone Adam at 4:30 each morning, at about the time Adam will have finished his breakfast in Madrid, to review any matters needing Adam's consultation. This would be much more convenient to Adam than a call three or four hours later, or in the early evening—arrangements that Adam may have had to live with on previous trips abroad. Similarly, if Betty's practice is devoted to covering for other doctors, she might attempt to persuade Adam that the risks of having another doctor in the community covering his practice are greater than Adam's initial perception (decrease Adam's Predictive Ability and thereby reduce the significance of Adam's perception of the Best Alternative to the Proposed Agreement) because he may risk that other physicians who cover for him may succeed in attracting away some of his patients.

In contrast with the exchange bargaining situation, in integrative bargaining, because the needs are common or compatible, an increase in one side's Offer to Meet the Other's Needs (OMON) should be accompanied either by an increase in the other side's OMON, if they are common needs, or no change in the other side's OMON, if the needs are compatible. As a result, we can see from Paradigm 4 that not only should there be no reduction in the prospects of reaching agreement, but to the extent that the parties' needs are common, an increase in OMON should be mutual and, therefore, also increase the prospects of settlement.

For example, assume that Al's Restaurant and Betty's bakery are in adjacent buildings and that Al has a new truck that he sends to the produce market every morning to pick up fresh supplies. Assume, too, that Betty has a new truck that she sends to a variety of shops and hotels every afternoon to deliver freshly baked dinner rolls, pies, and cakes. Assume further that neither truck is ever more than half full and that Al's truck has thirty percent more carrying capacity than Betty's. Finally, assume that they discuss an arrangement under which one of the trucks will be sold and the seller will rent the use of the other's truck for part of each day. Under these hypothetical circumstances, if the value and cost of operating the trucks is proportional to the carrying capacity, a proposal to sell Al's truck would clearly have the potential for increasing the value of each side's offer to meet the other's needs.

Of course, increasing the potential for meeting the other's needs does not ensure agreement. Each must still consider the elements on the right hand side of the Paradigm 4 diagram. Maximizing the parties' mutual benefits may not be enough to produce a settlement if one side has a very attractive alternative to the proposed agreement. For example, Betty may have an opportunity to use a delivery service at a very reasonable rate. Nor will maximizing the parties' mutual benefits achieve a settlement if one party perceives that it faces considerable costs in continuing to work out a potentially satisfactory settlement.

The reader will recall that the introductory chapter described the distinction between strategy and tactics. In the context of the above model of negotiating power (Paradigms 1 to 4), strategy involves the choice of which perceived bargaining strength element or elements the bargainer will attempt to alter, while tactics are the devices by which the bargainer attempts to modify the targeted perceptions. Hence the decision to increase Adam's perception of the value of Betty's offer to meet his needs is a strategic decision; the decision to accomplish that change in his perception by providing him with particular information or by reshaping the description of the offered services is a tactical decision. The next chapter describes ways in which the above models depicting negotiating power provide guidance respecting choices negotiators must make in selecting from among available negotiating strategies. Later chapters present models to guide the skilled negotiator's choice of tactics.

One last observation is in order regarding Paradigm 4 and the explanation of conditions conducive to settlement. One who has carefully analyzed the Paradigm 4 application of the bargaining strength model for determining when conditions are conducive to settlement, at first impression might think that there is a gap in the logic when applied to the situation in which either the Probability of Performance (POP) element or the Offer to Meet the Other's Needs (OMON) element has a perceived value of zero. It would at first glance seem reasonable to expect that a person who perceives either that the other side was offering nothing to meet his needs (OMON = 0), or that the other side was not going to perform on such an offer (POP = 0), would walk away from the transaction since it would seem to offer no benefit. Yet, Paradigm 4 indicates that such a person might still be prepared to settle if he perceives that he has already made a substantial investment of time, money, or effort in trying to negotiate a settlement (a high value placed on the Accrued Costs and Data Accuracy elements) and a low perception of the value of alternatives to the proposed agreement. Further analysis, however, removes this apparent deficiency in the bargaining strength model.

First, it must be remembered that bargaining strength is based on each side's perceptions. Generally, a person who has made a substantial investment of time, energy, or money in trying to negotiate a settlement (a high AC), is unlikely to be persuaded that that investment has been wholly futile. Hence, the situation involving a high perception of the Accrued Costs in fact will rarely be coupled with that person perceiving that the other side has a zero likelihood of performing or a zero likelihood of meeting his needs. Human nature inclines most people to find some virtue, some benefit in their own past deeds—a characteristic that some psychologists call cognitive dissonance. Having made a substantial commitment to finding a negotiated solution, most people will not allow themselves to reduce their perception of the potential benefit to zero.

Second, even in the unlikely event that a negotiator decides that he has invested substantial effort in bargaining with someone who will do nothing to meet his needs, the prospects for settlement are not necessarily wholly eliminated. This is because many negotiators, having made such an investment in bargaining with a particular party, will prefer to gamble upon unforeseen events or unknown information ultimately giving some value to the settlement rather than walking away from the situation and thereby making it certain that no benefit can come from the substantial investment in the bargaining effort.

B. The Flow of Interactions in Negotiations

Before exploring in more detail how the above paradigms of negotiating power can guide the skilled negotiator's strategic choices, it is important to place the opportunities for making such selections in a realistic context. A danger of abstracting conduct into descriptive models is that too often it oversimplifies to the point of misleading the user. As previously noted, the paradigms presented above are not intended to suggest a static situation; negotiating is anything but static. It is a dynamic process in which each change in the value or significance of a particular element can cause changes in perceptions of the values or significance of other elements.

Many efforts have been made to portray the dynamics of the negotiating process in terms of stages of particular types of activities. Here, too, the scientist's device of an abstract model offers a metaphor to help in understanding the characteristics of the process under scrutiny.

The dynamics of negotiating is a product of the activities of the negotiators and the environment and interests that affect them. Unskilled bargainers are liable to bypass or overlook steps that are essential to skilled negotiating. Therefore, the model presented below does not depict an inevitable flow of bargaining activity but rather offers a paradigm describing the dynamics of the process when generated by skilled bargainers.

In many ways the dynamics of skilled negotiating are similar to the process by which an experienced sailor navigates uncharted waters. Before choosing a course it is necessary to have a goal and gather information—observe and test the vessel, wind, sea, current, and horizon. The course is then taken; but that choice must be reassessed and corrected in light of the progress made and any changes in the elements. If the choice and adjustments are well chosen, and if the elements are favorable, the destination will be reached. However, there are times when ill winds or harsh currents force the navigator to abandon the original destination and return home or seek an alternative port.

So, too, in negotiating, the first stage of activity is to learn as much as possible about the elements that will shape the journey. The skilled negotiator does this by doing backgound research, observing and weighing the other side's words and conduct, eliciting information by asking questions and listening carefully (with eyes and mind, as well as ears) to all that is said. The goal of these Stage One activities, of course, is to gain understanding of the strength of the previously identified bargaining power elements.

Stage Two in negotiating is to confirm the negotiator's understanding of the other side's position, elicit additional information, and take or propose a course of action.

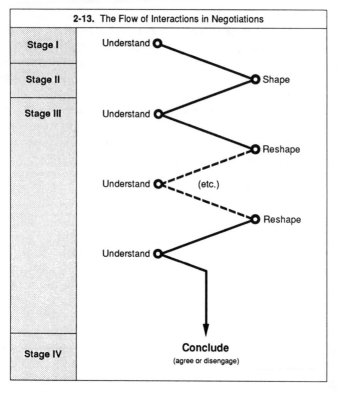

2-13. The Flow of Interactions in Negotiations

Stage I — Understand

Stage II — Shape

Stage III — Understand

Reshape

Understand (etc.)

Reshape

Understand

Stage IV — **Conclude** (agree or disengage)

Stage Three in negotiations involves reviewing the progress in light of the goal, reassessing the information, reassuring the other side, and making adjustments in the course of action or the goal. The flow of such action normally does not progress directly from one stage to the next. Just as the navigator often must tack from side to side or order a change in course so as to make headway or avoid hazards, so, too, skilled negotiators often must adjust and readjust their understanding and position in order to progress toward desired resolutions. Therefore, as symbolically indicated below, the flow of the negotiating process normally resembles tacking vessels as negotiators move back and forth seeking to enhance their understanding of the elements, shaping or reshaping their course, and then moving to a new level of understanding leading to further corrections and refinements in the course.

Finally, Stage Four is the conclusion. It is the realization and confirmation that the destination has been achieved or the goal is to be abandoned.

Chapter 3

Choosing the Most Effective Strategy

A. Introduction

This chapter further demonstrates how the bargaining strength model enables a negotiator to make sound strategic decisions. To do this we examine the manner in which the negotiator's strategic choice respecting the bargaining strength elements affect bargaining results. In this connection, it is worth noting that because a negotiator has the possibility of altering the other side's perception of any one or a combination of eight variable elements, there is a mathematical potential of 255 possible combinations of strategic approaches to increasing bargaining strength by altering the other side's perceptions. For example, one strategy is to concentrate efforts on altering the other side's perception of the bargainer's OMON (Offer to Meet Other's Needs) and POP (Probability of Performance) while also altering the other side's perception of its own BAPA (Best Alternative to the Proposed Agreement). Another strategy is to concentrate efforts on altering the other side's perception of the bargainer's OMON and the other side's own AC (Accrued Costs) and BAPA, or other element. Actually, there is a total of 256 variations because, as discussed below, one strategy concentrates on persuading the other side that it is incapable of altering any of the initiator's bargaining strength perceptions.

B. The Strategic Alternatives for Modifying Perceptions

The discussion that follows does not attempt to characterize or analyze every possible strategy. Instead, it looks at the more commonly encountered and discussed bargaining styles in order to offer some observations about them. However, the value of the bargaining strength model is not limited to an analysis of the strengths and weaknesses of particular bargaining styles. More important, these diagrams serve as a tool for strategic planning and for assessing the strategic status of an ongoing negotiation.

Negotiators cannot be expected to plot each step of their conduct in formal analytical terms. It is unrealistic—most of us are incapable of operating in so disciplined a manner. Nevertheless, the bargainer who settles for more is one who periodically takes the time and makes the effort to assess what point has been reached and what steps to take next. It is at such moments that the bargaining strength model provides its greatest worth. For, at such times, the model provides both a framework for reviewing what has transpired and a checklist for considering what avenues remain unexplored.

Let us review, therefore, ways in which the bargaining strength model can be used in the negotiator's strategic planning. Keep in mind that the purpose of such planning is to guide the negotiator in determining where to apply his energies.

We begin by examining, once again, Paradigm 3 (See Chapter 2), which portrays the relative bargaining strength of two negotiating parties. Paradigm 3, on the next page, helps us recognize the differences among the three basic types of strategies which A may use to alter A's relative bargaining strength by modifying perceptions.

One strategy, which we will call Type I, is for side A to reshape its perception of its own bargaining strength. A negotiator who settles for more realizes that his bargaining conduct is shaped in part by his perception of his own bargaining strength. The more confident the negotiator is in having a strong bargaining position, the more likely he is to hold out for offers that maximize meeting his needs and the more reluctant he is to modify his offers in an effort to increase the attractiveness of his offer to the other side. If we analyze the Type I strategy in terms of the paradigm of relative bargaining strength, what is happening is that A, by reassessing and reshaping his perceptions (the bottom scale in the diagram), insulates himself against the other side's (B's) ability to alter those perceptions. Thus, side B cannot increase its bargaining strength (the right hand side of the scales in the diagram) relative to the initiator's (A's) bargaining strength.

Later in this chapter we examine the hard nut bargaining style, the style of the bargainer who is super-tough, who alters proposals only with the greatest reluctance. We will see that an approach that rigidly resists accommodating the other side can achieve very favorable results but also increases the likelihood of not reaching a settlement. Therefore, a party that seeks to maximize its gains

3-1. A's Relative Bargaining Strength = B's Perception of:

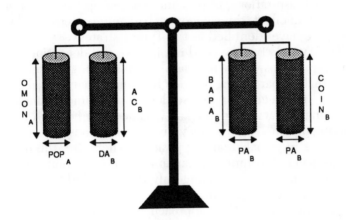

+
(Increase in A's Relative Bargaining Strength)

−
(Decrease in A's Relative Bargaining Strength)

PLUS
A's Perception of:

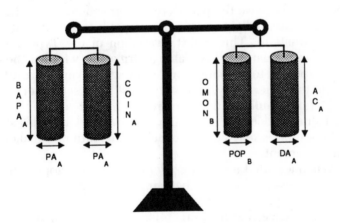

+
(Increase in A's Relative Bargaining Strength)

−
(Decrease in A's Relative Bargaining Strength)

OMON = Offer to Meet Other's Needs	PA = Predictive Accuracy
POP = Probability of Performance	BAPA = Best Alternative to the Proposed Agreement
AC = Accrued Costs	COIN = Cost of Impending Negotiations
DA = Data Accuracy	

with little regard for the risks of not achieving an agreement will try to bolster its own perception of its bargaining strength. Accordingly, some discussions of negotiating speak of the importance of having high aspirations, of psyching oneself up for the bargaining encounter. In effect, this category of bargaining advice is addressed to what we have identified as the Type I strategy.

The Type I strategy need not involve self-deception. A negotiator's aspirations will be increased by discovering information that reveals that his bargaining position is stronger than he had realized. However, the negotiator who settles for more understands that in negotiating, what you don't know sometimes helps you. If you probe deeply enough, you may discover previously unrecognized weaknesses in your bargaining position. Therefore, the negotiator who has decided to approach bargaining with maximum aspirations will direct efforts at expanding only that knowledge that is likely to give him encouragement.

But there is another approach to the Type I strategy. An alternative is for the negotiator to attempt to ensure that his perceptions approximate reality as closely as possible because: (a) there is reason to believe that little is available in the way of attractive alternatives to any proposed offer, or (b) because little time is available to seek alternative resolutions of the subject being negotiated, or (c) because the parties realize or should realize that their needs are essentially common or compatible (an integrative bargaining situation). This realist's variation of the Type I strategy requires investigating all available information, whether the results can be expected to encourage or discourage making more attractive offers to the other party. If a party must get a settlement, it must make its offer sufficiently attractive to the other side. Thus, the Type I strategy does not necessarily improve A's bargaining strength, but it does increase A's ability to achieve its ultimate goal of attaining a settlement.

When a skilled negotiator adopts the Type I approach of realistically assessing his own bargaining strength, he additionally enhances his prospects of success because the greater the negotiator's confidence that his perceptions closely approximate reality, the more difficult it is for the other side to alter those perceptions in a way that will increase its bargaining strength. Therefore, the two variations of the Type I strategy (seeking only those facts that increase the bargainer's aspirations or seeking as realistic an assessment of the situation as is possible) have a common characteristic of insulating the initiator against the other side's ability to alter the initiator's perceptions.

What we will call the Type II strategy involves increasing the initiator's (A's) relative bargaining strength by appropriately altering the other side's perceptions of the bargaining strength elements. If we look at the diagram for relative bargaining strength, we see that the upper scale represents A's bargaining strength paradigm and the lower scale represents B's bargaining strength paradigm. Thus, as shown in 3-2, A's relative bargaining strength is increased if B perceives A to have a higher Probability of Performance, or if B has an enhanced perception of the extent to which A's Offer will Meet B's Needs, or if B has a reduced perception of its Best Alternative to the Proposed Agreement, and so forth. Part C of this chapter, which describes typical bargaining styles, examines the Type II strategy in considerable detail.

The Type III strategy is the effort to increase relative bargaining strength by focusing on the other side's understanding of the initiator's (A's) bargaining strength perceptions. That is, the Type III strategy involves the awareness that side B will attempt to assess side A's sense of its bargaining strength and will respond not only to its own sense of strength or weakness but also to its perception of A's sense of strength or weakness. Accordingly, while our previous analysis explains B's bargaining strength in terms of A's perceptions, the Type III strategy is concerned, from A's perspective, with B's understanding of A's perceptions. Thus, if B thinks A perceives B as offering little to meet A's needs ($OMON_B$), in order to improve its bargaining strength B will try to persuade A to increase its perception of B's offer. One way to do that is to sweeten the pot—the very type of persuasion that A is seeking when A uses the Type III strategy. The essence of the Type III strategy, therefore, is to alter the other side's understanding of your own perceptions. By doing this successfully you alter its understanding of its own relative bargaining strength and, thereby, effectively increase your relative bargaining power.

There are two approaches to the Type III strategy. One is to help the other side understand why your perceptions of the various elements of its bargaining strength make its offer less attractive to you than it otherwise might expect. The other approach is to deceive the other side into thinking that you perceive its offer to be less attractive to you than it actually is.

There is a basic danger in the deceptive approach to the Type III strategy. If the other side detects that attempted deception, the initiator of the strategy loses credibility. Not only does the Type III strategy fail, but the loss of credibility also reduces the initiator's ability to employ the Type II strategy—a strategy that

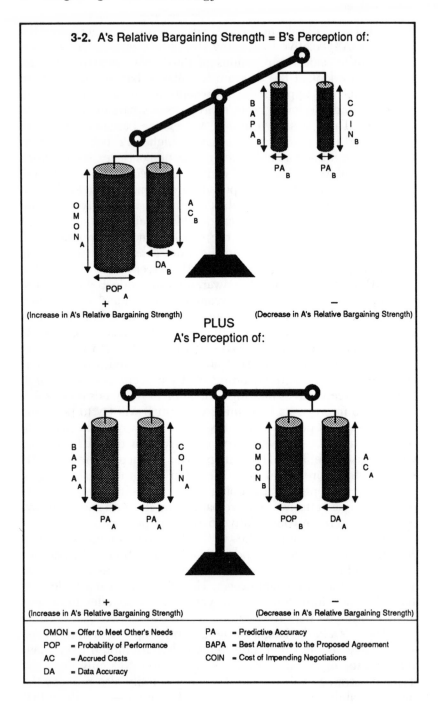

3-2. A's Relative Bargaining Strength = B's Perception of:

(Increase in A's Relative Bargaining Strength)

(Decrease in A's Relative Bargaining Strength)

PLUS
A's Perception of:

(Increase in A's Relative Bargaining Strength)

(Decrease in A's Relative Bargaining Strength)

OMON	= Offer to Meet Other's Needs	PA	= Predictive Accuracy
POP	= Probability of Performance	BAPA	= Best Alternative to the Proposed Agreement
AC	= Accrued Costs	COIN	= Cost of Impending Negotiations
DA	= Data Accuracy		

does not rely on deception. In addition, as noted in the introductory discussion of the POP element, having lost credibility, the other side is likely to have a diminished perception of the initiator's Probability of Performance. Looking at the bargaining strength diagram, we can see that this reduces the initiator's bargaining strength. Therefore, the Type III strategy, used by itself or in combination with the Types I and II strategies, is another means of settling for more. However, when the deceptive approach to this type of strategy is executed unsuccessfully it involves considerable risk of undermining the entire negotiating effort.

To summarize, then, the three basic types of strategies for modifying perceptions are Type I, which involves reshaping your assessment of your own bargaining strength; Type II, which involves efforts to increase your strength by altering the other side's perceptions; and Type III, which involves efforts to increase your strength by altering the other side's understanding of your perceptions. Within each of these three categories is the full range of alternatives respecting which elements of bargaining strength will receive the negotiator's attention.

Let us look at an illustration of the differences in the three basic types of strategic approaches to increasing bargaining strength by modifying perceptions. Suppose a buyer must obtain a supply of wing nuts. He, of course, must know the needed size, the acceptable quality requirements, the projected quantities needed for adequate inventory, and the like. These specifications are his needs. Not all of them are absolutes; there may be flexibility in some of them. Thus, in order to accurately assess how well a potential supplier's offer meets his needs, the buyer must be aware of what variations are acceptable. His engineering department, for example, may have identified the item using standards pulled from a catalog. Yet, the actual engineering needs for the particular use may allow for greater flexibility than those indicated by the catalog description of the wing nuts. If the buyer has not made the effort to find out from the engineers what the "real" requirements are, his perception of his needs may cause him to misconstrue his best alternative to a proposed agreement as well as incorrectly assess the worth to him of the prospective seller's offer. Therefore, the buyer may end up insisting on delivery of a more costly item than is necessary. Deciding to attempt to fully understand those real needs constitutes what we have described as the Type I strategy— the buyer is reshaping his own perceptions of the bargaining elements in order to be certain that they accurately reflect reality.

Looking just at our hypothetical buyer's need for wing nuts, suppose that the potential seller makes an offer that falls within the definition of what meets the buyer's needs but the offered items do not fit the catalog standards. The Type III strategy suggests that to the extent that the buyer views the transaction as an exchange negotiation (your gain is my loss), he should avoid revealing the extent to which the potential seller's proposal fully satisfies his needs. For example, he might express concern about the engineering or assembling adjustments that might be necessary or concern that there will be an increase in customer rejections. If the potential seller is persuaded that the buyer is not fully satisfied with the specifications of what has been offered, the potential seller may decide that it is necessary to sweeten the pot by lowering the price or offering more attractive delivery or payment terms.

How would what we have identified as the nondeceptive Type III strategy be used in our hypothetical effort to buy wing nuts? Concentrating only on the issue of the extent to which the offer meets the buyer's needs, we can see that if the seller is persuaded that in fact her wing nuts are not the best quality available and that the buyer realizes this, the potential seller's bargaining strength will be reduced and she is more likely to decide that it is necessary to do something else to improve her ability to meet the buyer's needs — such as lowering the price or offering more attractive delivery or payment terms.

Now, using the same hypothetical effort to buy wing nuts, let's see how the buyer might use the Type II strategy. If we continue to limit ourselves to the OMON element, the Type II strategy requires the buyer to enhance the seller's perception of the buyer's offer to meet the seller's needs. A simple way to do this is to offer a higher price; generally, however, that is not a good route to settling for more. Rather, the negotiator who settles for more recognizes that the seller likely has other needs that might be less costly to meet. For example, the buyer might call the seller's attention to the possibility that the increased level of production required to meet the buyer's order will reduce the marginal cost of production and thereby enable the seller to operate at a higher profit margin. Or, the buyer might offer to list the seller in trade publications as one of his suppliers and thereby improve the trade stature of the product. As can be seen in the diagram of relative bargaining strength, set out as 3-3, both of these suggestions are designed to increase the seller's (B's) perception of the value of the buyer's (A's) offer to meet the seller's needs. If successful, there-

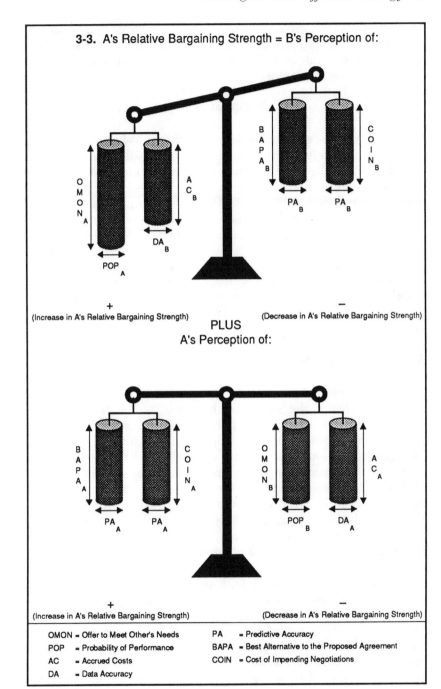

3-3. A's Relative Bargaining Strength = B's Perception of:

+
(Increase in A's Relative Bargaining Strength)

−
(Decrease in A's Relative Bargaining Strength)

PLUS

A's Perception of:

+
(Increase in A's Relative Bargaining Strength)

−
(Decrease in A's Relative Bargaining Strength)

OMON	= Offer to Meet Other's Needs	PA	= Predictive Accuracy
POP	= Probability of Performance	BAPA	= Best Alternative to the Proposed Agreement
AC	= Accrued Costs	COIN	= Cost of Impending Negotiations
DA	= Data Accuracy		

fore, they will improve the buyer's relative bargaining strength. Of course, if the buyer successfully executes tactics to carry out all three types of strategies, the buyer's relative bargaining strength will be that much greater.

C. Bargaining Style

Successful negotiators have many styles. What we call negotiating style largely represents a conscious or subconscious choice of strategy for altering the other side's perceptions. A negotiator need not adhere to a single style for all transactions nor even for the full course of a single transaction. Accordingly, the negotiator who settles for more should not be wed to one bargaining style but rather should be prepared to adjust his style to meet his goals.

To improve bargaining effectiveness a negotiator should become familiar with a variety of the more common negotiating styles and understand how they relate to the elements of bargaining power. This provides insight into the strategic use of bargaining power and offers guidance in selecting the bargaining style most appropriate to any particular occasion.

1. The Hard Nut Negotiator

A style often encountered in negotiating is the Hard Nut approach. This is the super-tough stance, which the negotiator modifies only with the greatest reluctance—if at all. In terms of the previously described model of bargaining strength, the Hard Nut negotiator emphasizes what can be called the negative elements in the bargaining power paradigm. These elements are the BAPA (Best Alternative to the Proposed Agreement), PA (Predictive Ability) and COIN (Cost of Impending Negotiation), the elements on the right hand or minus half of the bargaining strength diagram. Illustrated in 3-4 is party A's successful execution of the Hard Nut bargaining style as reflected by appropriate changes using the bargaining strength paradigm.

As an example of this style, suppose Adam has a piece of land on the edge of town that Betty is interested in acquiring. Assume, also, that Adam has a Hard Nut style of bargaining. One way Adam might demonstrate his bargaining style would be to name a price, not budge from it and, in addition, tell Betty that the price is going up $5,000 a week for the next five weeks.

The tactic Adam has employed, pursuant to his Hard Nut bargaining style, effectively increases his relative bargaining strength

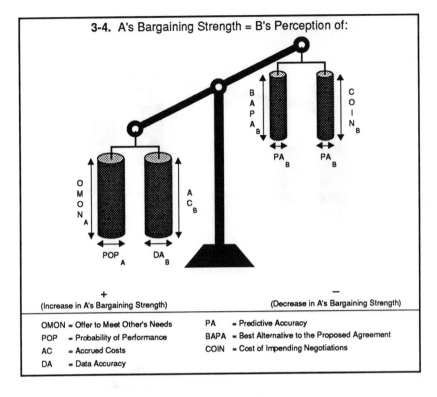

3-4. A's Bargaining Strength = B's Perception of:

+
(Increase in A's Bargaining Strength)

−
(Decrease in A's Bargaining Strength)

OMON = Offer to Meet Other's Needs	PA = Predictive Accuracy
POP = Probability of Performance	BAPA = Best Alternative to the Proposed Agreement
AC = Accrued Costs	COIN = Cost of Impending Negotiations
DA = Data Accuracy	

if Betty is persuaded that Adam means what he says. One reason for this is revealed by examining the paradigm of Adam's bargaining power. If in the bargaining strength diagrams presented in 3-5 we assume that Adam is party A and Betty is party B, Adam, as we can see, has conducted himself as though his own Best Alternative to the Proposed Agreement has a very large value. His conduct also conveys the assessment of Betty's Best Alternative to the Proposed Agreement as being of small value. Diagram 3-5 shows that if Adam thinks he has attractive alternatives to the proposed agreement, this reduces Betty's bargaining power. ($BAPA_A$ produces greater weight in the lower scale, the balance scale showing Betty's bargaining strength.) Similarly, if the approach Adam takes persuades Betty that there is little value in her alternatives to his proposal, Adam's bargaining strength is increased. ($BAPA_B$ produces less weight in the upper scale, the balance scale showing Adam's bargaining strength.)

Of course, Betty might decide that Adam is bluffing. If Betty waits a week in order to test the accuracy of Adam's statements and Adam then fails to raise his price, Adam's bargaining strength

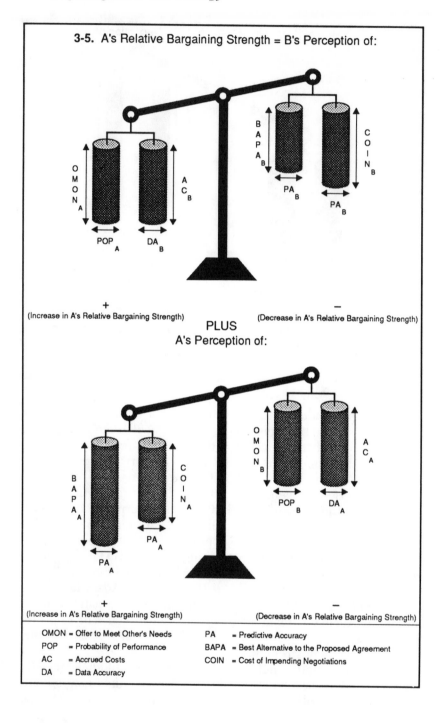

3-5. A's Relative Bargaining Strength = B's Perception of:

(Increase in A's Relative Bargaining Strength) — +
(Decrease in A's Relative Bargaining Strength) — −

PLUS
A's Perception of:

(Increase in A's Relative Bargaining Strength) — +
(Decrease in A's Relative Bargaining Strength) — −

OMON	= Offer to Meet Other's Needs	PA = Predictive Accuracy
POP	= Probability of Performance	BAPA = Best Alternative to the Proposed Agreement
AC	= Accrued Costs	COIN = Cost of Impending Negotiations
DA	= Data Accuracy	

is diminished because his conduct reveals that his perception of his BAPA is not as large as he had tried to bluff Betty into thinking it was. Moreover, having been caught bluffing, Adam will find it much more difficult in the future to persuade Betty to change her perceptions respecting any other aspect of their relative bargaining strength. On the other hand, if Adam does raise his price at the end of the week, this will make Adam's apparent perception of his BAPA more persuasive with the result that his bargaining power will be further enhanced.

The Hard Nut bargaining tactic that Adam used in the above illustration additionally suggests to Betty that she may have excessive confidence in her Predictive Accuracy (PA) respecting the value of her own Best Alternatives to the Proposed Agreement. Betty's alternatives probably include buying a parcel from someone else or holding on to her money and waiting for a better opportunity. Adam's prediction that the price is going up next week suggests to Betty that she may have misread the local real estate market and incorrectly projected its future. Thus, as the diagram of Adam's bargaining strength shows, if Adam succeeds in getting Betty to reduce her perception of the accuracy with which she has predicted alternatives to the proposed agreement, the impact will be to enhance Adam's bargaining power.

We can further examine the Hard Nut bargaining style using Paradigm 4 (see Chapter 2) to gain a better understanding of the impact of this approach on the prospects of reaching an agreement. Paradigm 4 shows each side's perception of the bargaining strength elements in relation to whether these elements constitute a situation conducive to reaching agreement. Therefore, in our example, we can see that if Adam succeeds in persuading Betty that he can afford to raise his price if Betty does not immediately accept Adam's proposal, it in effect means that Betty has been persuaded that her Best Alternative to the Proposed Agreement is worth less than she originally assumed. That is, Betty has a reduced perception of the size of her $BAPA_B$. In terms of the Paradigm 4 formula representing conditions favorable to a negotiated resolution as shown in 3-6, this results in Betty's balance scale (the lower scale in the diagram) being weighted more in the direction of accepting the proposal.

On the other hand, if Adam's Hard Nut approach induces Betty to respond in kind (e.g., "my offer goes down \$1,000 for every day you delay in accepting it"), then instead of having the effect of reducing Betty's $BAPA_B$, it increases Adam's $COIN_A$ (Cost of Impending Negotiations), reduces the future value of Betty's

3-6. Conditions Conducive to Settlement = A's Perception of:

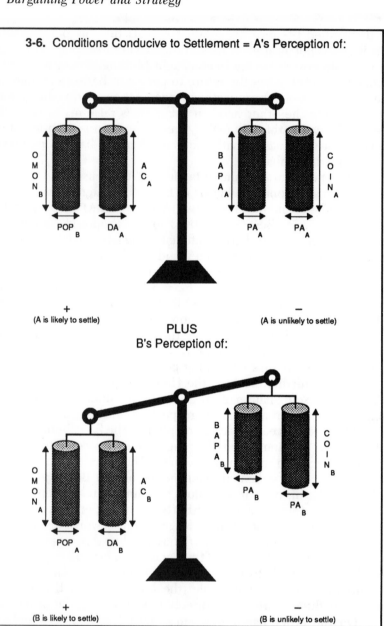

OMON = Offer to Meet Other's Needs   PA = Predictive Accuracy
POP = Probability of Performance   BAPA = Best Alternative to the Proposed Agreement
AC = Accrued Costs   COIN = Cost of Impending Negotiations
DA = Data Accuracy

offer to meet Adam's needs ($OMON_B$), and takes the parties further away from the conditions for settlement.

Moreover, to settle for more, a negotiator must weigh the emotional level of the impact of a Hard Nut bargaining strategy. Such an approach raises the level of stress in the parties' interaction. The classic stress syndrome is a response of flight or fight. The Hard Nut counterproposal is an example of a fight response to the increased stress whereas giving in to the implications of Adam's Hard Nut proposal is an example of a flight response. However, there is an alternative stress response and that is to modify one's perceptions so as to rationalize walking away from the stressful situation. Betty could do this either by persuading herself that she does not find Adam's property very desirable after all (decreasing Betty's perception of the potential of Adam's offer meeting her needs), or by persuading herself that the alternatives to a settlement with Adam are more attractive than she originally thought (increasing Betty's perception of her BAPA). In either event, such a response to the stress created by Adam's negotiating style would reduce the prospects of a settlement.

Additionally, it is worth noting that if, as we have suggested, the essential characteristic of Hard Nut bargaining is emphasis upon the negative side of the bargaining strength paradigm, then there are seven combinations of ways this can be accomplished in terms of the choice of bargaining strength elements the initiator might attempt to alter in relation to the other side's perceptions that affect the initiator's bargaining strength. Hence, the Hard Nut negotiator A can attempt to alter side B's perception of:

1. its PA
2. its BAPA
3. its COIN
4. its PA and BAPA
5. its PA and COIN
6. its BAPA and COIN
7. its PA, BAPA and COIN

In summary, therefore, using the paradigms of bargaining strength and the model for determining whether bargaining conditions favor an agreement, we see that there are a number of ways to press one's position in the style of Hard Nut bargaining and that the technique can lead promptly to a successful conclusion for the party who takes that approach. However, it also poses increased danger that there will be no deal.

2. The Nice Guy Negotiator

The opposite of the Hard Nut negotiator is the bargainer who concentrates on making the other side feel happy about what has been proposed. Just as the Hard Nut negotiator typically follows a strategy that in effect emphasizes only the minus half of the bargaining strength paradigm, the Nice Guy negotiator typically emphasizes only the plus side of the model—the POP, OMON, DA, and AC. Thus, if party A uses the Nice Guy style, its potential to increase its bargaining strength by altering side B's perceptions are reflected in bargaining strength diagram 3-7.

For example, once again suppose that Betty is interested in purchasing a parcel of land from Adam. This time, however, assume that Adam has a Nice Guy style of negotiating. Accordingly, as an extra inducement to accept his offer, Adam might propose to provide Betty with a landscape architect's plans he had drawn for the parcel. Or, he may offer to vacate the premises early so that Betty can repaint the interior before moving in. In this instance, the

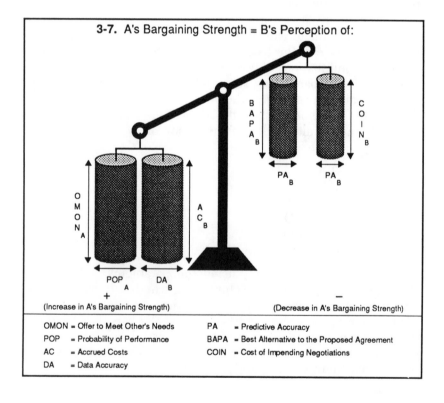

3-7. A's Bargaining Strength = B's Perception of:

OMON = Offer to Meet Other's Needs	PA = Predictive Accuracy
POP = Probability of Performance	BAPA = Best Alternative to the Proposed Agreement
AC = Accrued Costs	COIN = Cost of Impending Negotiations
DA = Data Accuracy	

paradigm of Adam's bargaining power shows that Adam is attempting to enhance his bargaining strength by increasing Betty's perception of the value of Adam's offer to meet Betty's needs ($OMON_A$).

Nice Guy efforts to alter the other side's perceptions can focus on any one of, or a combination of, the four positive elements of bargaining strength. Therefore, as with the Hard Nut approach, this offers several possible combinations of execution strategies to alter the other's perceptions of the initiator's bargaining strength. It is important to note that some of these strategies are likely to be much more costly than others. Thus, playing Nice Guy by increasing the other side's perception of the value of the offer to meet the respondent's physical or fiscal needs ($OMON_A$ in the previous diagram), is likely to be more costly—unless the needs are compatible or common with those of the one offering the bargain. (For example, if Adam plans to move out early anyway.) Playing Nice Guy by increasing the other side's perceptions of the offer's value in meeting the respondent's emotional needs, on the other hand, usually involves little or no cost. In addition, it is often possible for Nice Guy efforts to concentrate solely on increasing the respondent's perception of the initiator's Probability of Performance (POP_A) and of the respondent's own Accrued Cost (AC_B) of participating in the negotiation. These efforts, too, need not be costly to the initiator.

To put it another way, Nice Guys need not finish last. It is possible to take a Nice Guy approach to negotiating without giving away the store. But to do so successfully, the negotiator must realize which bargaining strength elements deserve attention and which pose a danger of a less than optimal result.

3. Building Block

The negotiating style that we will call Building Block is the approach of dealing with easy issues first. The goal is to establish the ability to come to terms on at least some matters in order to form a basis for gaining mutual respect and a constructive working relationship. This style is appropriate for use by negotiators who approach the bargaining table either as suspicious strangers, as long-term antagonists, or as parties seeking to avoid sharing confidential information unless an agreement that preserves those confidences is almost certain.

One illustration of this style is the typical scenario followed when hiring someone to work at a professional or executive level.

Usually, before the first meeting each side has gathered considerable information to determine whether the other is likely to meet its needs. The potential employer normally has received a resume detailing the job candidate's education and work experience and checked with references; the candidate likely has gathered information about the company's or firm's operating policies, status in the industry or profession, and the like. When the parties finally meet, the initial discussions are occupied not with exchanging proposals, but with trying to assess the respective personalities, expectations, ambitions, and idiosyncrasies. Meals might be taken together, social events attended, and eventually, if things seem to be going smoothly, some proposals may be exchanged—often beginning with an overview of benefit policies. Eventually, if there is a mutual perception that a long-term relationship is feasible, they may finally begin discussing the details of compensation.

Another example of Building Block is the process of deescalation often followed in international relations. Thus, when nations are at war, the first step toward peace is a truce followed by a pullback from battle lines. If that situation stabilizes, the parties may then attempt to discuss a more permanent disengagement from hostilities and adjustments in the conflicting interests that provoked armed conflict.

Looking again at the bargaining power paradigms, we can see that the emphasis in the Building Block style is upon strengthening each side's sense of the other's POP and reducing each side's COIN. That is, the Building Block approach provides an opportunity for each side to demonstrate its willingness to resolve issues through negotiation. If the parties are responsive to that opportunity, an atmosphere of trust may develop with the result that each will perceive a greater likelihood that the other will perform what it promises. At the same time, by demonstrating its willingness to resolve issues through negotiations, each side reduces the other's fear that the time, effort, and expenses of continued negotiations will be wasted. Hence, the cost of impending negotiations looms as less of an obstacle.

From diagram 3-8 we can readily see that the Building Block approach makes little sense if the parties come to the bargaining table with a favorable perception of their respective probabilities of performance. Similarly, analyzing the strategy with the guidance of Paradigm 4 (see Chapter 2), the model showing the power conditions favoring a negotiated resolution, we can also see that this strategy is undesirable if the prospective OMON is unknown or is

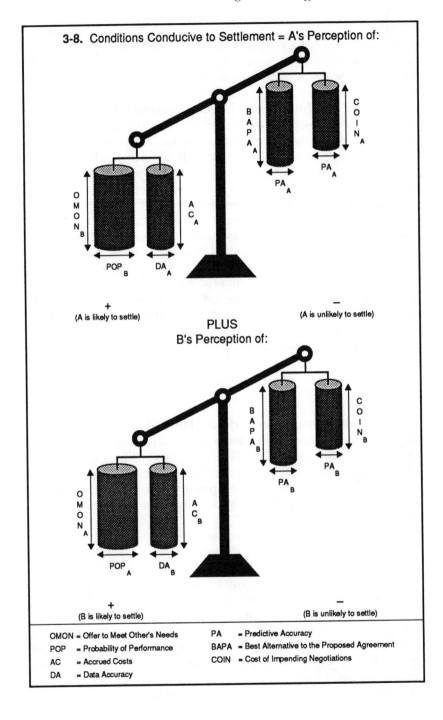

3-8. Conditions Conducive to Settlement = A's Perception of:

+ (A is likely to settle)

− (A is unlikely to settle)

PLUS
B's Perception of:

+ (B is likely to settle)

− (B is unlikely to settle)

OMON	= Offer to Meet Other's Needs	PA = Predictive Accuracy
POP	= Probability of Performance	BAPA = Best Alternative to the Proposed Agreement
AC	= Accrued Costs	COIN = Cost of Impending Negotiations
DA	= Data Accuracy	

known to be small. In the latter case, the effort to build up the POP likely will increase the other side's perception of its cost of impending negotiation (there are still all of the core issues to be negotiated) without providing an OMON adequate to produce a likelihood of settlement.

Finally, the Building Block style requires reciprocation by the other side. Both parties must be willing to expend their early efforts trying to resolve some easy issues. Thus, if it is to succeed, the initiator of this approach must persuade the other side to alter its negotiating style so as to give the parties an opportunity to demonstrate their ability to resolve their differences and operate with mutual trust.

In a sense, Building Block is a courtship strategy. Reassurance and trial runs provide an opportunity to reassess mutual perceptions and the prospects for mutual benefit. Thus, it has proven to be a successful bargaining style in international negotiations among unfriendly nations, in domestic relations disputes, and in rehabilitating other shattered relationships such as among business partners. Often, for this bargaining strategy to succeed, it helps if a mediating party is available to encourage the experiment and provide credibility to each party's representations.

4. Tough Issues First (TIF)

This is the counterpart to the Building Block style. The Tough Issues First approach (TIF) seeks to quickly determine whether there is a likelihood that a settlement is attainable. This approach places great weight on reducing the costs of negotiating—both the AC and the COIN—as well as promptly determining the extent of the parties' mutual ability and willingness to meet each other's needs.

For example, suppose a general contractor for a construction site on which the work has begun discovers that the electrical subcontractor has died and there is no one to run the business. Any significant delay in bringing a new electrical subcontractor on the job will throw the whole project off schedule. The general contractor knows a number of electrical contractors who can do the job, but the general contractor has two primary needs. First, get the electrical work started promptly; second, get it done at something close to the planned price. Since anyone in the business is almost certain to know that the deceased subcontractor had the job and that as a result of his death the general contractor is in a bind to find someone quickly, there is no purpose in trying to hide the fact that a premium will be paid, if necessary, to get a subcontractor on the job immediately. Hence, the Tough Issues First style is an appropriate choice for the general contractor. Issue number one—what assurance can you give me that you will be able to have some electricians on the job before the week is out? If the answer to that question is satisfactory, the second question is—will you do the work for the previously negotiated price? If the answer is "no," the next question is—how much more? Of course, before reaching that last question, the general contractor will want to point out that the subcontractor has needs to be met other than just a large profit on this job (such as future contracts with the general contractor). In other words, by helping the subcontractor to take a more expansive perspective of its needs, the general contractor increases its opportunity to meet the subcontractor's needs without having to pay an excessive price. The point is, however, that the general contractor must deal with the tough issues first so that it can quickly turn to other potential subcontractors if it appears that the one it is dealing with is going to try to take undue advantage of the situation or is unable to meet the job schedule.

Analyzing the nature of this strategy in terms of Paradigm 4 showing the conditions conducive to settlement, its use makes a great deal of sense if the parties come to the bargaining table with little understanding of their respective abilities to meet each other's needs or if the costs of negotiating can be expected to become significant. This is shown in 3-9. However, the Tough Issues First approach makes little sense if each sides's ability to meet the other's needs is known to be strong from the start but they do not have an established relationship or known favorable reputations. It is especially inappropriate if, in addition, the costs of negotiation are not expected to be significant and each side lacks attractive alternatives to agreement with the other.

As noted, the Tough Issues First bargaining style in effect seeks to keep the costs of bargaining low. However, if the tough issues are not promptly resolved, the strategy can raise uncertainties as to whether the bargaining proposals will ever meet the other's needs. As a consequence, the parties' perceptions of the prospects of reaching agreement may diminish prematurely with the result that there will be a deadlock before all potential solutions have been discovered and explored.

Another characteristic of the Tough Issues First bargaining style is that its primary focus is upon the bargaining agenda. Unless

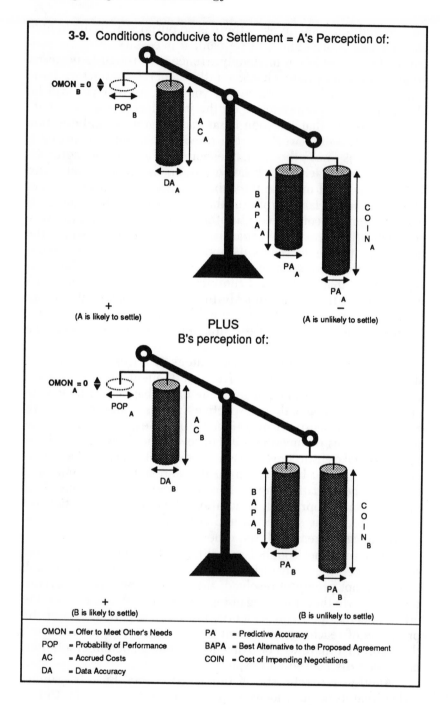

3-9. Conditions Conducive to Settlement = A's Perception of:

+
(A is likely to settle)

PLUS
B's perception of:

(A is unlikely to settle)

+
(B is likely to settle)

(B is unlikely to settle)

OMON = Offer to Meet Other's Needs	PA = Predictive Accuracy
POP = Probability of Performance	BAPA = Best Alternative to the Proposed Agreement
AC = Accrued Costs	COIN = Cost of Impending Negotiations
DA = Data Accuracy	

the other side accepts a Tough Issues First agenda, there is risk of a deadlock over the agenda issue without having an opportunity to explore the prospects of a mutual accommodation regarding the underlying substantive matters.

5. Best Offer First (BOF)

The Best Offer First, or priced as marked, bargaining style, like the Tough Issues First style, is designed to minimize the costs of negotiating. However, it does this by attempting to convince the other side that it cannot alter the initiator's perceptions. This is done by taking a wholly rigid bargaining position—making an offer and doing everything to demonstrate to the other side that nothing said or done in negotiations will alter that offer. Thus, a Best Offer First negotiator, by insisting that he will put forward one offer only, emphasizes the perception element in the bargaining strength equation.

For example, suppose a coin collector is at an antique fair during her lunch break and spots a rare coin that would make a nice addition to her collection. After inspecting the coin she asks the price, hoping that the seller may not be aware of its true value. The seller's price, $120, though not outrageous, is higher than our collector would like to pay. She then explains to the seller: "I am on my lunch break and don't have time to bargain. The coin is worth $85 to me and that is all I am willing to pay. Will you accept?" If the seller declines, the collector responds: "Thank you for considering my offer. I'll be looking in some other booths for a few minutes and will come back by here on my way out in case you change your mind and decide to accept my offer." She then leaves and later passes by. She has preserved her opportunity to spot some other bargains and, assuming that the offered price was reasonable, still has a good prospect of purchasing the coin on her way out for the offered price—or just a few dollars more.

The Best Offer First style is often used in situations in which the party making the offer has reason to assume that the other side perceives that few, if any, other proposals (the Best Alternative to the Proposed Agreement) are likely to be received. Thus, this style is often used by buyers in the closing hours of a trade exhibit at which activity has been slow.

Because it assumes that there is nothing the other side can say or do that could alter the initiator's perceptions, Best Offer First can be characterized as an arrogant bargaining style. In a sense it is not bargaining at all but rather an ultimatum demanding that the other side accede to the initiator's unilateral action. Such negotiating conduct often generates resentment and substantial resistance; it is considered by many to violate mores of acceptable business or social interaction. But, while our society generally frowns upon arrogant conduct, at times the Best Offer First bargaining style proves successful. Sometimes the self-assurance, the certainty and firmness with which the initiator sticks to the first and only proposal shakes the other side's sense of the Predictive Accuracy (PA) of its Best Alternative to the Proposed Agreement (BAPA). Moreover, if the initiator uses tactics designed to placate the other side's ego, such as giving the other side a sense of participation in shaping the Best Offer First proposal, or if the initiator in a quiet nonthreatening manner demonstrates the soundness, reasonableness, and attractiveness of the offer, or the need to immediately get to the bottom line, it is less likely to be perceived as an ultimatum and is more likely to be accepted as a thoroughly considered, equitable proposal.

Best Offer First bargaining, unlike some other bargaining styles such as Building Block and TIF, is not dependent upon a reciprocal approach by the other side. However, similar to the Hard Nut approach, it is likely to lead quickly to a deadlock if the other side adopts the same bargaining style. Moreover, if the other side's perceptions of the value of the offer are significantly different from the initiator's, or if the other side has good reason to place a high value on its ability to accurately predict its BAPA and COIN, the initiator can anticipate encountering considerable difficulty in altering the other side's perceptions. Thus, unless the other side is prepared to accede to the unilateral action of the Best Offer First negotiator, the approach is unlikely to lead to a settlement.

6. Give and Take (G&T)

The Give and Take negotiating style, in contrast with Best Offer First bargaining, implicitly acknowledges that the bargainer does not have perfect knowledge respecting the variable elements affecting the transaction under consideration. It also acknowledges that the transaction involves at least some exchange (or distribution) interests concerning which a compromise will have to be reached or some integrated elements regarding which an optimal solution must be developed through mutual efforts.

Give and Take negotiating is the style of the bazaar and the flea market. Thus, in the previous example involving the rare coin collector, a typical Give and Take bargaining style response to the seller's offer would have been to protest that there must be a mistake, $120 must be the price for some other coin, and offer $60. When the seller, after proclaiming the fine condition and rare quality of the coin, counters the offer with $110, the collector might point out a flaw in the coin's condition but suggest that out of sheer generosity she is willing to pay $65. After two or three more offers and counteroffers either agreement will be reached or the parties will realize that they are deadlocked.

Some people have cultural or subcultural values that cause them to prefer this style, while the background of others conditions them to think there is something undignified or unsavory about this sort of bargaining. Indeed, negotiators tend to engage in Give and Take bargaining with less pretense than is used in some other styles of bargaining. Probably, there is less pretense because the parties implicitly acknowledge that they do not have a firm idea of what is a reasonable solution. But, acknowledgement of limited information is not of itself undignified and the Give and Take style is appropriate in many negotiating situations. Thus, cultural values that inhibit a negotiator from engaging in this style of bargaining may reduce the negotiator's potential effectiveness in dealing with some types of bargaining situations.

In adopting the Give and Take approach it is essential to discover what accommodations might be available to the parties and to gain a better understanding of how those potential accommodations stack up against the Best Alternative to the Proposed Agreement. Therefore, using our paradigms of bargaining strength, we find that the Give and Take negotiating style involves giving special emphasis to the OMON (Offer to Meet the Other's Needs) and BAPA (Best Alternative to the Proposed Agreement) elements.

The Give and Take negotiating style is intended to be one of reciprocation. Each side is expected to do some giving as well as some taking in an attempt to find a mutually satisfactory resolution. Without reciprocation, the strategy evolves into the Nice Guy style. Although, as previously discussed, a Nice Guy strategy can be a means of settling for more, it will not achieve that result if the element receiving attention is solely the initiator's offer to meet the other's needs. Thus, for the Give and Take bargaining style to succeed, the initiator must insist upon reciprocation.

7. Honey and Vinegar

Previously it was noted that when looking at Paradigm 4, the diagram of the conditions that are conducive to settlement, the left hand side of the diagram is the plus part, the elements that entice the negotiator to accept a settlement. In contrast, the right hand side of the diagram is the minus half, the elements that dissuade the negotiator from reaching a settlement. In a study of the decision making process involved in collective bargaining, *Strategy and Collective Bargaining Negotiation*,[1] Carl M. Stevens contends that bargaining strategies that emphasize the affirmative—the potential benefits of settlement—reduce the stress level of the negotiators. However, those strategies that emphasize the negative—the undesirable consequences of failing to reach agreement—increase the parties' stress level.

Stevens suggests that changes in a negotiator's stress level have an important impact upon the negotiator's decision making behavior. Thus, increasing a negotiator's stress can lead to the previously discussed "fight or flight" response. As already noted, one form of flight from bargaining stress is to accept the other side's proposal and thereby eliminate the stressful situation. A different form of flight is to disengage from the transaction; that is, to declare no deal by seeking some other way to meet the negotiator's needs. The alternative response of fight likely means discontinuing any efforts to be accommodating and demanding, instead, that any further concessions must come from the other side. Although Stevens' analysis suggests that emphasizing the negative poses risks, he points out that it also holds out the prospect of an accelerated resolution—a prompt decision from the other party, whether favorable or unfavorable.

Emphasizing the affirmative, Stevens further explains, can also affect the bargainer's stress level by reducing the level of stress. This tends to keep the other side at the bargaining table, though it also reduces the prospect of a prompt decision to settle or disengage.

Based upon his analysis, Stevens counsels that maximum gains can be attained by using a strategy that gives comparable emphasis to both the affirmative and negative aspects of the negotiation. For obvious reasons, such a strategy can be called the Honey and Vinegar style of bargaining. If we look at the impact of the Honey and Vinegar style in terms of the bargaining strength paradigm, we can readily see confirmation of Stevens' contention that this

---

[1]Greenwood Press (1978).

approach should maximize the negotiator's results. For example, suppose that a company is negotiating a new collective bargaining agreement with the labor organization that represents its employees. Both sides come to the bargaining table with proposed changes in the terms and conditions of employment. A way for the company to use the Honey and Vinegar approach would be to accompany each partial concession to a union demand for increased benefits (an increase in the union's perception of the value of the company's offer to meet the employees' needs) with a reminder that unemployment rates are high and striking workers cannot collect unemployment benefits (thereby hoping to reduce the union's perception of the value of the employees' best alternative to the proposed agreement). This is shown in diagram 3-10.

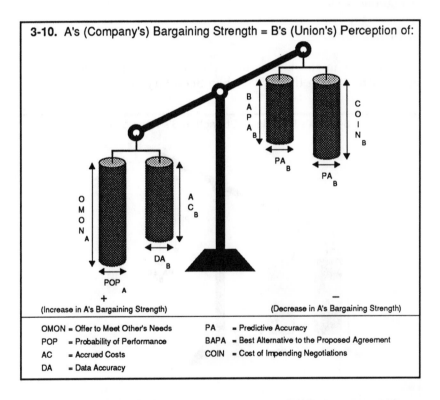

3-10. A's (Company's) Bargaining Strength = B's (Union's) Perception of:

(Increase in A's Bargaining Strength)   (Decrease in A's Bargaining Strength)

OMON	= Offer to Meet Other's Needs	PA	= Predictive Accuracy
POP	= Probability of Performance	BAPA	= Best Alternative to the Proposed Agreement
AC	= Accrued Costs	COIN	= Cost of Impending Negotiations
DA	= Data Accuracy		

Although the above depiction of the Honey and Vinegar bargaining style indicates emphasis on two elements that are affected by the negotiator's perceptions, conceptually the same label should be applied any time there is a balance of emphasis upon a right hand and a left hand element or elements in Paradigm 4 (see

Chapter 2), the diagram showing the conditions conducive to settlement. For example, a negotiator who presses for a settlement by bolstering the other's perception of his Probability of Performance (POP) is using a Honey and Vinegar approach if he combines that effort with demonstrating to the other side that its assumptions respecting its alternatives to the proposed agreement are based on unreliable data (reduced Predictive Accuracy).

Defining the Honey and Vinegar bargaining style as a balance of accentuation of affirmative and negative elements in the bargaining strength model, we find that this strategic approach has considerable flexibility. It presents a potential of many different variations in the balanced combination of elements. Interestingly, one of these variations is the previously discussed Building Block bargaining style.

8. Brinksmanship

Interest in the nature of bargaining strategy gained considerable attention in the 1950s when Secretary of State John Foster

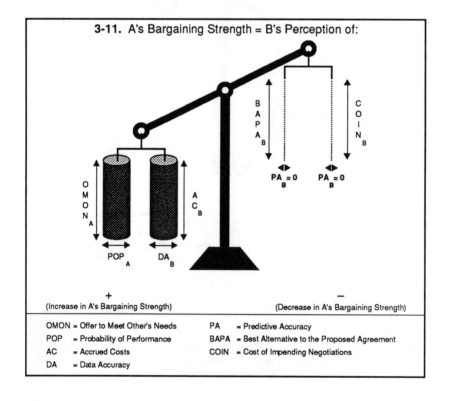

3-11. A's Bargaining Strength = B's Perception of:

OMON = Offer to Meet Other's Needs	PA = Predictive Accuracy
POP = Probability of Performance	BAPA = Best Alternative to the Proposed Agreement
AC = Accrued Costs	COIN = Cost of Impending Negotiations
DA = Data Accuracy	

Dulles portrayed his own bargaining style as one of Brinksmanship. Brinksmanship is a particular type of Hard Nut approach to bargaining. Thus, it places its emphasis upon altering the other side's perceptions respecting the negative side of the bargaining strength equation. As illustrated in diagram 3-11, in the case of Brinksmanship, the initiator attempts to reduce to zero the other side's sense of predictive accuracy respecting its BAPA and COIN. If the practitioner of the Brinksmanship approach succeeds, the other side becomes convinced that it has no choice but to accede to the Brinksman's offer. Dulles, for example, asserted that the only way to negotiate successfully with the Soviet Union was to lead them to the brink of nuclear war in support of our demands. He counted on the underlying rationality of the Soviets, and their acknowledgement that we were the superior military power, to cause them to back down rather than lead both sides over the precipice—a risk that Dulles' detractors thought was excessive and that accomplished little other than to accelerate Soviet armament improvements.

In more recent times, the Brinksmanship bargaining style of domestic and international terrorists has become all too familiar. The terrorist tries to create a situation in which no matter how unattractive his offer to meet your needs, there is no acceptable alternative to the proposed agreement. For example, a typical group of political terrorists might demand a $10 million contribution to their cause and the release of their imprisoned terrorist brethren. Their demand might be accompanied by a threat to blow up a commandeered planeload of civilians if their demand is not met by a specified time. To ensure against a rescue attempt—one alternative to the proposed agreement—they might attach explosives throughout the commandeered plane.

The terrorist, as with other Hard Nut negotiators, is counting on the stress of the situation resulting in a flight rather than a fight response. One counterstrategy, of course, is a one-upsmanship type of reverse terrorism. To illustrate, it is reported that in the mid-1980s one of the factions in Lebanon decided to impose pressure to get more overt support from the Soviet Union by kidnapping a couple of Soviet Embassy officials. A few hours later, a car stopped in front of a mosque that was a center of the faction's supporters. Two burly men opened the trunk of the car, ceremoniously pulled a large burlap bag from the vehicle, dumped it in the street, and drove off. Within a short time a crowd gathered around the bag, which had been opened. Inside were the crudely rearranged, cut-up portions of the body of one of the faction's lower echelon leaders.

A short time thereafter, the kidnapped Soviets were safely back at their Embassy—or so the story goes.

D. Bargaining Strength Model as a Guide for Controlling Information Flow

In addition to helping us understand the nature and characteristics of the alternative types of strategies, the bargaining strength model can help the negotiator make the strategic choice of what information should be shared with the other side. Many negotiators make the mistake of assuming that the less the other side knows the better off you are. This is wrong. Often in negotiation, the more the other side knows, the better off you are. Some information can help you; some can hurt you. The bargaining strength paradigm is a tool that provides guidance respecting what information should be shared readily with the other side and what information should be held in confidence. To examine this dimension, let us again look at the diagram of individual bargaining strength presented in 3-12.

The paradigm shows us that one way for A to increase its bargaining strength is to increase B's perception of A's probability of performance (POP). Thus, information demonstrating A's reliability, integrity, status, stability, and the like, should be readily shared by A. On the other hand, A clearly should avoid sharing any information that is likely to detract from B's good impressions of A's reliability. Looking at the next element, OMON, we can see that A should share information that is likely to make B realize that it has the type of needs that A is offering to satisfy. For example, if B was injured in an accident and A is the insurance company that represents the party being sued by B, A can increase its bargaining strength by educating B to the need for the type of rehabilitation training that A's medical consultants are prepared to provide.

The bargaining strength paradigm demonstrates that A should also share information that will increase B's awareness of the extent to which B has already expended time, energy, and funds in seeking a negotiated solution with A. Therefore, again assuming that A is the insurance company, A might want to expressly note the number of hours and amount of correspondence exchanged and observe that it would be satisfying if all of that effort could lead to a settlement.

Shifting, now, to the right hand side of the diagram showing A's bargaining strength, it is obvious that A should share any infor-

3-12. A's Bargaining Strength = B's Perception of:

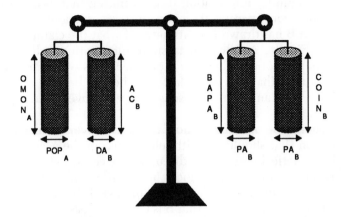

+
(Increase in A's Bargaining Strength)

—
(Decrease in A's Bargaining Strength)

B's Bargaining Strength = A's Perception of:

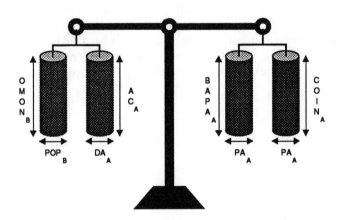

+
(Increase in B's Bargaining Strength)

—
(Decrease in B's Bargaining Strength)

OMON = Offer to Meet Other's Needs	PA = Predictive Accuracy
POP = Probability of Performance	BAPA = Best Alternative to the Proposed Agreement
AC = Accrued Costs	COIN = Cost of Impending Negotiations
DA = Data Accuracy	

mation that would indicate that B has an unfavorable BAPA—for example, a recent dismissal of the law suit or a low award by a jury in a similar case. Or, that B's sources of information are unreliable—for example, information demonstrating that local juries are much more conservative than are juries in sections of the state from which B has drawn his estimates of what the claim is "worth" in court. Finally, A will want to share information indicating that any further negotiating will be more costly, as would be the case if A announces that this is the last offer he will be able to make by telephone, and any further discussions will have to take place at A's office.

It should be obvious by now that the converse rules apply to information that should be withheld. Thus, in the accident insurance hypothetical case being discussed, A certainly will not want to draw attention to recent local jury verdicts if they have been generous to claimants similar to B, nor reveal that it relies on the same sources of information that B is using (increases B's confidence in B's Predictive Accuracy), nor note that the insurance commission has under consideration a regulation that, starting at the beginning of next year, will require companies to pay interest on all new claim settlements.

Thus, when assembling information, it is useful for a negotiator to assess which element of bargaining strength the data affects and whether its likely impact upon the other side's perceptions will be to increase or reduce the weight that will be attached to that element. In this way, sound judgments can be made respecting whether and when particular information should be shared.

Part II

Bargaining Tactics

Chapter 4

Transactional Analysis: A Foundation for Tactical Actions

The negotiator who settles for more must master the techniques of assessing and modifying human behavior. Such techniques enable a bargainer to alter the other side's perceptions regarding the previously discussed elements of bargaining strength (OMON, POP, AC, DA, PA, BAPA, COIN).

Managing human behavior is an ancient art. Insights into its mastery can be found in such diverse sources as the Bible's Book of Proverbs, Machiavelli's *The Prince*, much of Shakespeare's works and Ben Franklin's *Poor Richard's Almanac*. However, such collections of practical wisdom do not offer a clearly defined structure for tactical analysis or planning. They lack the convenience that scientific type models offer to guide the collection of information and the decision regarding the use of that information in each unique set of circumstances.

In recent decades, behavioral scientists have dedicated much effort and brilliance to designing models for analyzing and modifying human thought and behavior. Although their efforts have not matched the precision achieved by physicists and biologists in defining cause-effect relationships and predicting events, behavioral scientists have made impressive strides. They have developed models that enable practitioners to deal on the individual level with behavioral disorders and on the group level with such things as consumer and voting behavior. Their behavioral models are sufficiently successful so that the better practitioners are able to command high fees for their services. These same behavioral models have the potential of serving the negotiator who is determined to settle for more. One such model for understanding behavior is a system called Transactional Analysis, or TA.

Transactional Analysis is a school of psychotherapy derived from psychoanalysis. While that may sound a bit intimidating, a central purpose of TA is to describe human behavior in simple, clear, readily understandable, everyday language. Through such language, TA provides a means for analyzing the stimulus-response patterns of human interactions so as to enable people to better understand what they are doing when they interact with others and how they can change what they are doing if change is desired.

Transactional Analysis was much in fashion from the mid 1960s through the late 1970s. It was sufficiently popular so that some of its terminology—e.g., "different strokes for different folks"—became part of our everyday language. As so often happens with popular concepts, in time TA suffered from its own success. On one hand, some people became so fanatically attached to the concept that they treated it as a cure for all problems. Disappointments were inevitable. On the other hand, new generations of behavioralists viewed TA as the old orthodoxy, thus making it a target for the criticism of the ambitious. Still others never became comfortable with TA's lack of the mystique of a technical vocabulary or with its failure to use the symbols of higher mathematics and other trappings of the hard sciences. Nevertheless, those seeking practical tools for mastering the bargaining process will find that TA is a very useful technique, a tactical tool for achieving the goal of settling for more.

A. The Three Ego States That Structure Personality

The starting point for Transactional Analysis is the proposition that *human personality is composed of three ego states, which generate all human physical, emotional, and communication conduct.* One of these ego states is called the Parent. (The P is capitalized to distinguish this special use of the word from its normal usage.) The second basic ego state is called the Adult and the third is called the Child.

The Parent ego state (referred to simply as "the Parent") is the part of our thinking and emoting—our personality—that accepts certain assumptions and responsibilities as unquestionable truths. It is the Parent that directs us to place a fork to the left of a plate, it is the Parent that directs us to brush our teeth in the morning, it is the Parent that directs us to deal honestly with friends and associates.

There are two distinguishable parts of the Parent ego state. One is denoted as the Nurturing Parent, the other as the Critical Parent. The Nurturing Parent is that part of the personality that is sympathetic and offers protective love for others. It represents, for example, those ethical commands or natural instincts that direct parents to protect, feed, clothe, and educate their children; that reminds us to visit sick friends; or to help strangers in distress. The Critical Parent, in contrast, is that part of the personality that involves prejudice and moral imperatives and that seeks to repress all that conflicts with such prejudgments or unquestionable truths. For example, it is the Critical Parent dimension of personality that causes people to raise their children to be members of the parents' religious group. The Critical Parent, similarly, is the side of our personality that causes most of us to select particular modes of dress and to avoid using crude language in the presence of young children or members of an older generation.

There is obvious danger for the negotiator whose Nurturing Parent ego state is in control when formulating what fiscal and physical benefits to offer the other side. On the other hand, a negotiator's Nurturing Parent ego state is best equipped to meet the other party's emotional needs in a sincere and, therefore, convincing manner. The Critical Parent ego state can be given full rein if a negotiator has decided to employ one of the more competitive bargaining styles such as Tough Issues First, Best Offer First, or Brinksmanship. But in most other situations, the rigidity of the Critical Parent aspect of personality can be expected to interfere with effective strategic and tactical planning and the successful execution of bargaining skills.

The Adult ego state, in contrast with the Parent, is the organized, rational, objective part of our personality. It seeks relevant facts, gauges the reliability and adequacy of information, examines alternatives, and weighs the probable outcomes of prospective decisions. In a sense, the Adult functions like a computer. Clearly, to settle for more, one's Adult ego state should be in control when doing background preparation for bargaining, when making strategic and tactical choices, and when weighing alternative proposals in an integrative (problem solving) bargaining situation.

The Child ego state is the sensuous part of our personality. It feels pleasure and pain and acts spontaneously or impulsively as well as coyly. There are three components to the Child ego state. One is the Natural Child. This is the curious, impulsive, feeling, self-centered, affectionate, playful part of the structure of personality. The Natural Child can also be rebellious, fearful, or aggressive. The second component is the Adaptive Child—the unassertive, compliant, inhibited, cautious part of personality. The Adaptive Child seeks to please others, to get along, to gain acceptance, to survive. Finally, the third aspect of the Child ego state is the Little Professor. The Little Professor is the shrewd, intuitive, creative, fantasizing and improvising part of personality. For example, it is the Little Professor that responds trustingly to some people but with distrust toward others. While the Natural Child side of personality enjoys humor, the Little Professor side often is the creator of humor. It has been suggested that the Adaptive Child is the Parent quality of the Child ego state while the Little Professor is the Adult quality.

As with other ego states, the variations of the Child dimension of personality offer opportunities for exploitation by the bargainer who seeks to settle for more. Thus, the intuitive and creative qualities of the Little Professor ego state can aid in accomplishing such tasks as assessing the other party's sincerity and in developing alternative solutions for resolving integrative bargaining problems. The Natural Child ego state often provides the most effective means of satisfying the other side's emotional needs and of triggering changes (through humor, distraction, persuasive anger, etc.) that alter which ego state is in control of the other side's conduct. In contrast, the negotiator generally wants to avoid bargaining when in his Adaptive Child ego state because it is the submissive dimension of personality. Nevertheless, the negotiator's Adaptive Child ego state can play a constructive role in providing needed flexibility when seeking solutions to maximize mutual benefits in resolving integrative bargaining problems.

In abbreviated form, Transactional Analysis offers the following model to describe the structure of personality. The terminology is intended to describe the structure of personality but not to make value judgments. Each ego state has appropriate and valuable contributions to make to healthy human behavior. There are times, for example, when it is best for the Natural Child to be in control of the behavior of an adult—such as when making love, listening to music, or greeting your child who has just returned home from camp. At other times—such as when driving a car in heavy traffic— it may be best if the Critical Parent is in control. Similarly, as previously suggested, each ego state can operate constructively for the effective bargainer.

Transactional Analysis theory postulates that all individual personalities are a composite of Parent, Adult, and Child ego states

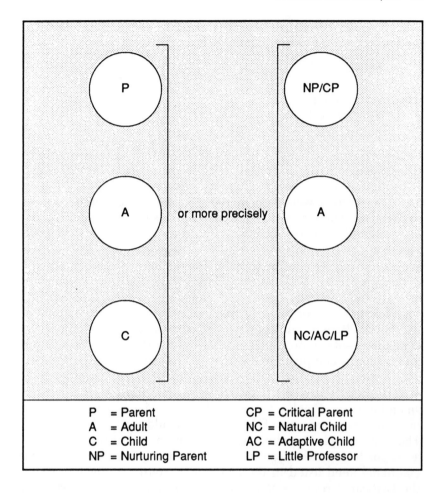

P	= Parent	CP	= Critical Parent
A	= Adult	NC	= Natural Child
C	= Child	AC	= Adaptive Child
NP	= Nurturing Parent	LP	= Little Professor

whatever a person's age. The particular character of each personality is shaped by the frequency with which the different ego states control that person's behavior. Thus, a person whose Adult is most often in control likely would be described as serious, humorless, even-tempered, fair, and efficient. A person whose Nurturing Parent is the dominant ego state probably would be described as generous, soft-hearted, emotional, and, perhaps, overbearing.

Settling for more is facilitated by understanding your own personality structure and that of the other side's bargaining agent. Recognizing what ego state dominates a personality enables a negotiator to better anticipate responses to planned tactics and to spot when reactions are uncharacteristic and, therefore, more likely to be a ploy designed to mask the party's true feelings.

Chapter 1 used the acronym SLAPS to summarize the five general categories of emotional needs.

S Security
L Love
A Amusement
P Personal achievement
S Status

Examining the TA model of personality reveals how those emotional need categories correlate with the previously described ego state dimensions of personality. Accordingly, the emotional need for Security is a reflection of the Adaptive Child dimension of personality. The emotional need for Love is encompassed by two ego states: the Nurturing Parent ego state reflects the protective aspect of Love while the Natural Child ego state reflects the passionate side of Love. Similarly, the emotional need for Amusement finds its source, as well, in the Natural Child aspect of personality whereas the emotional need for Personal Achievement is of a more complex nature. For some people that need is centered largely in the Critical Parent. Such people seek accomplishment with a sense of mission—of compulsion to prove their worth. In others the need for personal accomplishment is largely a reflection of their Adaptive Child. For this type of person, achievement is a means of gaining or retaining security, love, or meeting some other need—it is not an end in itself. Finally, there are those for whom personal accomplishment is an exercise of their Natural Child and Little Professor. These are people for whom accomplishment is but the payoff of a game for testing what can or cannot be done. The one remaining emotional need listed in the acronym is Status. Status fits within the Critical Parent's preference for order and rules. Status has a mirror image—embarrassment (sometimes called loss of face). Embarrassment occurs when a person perceives others as having discovered that he is not conforming to the rules acknowledged by his Critical Parent.

We will return to this comparison between the factors that comprise the Offer to Meet the Other's Needs element of bargaining strength and the ego state elements of the TA model. First, though, we need to complete our understanding of the Transactional Analysis model.

In order to put the TA model to work, we must develop our ability to determine which ego state is in control of a person's behavior at any given time and learn how to get someone to shift to a different controlling ego state. This is important because the second basic proposition of Transactional Analysis is as follows: *The ego state in command at a particular time governs the response to a stimulus*.

Determining which ego state is in control is greatly facilitated by the very descriptive nature of the terms used to label the different parts in the structure of personality. Thus, to determine whether one is in the Child ego state we ask whether that person's facial expression, posture, voice tone and volume, choice of words, and conduct are similar to the stereotypical characteristics of a child. When the Child is in control, posture is more likely to be relaxed and informal, the voice tone is more likely to be high pitched and animated, and the words are likely to be accompanied by giggles, laughter, sighs, whining, or the like. The voice volume in the Child ego state often is louder or softer than a normal conversational tone (e.g., boisterous or meek) and there is greater likelihood that the content will include mild obscenities, imperatives, exclamations, and simple rather than complex words and grammatical structures.

In contrast, the Parent ego state posture tends to be stiff, erect, and formal in the Critical Parent but forward leaning and open in the Nurturing Parent. Similarly, voice tone has a deeper pitch and is authoritative (and often is quite loud) in the Critical Parent but is softer, sympathetic in tone, and cajoling or loving in content in the Nurturing Parent. The Nurturing Parent uses words of encouragement and comfort and offers of help ("let me . . ., I'd be happy to . . ., wouldn't you like . . ."), whereas the Critical Parent uses imperatives and words of judgment or control ("you'd better . . ., don't . . ., I don't appreciate . . ., I'll not tolerate . . .").

In the Adult ego state facial expression generally is mild though serious (the Critical Parent is dead serious) and the voice tone is conversational, clear, and unaffected. The body posture tends to be moderately relaxed and word content is organized, explanatory, descriptive, or interrogatory.

The descriptive nature of the Parent-Adult-Child terminology used to define the TA model of personality facilitates not only recognition of which ego state is in control of the other person, but also which aspect of our own personality is in control at a given moment. It also enables the skilled negotiator to more cogently gauge the timing of particular tactical moves. For example, the negotiator who settles for more realizes that when the other party's

Nurturing Parent is in control, he is less likely to storm out of the bargaining session upon being asked to reopen a previously resolved term of agreement than he is when operating in the Critical Parent ego state. Similarly, a proposal to do something a particular way because it has been done that way in the past (precedent) is more likely to be accepted by an adversary whose Adaptive Child or Critical Parent is in control than by one who is in a Natural Child or Adult ego state. Therefore, in order to settle for more, the negotiator who has strong precedent on his side should make special efforts to encourage the other side to "turn on" his Adaptive Child or Critical Parent.

Of course, more difficult than ascertaining which ego state is controlling another person's conduct at a particular time is the problem of how to alter the controlling ego state—how to "hook" or "turn on" a particular ego state. Here, again, TA's terminology and definitions are helpful. If one wants to turn on the other side's Adult, it is useful to ask questions or state information, speak in a calm voice, and offer reasonable explanations for assertions—that is, to address one's communication to the other side's Adult. Similarly, to turn on the other side's Natural Child, it helps to tell a joke, smile, laugh, speak playfully, and the like.

The environment in which we interact also influences the ego state that is likely to control a party's behavior. For example, in recent years research has demonstrated that many people get depressed if they go for long periods without exposure to sunlight or full spectrum artificial light. In such a state, a person is less likely to operate from his or her Nurturing Parent or Little Professor ego states. On the other hand, going from a very brightly lit environment into a dimly lit atmosphere can have a momentary quieting effect. Hence, the uproar of interactions coming from conflicting Critical Parent ego states may be successfully modified to an Adult-Adult interaction by moving the discussion from a conference room's bright fluorescent lighting to a restaurant's more subdued atmosphere.

Of course, lighting is not the only environmental factor that may influence which ego state is in control. Colors of walls and furnishings, the shape of and materials used in furniture, and even the negative or positive ionization of the air all have been found to have their impact on behavior. Obviously, a person sitting in an uncomfortable position on a hard chair, at a corner of a twenty-foot ebony table facing a marble wall, is less likely to operate from the Nurturing Parent ego state than if seated in a plush, comfortable chair placed at the head of a six-foot oak table facing a pastoral scene.

Our ego state can be influenced not only by what surrounds our bodies but by what enters them as well. For a nonsmoker, inhaling the air in a smoke filled environment often creates discomforts that can distract one from an Adult ego state or constitute an irritant barrier to operating from the positive aspects of the Natural Child (good humored) or Nurturing Parent ego states. For a smoker, being nicotine deprived for an extended period can have the same impact. Alcohol tends to repress the Adult ego state. Taken in small amounts it is likely to assist positive aspects of the Natural Child ego state to take control of behavior; taken in large amounts it is likely to call up the Critical Parent or negative aspects of the Natural Child (aggressive) dimension of the drinker's personality. Some foods have similar, though usually less dramatic effects. Thus, the energizing effects of recent consumption of significant amounts of sugar or caffeine can be expected to have its impact, as well, on whether a person is more likely to engage in quiet reasoning or vigorous emoting.

Let us now return to the relationship between emotional needs (SLAPS) and the TA model so that we may further our understanding of how TA can be a practical tool in the hands of a negotiator who has mastered the skills of settling for more.

Our bargaining strength model reveals that offers that meet the other side's emotional needs increase the offeror's bargaining power. Transactional Analysis provides a means of identifying when conduct is being predominantly influenced by the emotional dimensions of personality—the Parent and Child ego states. It also suggests a linkage between particular emotional needs and particular ego states. Finally, TA alerts us to the fact that if we are to successfully alter perceptions respecting emotional needs, we either must time our efforts to correspond with the appropriate ego state that is in control or must find a way to "turn on" the appropriate ego state prior to making the particular emotional appeal.

Before illustrating this last point, it should be noted that these observations are as important to guiding the defensive efforts of the negotiator (keeping one's own perceptions in line with functional reality—Type I strategy) as they are to guiding the negotiator's tactical efforts to alter the other side's perceptions—Type II strategy.

An illustration of the use of TA in altering perceptions of how well a proposal meets the bargainer's emotional needs is the situation of a new business seeking a loan from a local bank. The bank, of course, has functional needs for income and for the eventual return of the loaned principal. But the bank is an artificial entity; its decisions are made by the operating officers. Unlike the abstract entity, the operating officials have emotional as well as functional needs. By reviewing those emotional needs, the prospective borrower can better assess how to frame its proposal. Using the acronym SLAPS (Security, Love, Amusement, Personal achievement, Status) as a guide, the borrower's bargaining representative is likely to conclude that there is no way to meet the Status needs of the officers—unless it can find a way to offer public commendation to the bankers' progressiveness and leadership in encouraging expansion of the local economy. Love is another emotional need that our hypothetical borrower's bargaining representative is likely to discard—unless it can turn on the bank officers' Nurturing Parent to help this promising venture through the inevitable rough spots of forging a new enterprise.

Amusement, too, might seem too far removed from the parties' concerns to hold promise as a negotiating tool—unless the borrower can meet the lending officer's amusement needs through wit, hospitality, entertainment, or sport. Does this not help explain the extent to which business activities are conducted over lunch or dinner, at parties, on golf courses, at pregame gatherings, on yachts, and so forth? In such settings the negotiator has a better chance of dealing with the Natural Child aspect of the other side's personality and, thereby, has an opportunity to elicit a "sure, what the hell, let's give it a try" type response to a functionally risky proposal.

The emotional need for Personal Achievement finds its source in the Critical Parent, Adaptive Child, or Little Professor. If the borrower in our hypothetical problem seeks a loan from his actual parent, there might be a chance to strengthen the OMON by appealing to the parent's Critical Parent. (E.g., "Dad, you always told me I should go into business for myself. I need the $25,000 to be able to follow your advice.") However, one must be cautious about turning on a banker's Critical Parent since that aspect of the banker's personality may remind the banker to abide by rules such as "collateral must equal at least fifty percent more than the amount of the loan." Nor, in most situations, is it possible for a prospective borrower to turn on a banker's Adaptive Child. (There have been notable exceptions that have created serious difficulties for some bankers. This has occured, for example, when the bank previously made unsound loans to the borrower and the borrower demanded further credit in order to maintain a semblance of financial stability, threatening to declare bankruptcy if the additional loan was not made.) Generally, however, there is some prospect of meeting the banker's need for Personal Achievement by appealing to the banker's Little Professor. This may be achieved, for example, if the borrower infects the banker with the sense of excitement or adventure of seeing new ideas transformed into reality.

Continuing with the analysis of our hypothetical from the perspective of finding ways to meet the lender's emotional needs, we turn, finally, to the banker's need for Security—a need that, in TA terms, comes from the banker's Adaptive Child. Because this ego state will focus on such concerns as the borrower's credit rating and the marketability of the collateral, most often it probably is best to avoid appeals to a banker's Adaptive Child. However, in the right circumstances, addressing the lender's Adaptive Child may offer a means of meeting his emotional needs. For example, assuming that the borrower has adequate collateral but is looking for a low interest rate, turning on the banker's Adaptive Child might facilitate playing off the lender's need for Security against the borrower's request for a lower interest rate.

B. Strokes

Dissecting personality and conduct in terms of the Parent-Adult-Child ego states is but the beginning of the TA model for analyzing interpersonal transactions. Transactional Analysis additionally adopts the proposition that *some human needs are met by the very process of interaction.*

In TA terminology, a "stroke" is any verbal, physical, or symbolic interaction by which a person's existence is acknowledged. A stroke can be affirmative or supportive such as an affectionate pat on the back, a hug, a kiss, a smile, words of praise, words of encouragement, and the like. A stroke also can be negative or rejective such as a hard kick in the pants, a sharp slap in the face, a sneer, words of criticism or words of threat. As we pass from childhood to adulthood, verbal strokes frequently substitute for physical ones. We even use phrases that make such substitutions. (E.g., "I could kiss you for that;" "that was a real pat on the back.")

Transactional Analysis theory assumes that every person needs a minimal amount of stroking to exist. This assumption is supported by laboratory experiments with animals and clinical data respecting isolated human infants. It also explains the resort to solitary confinement as the most severe form of prison discipline, which has been vividly dramatized by accounts of political prisoners. Thus, Jacobo Timerman, imprisoned and tortured in the late 1970s by the Argentinian military dictatorship, recounts in poetic terms the comfort gained one night from merely being able to look into the eye of an unknown fellow prisoner as each pressed against the steel doors of their respective cells and silently peered across a corridor through open peepholes.

Bargaining behavior, accordingly, is affected by the stroking conduct and stroking characteristics of the participants. Strokes can become part of the barter of negotiations and, therefore, constitute a particular type of need that should be included in the skilled negotiator's assessment of ways to increase bargaining power by increasing his Offer to Meet the Other's Needs (OMON). The theme of the ancient Greek comedy *Lysistrata*, in which the women conspire to bring peace to the land by withholding sexual favors from their warring soldier husbands, suggests the power of this form of stroking. In less dramatic and less apparent fashion, strokes commonly are used by negotiators to bring the other side to the bargaining table and to provide that little extra inducement needed to close a deal. Such stroking might take the form of buying the other side dinner during which the closing stages of the bargaining take place, or it might consist of overt acknowledgement of the other side's accomplishments, skills, or status.

Similarly, one who has mastered the art of negotiating insulates himself from the other side's attempts to increase its bargaining power by meeting his needs for strokes. This becomes particularly important when negotiating in strange surroundings, when negotiating while away from home, or when outnumbered at the bargaining table. In each of these situations, the negotiator is likely to be isolated from normal sources of strokes, thereby making the bargainer susceptible to the other side trading on his stroking needs. By being conscious of this need, the negotiator is better able to distinguish between offers to meet the functional needs of the transaction and offers aimed at the negotiator's personal needs. The negotiator who settles for more can seek protection from the latter tactic by doing such things as having a luxurious meal, telephoning family and friends during leisure moments, making time for relaxation, bringing along a cassette player and tapes of favorite pieces of music, looking up old friends who live in the area, and the like.

Stroking also serves as a tactical tool when used as a device to influence which ego state (Parent, Adult, Child) is in control of the adversary's behavior at a given moment. Thus, often it is possible to elicit responses from the other's Critical Parent by using honorifics (Sir, Mr., Dr.) and offering praise or showing awareness respecting the other's status in the community or profession. In contrast, telling a joke or story that evokes a laugh is a form of stroking which is likely to turn on the other side's Natural Child.

C. Personal-Social Orientation (Existential Position)

As we age, we form impressions respecting our relationship to our social environment. There are at least two dimensions to these impressions: what we perceive to be our status in relation to the rest of society and what we believe to be the status of the rest of society. In Transactional Analysis, the dominant impact of these impressions is summed up as being "OK" or "Not OK." Accordingly, there are four initial combinations of one's dominant impressions concerning a person's place within society:

	Abbreviated As
I'm OK—You're OK	I + U +
I'm OK—You're Not OK	I + U −
I'm Not OK—You're OK	I − U +
I'm Not OK—You're Not OK	I − U −

These four combinations are used to summarize the basic "existential positions" or "life views" by which people perceive their relationships with others. Further, TA theory postulates that those who have an I'm OK existential state are more likely to solicit positive strokes than are those with an I'm Not OK position. The latter, as to be expected, are prone to solicit negative strokes. Similarly, those with a You're OK position tend to give positive strokes; those whose life views are You're Not OK mainly give negative strokes.

People who have an I'm OK—You're OK (I + U +) existential position are, in everyday language, those who have self respect and respect for others. Characteristically, they are optimistic, patiently accept defeat, recover from disappointments quickly and without rancor, admire and readily and sincerely acknowledge the accomplishments of others.

The I'm OK—You're Not OK (I+ U−) person is characteristically highly manipulative, self-centered, and amoral. Dr. Eric Berne, the guru of TA, called it the arrogant position. Such persons can be very difficult to deal with at the bargaining table because they often play the aggressive role in destructive social games.

Those who have an I'm Not OK—You're OK (I− U+) existential state have the insecurity characteristic of small children. Such people wait upon the favor of others, blindly follow leaders, accept the status quo, and are very respectful of precedent.

The position of I'm Not OK—You're Not OK has been called the futility position. At the extreme, it is the existential state of schizophrenics.

While the above four existential positions provide the basic paradigm for understanding how people perceive their relationship with society, Berne postulated that there are additional dimensions. He suggested that often people draw a distinction between their closer associates and the rest of the world. A snobbish person might, for example, have an existential position of I+ U+ They−. A variation of the highly manipulative personality might be characterized as I+ U+/− They 0. That is, such a person is ready to deal with you (or anyone else) as a friend or foe, as his needs dictate, and does not have any concerns about what the rest of the world is like.

A negotiator who understands his own existential position should have a better understanding of the emotional needs he may be seeking to fulfill in the course of the bargaining transaction. This, of course, reduces the prospect that the other side will be able to effectively trade upon those needs. A highly skilled negotiator also tries to understand his client's or principal's stroking needs and existential position in order to understand why certain seeming distortions of functional self-interest are present in the client's or employer's articulated goals or in the client's or employer's response to the other side's proposals. It also facilitates effective counseling of the client whose self-interest is being undermined by emotional needs. And, of course, such insight respecting the other side's stroking needs and existential position provides valuable guidance concerning the style of behavior that is most likely to succeed in altering the other side's perceptions respecting the various elements of bargaining strength.

Understanding the other side's existential position should be especially helpful in assessing the prospects and means of modifying the other side's perceptions of the initiator's Probability of Performance (POP) and the other side's confidence in its Predictive Accuracy (PA). For example, those with an I'm OK (I +) existential position can be expected to be more resistant to attempts to change their perceptions of their Predictive Accuracy than are those with an I'm Not OK (I −) existential position. Thus, when bargaining with the latter type of person, one can anticipate greater success with tactics aimed at modifying the other's PA than when dealing with an I'm OK personality type. Conversely, the negotiator can anticipate better success in trying to alter the other side's perception of the initiator's Probability of Performance if the other side has a You're OK (U +) existential position than if the other side is a You Don't Matter (U +/−) or, even more difficult, if the other side is a You're Not OK (U −) personality type.

D. Personal Scripts

According to TA theory, a script is a subconscious life plan shaped by a combination of a person's genetic inheritance and early stroking experiences. It is the means by which the Adaptive Child adjusts to the perceived existential state and becomes the plan by which a person structures long periods of time. Scripts play a central role in human behavior. As a result, in TA therapy unraveling the script is of primary importance in helping people gain better understanding of their conduct and in enabling people to better adjust their lives to their circumstances. However, complicating the task of unraveling a person's script is the phenomenon of counterscript—a pattern of conduct that represses the script through behavior that is the converse of what is called for by the script. To illustrate, the late comedian Jack Benny cultivated a stage caricature of himself as a stingy, egocentric, socially awkward person. Off stage, Benny was generous, cultivated, and relatively low-keyed. Here was a script and counterscript. But whether his private life followed his true script or a counterscript could only be determined after extensive examination of Benny's childhood experiences.

It is, of course, very useful for a negotiator to understand his own script and would be extremely valuable to understand the other side's script. But this is probably asking too much except, perhaps, in very long term bargaining relationships. However, TA specialists have identified many common themes or "currencies" that motivate people in playing their particular scripts, and familiarity with these currencies, sometimes called "trading stamps" in TA jargon, itself might provide useful insight into ways to modify a negotiating party's perceptions.

To illustrate, "uniqueness" is an appropriate currency for someone in an I+ U− existential state. Such people often seek uniqueness through conduct such as collecting one-of-a-kind items, in the manner in which they dress, the vocabulary they use, their recreational activities. Uniqueness is an aspect of such a person's sense of personal achievement. Thus, the bargainer who settles for more recognizes when the other side uses such trading stamps and tries to meet this emotional need by formulating a proposal that gives the transaction an appearance different from others of its genre.

Another currency identified by TA analysts is called "One and Only." This refers to an overwhelming dedication to the quality of loyalty. Such people tend to buy the same make of car time after time, shop at the same stores, eat in the same restaurants, use the same physician, keep within the same circle of friends, and the like. One and Only indicates a very strong Critical Parent component in the personality. Therefore, a negotiator dealing with a person whose script currency appears to be One and Only will want to particularly rely on precedent to show the value of the initiator's OMON and the deficiencies in the other side's BAPA.

In addition to individual scripts, likely we are all influenced by cultural scripts. Psychologists have observed that shame is a particularly powerful human emotion. One way to explain shame is that it results when one perceives oneself as violating a cultural script. For example, if someone asks for a wage increase and feels shamed when told "we're not here to give charity," that person likely follows a cultural script of "be poor but proud."

E. Redefining

An important proposition for the transactional analyst is that *people alter their perception of stimuli to fit the frame of reference which has been shaped by their existential state and script.* The process of fitting stimuli, such as information or proposals, into one's own perceptions of life (one's personal and social orientation and one's script) is a major source of distorted communications, and is called "redefining." Redefining is sometimes characterized by long directionless or circular discussions or by diversions from the original stimulus. For example, if negotiations have turned to the question of who will bear the risk of loss and the other side suddenly goes off on a tangent discussing the problem of finding a desk chair that doesn't squeak, there is a good chance that that person follows a script of "play it safe." That realization should cause the negotiator who settles for more to reexamine the proposal in order to find a way to absorb, and more than offset, the cost of the risk so that the risk adverse person need not be overtly designated as the risk taker.

Another form of redefining, called discounting, involves reducing the significance or extent of viability or variability of a stimulus. For example, a person might say "I am delighted to see you." Alternatively, that person could have said "It is good to see you." The second expression is a discount because it partially detaches the speaker from the statement ("It" instead of "I"). The significance of the discount is that it indicates something less than genuine, undiluted joy at the encounter.

Redefining also can take the form of aggrandizement—the converse of discounting. Aggrandizement is the exaggeration of the extent, significance, variability or viability of the stimulus. An example would be to say to a casual acquaintance: "I have greatly missed your company." The more obvious the redefining of the aggrandizement variety, the more likely we are to characterize it as sarcastic or patronizing.

Finally, redefining can also take the form either of excessive attention to detail or of engaging in excessive generalization.

Redefining is especially troublesome to the negotiator because it distorts meaning. In the TA terms discussed below, it inhibits Adult-Adult transactions. While redefining can provide insight into the true hierarchy of the other's needs, such psychoanalytic efforts carry considerable risks of error. An alternative, therefore, is to try to overcome the redefining and get communications back to reality. One approach is to explicitly, though diplomatically, call attention to the impact of the redefinition and indicate your desire for neutral information. An example of such a response would be a statement along the lines of: "I think we both have been speaking in overly broad terms. It probably would be useful if we could now be more specific . . . ." Or, "I am uncomfortable with what has been said because I think it is more important to _____ than we have have acknowledged . . . ."

F. Transactions

Transactional Analysis defines a "transaction" as a unit of social action. A transaction is a stimulus and response between two people carried on verbally, physically, or symbolically. It can be, and often is, a combination of these. To describe a transaction we return to the initial diagram of personality structure because TA analyzes a transaction not in terms of the composite interacting personalities but rather in terms of the respective ego states, the separate dimensions of the respective personalities that are involved in the transaction. Thus, a parallel, or complementary transaction, is one in which the ego state that is addressed by the person providing the stimulus responds to the ego state that provided that stimulus. For example:

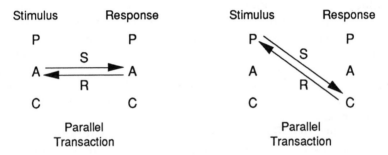

A parallel or complementary transaction is considered the purest form of communication. It is not encumbered by any structural difficulties. In common parlance, it is straightforward talk.

Another form of communication is the crossed transaction. This occurs when the response comes from an ego state other than the one that offered the stimulus. For example, a child asks: "Mom, have you seen my skateboard?" The response, "No, have you looked in the hall closet?" would be a parallel transaction because the stimulus and response came from the respective parties' Adults. A crossed transaction, on the other hand, might sound something like: "Why don't you ever put things where they belong!" Instead of the response coming from the same ego state as the stimulus, the Adult, it came from the Parent (the Critical Parent, to be more precise). The above crossed transaction can be diagramed as:

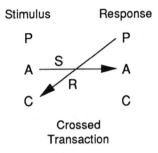

Crossed
Transaction

Berne calculated that there are nine possible types of parallel transactions but 72 possible types of crossed transactions. Perhaps that explains the frequency with which potentially constructive human interaction falls victim to communications breakdowns because an important proposition of TA theory is that *crossed transactions block communications.* Moreover, everyday observations reveal that crossed transactions can generate a state of uproar or be the prelude to an emphatic leave taking.

In parallel and crossed transactions no one is hiding anything. The ego state in control is the one that is apparently speaking or acting. However, many transactions have an ulterior dimension. At the overt level the communication comes from one ego state but at the ulterior level a different ego state either is subconsciously in control or is consciously engaged in deceiving the other party. For example, at the overt level the child may report to her mother "I looked everywhere and still can't find my skateboard." Overtly this is an Adult-Adult transaction. However, if the child's goal is to elicit the mother's offer to help in the search, at the ulterior level the transaction is from the child's Adaptive Child to the mother's Nurturing Parent. If the response is, "Well, in that case, I'd better help you find it," the communication is successful even though at the overt level it is a crossed A-A/NP-AC transaction. On the other hand, the response, "That's unfortunate. If I see it I will let you know," is a parallel transaction at the overt level but crossed at the ulterior level with the result that the ulterior effort was unsuccessful.

Negotiations often proceed largely at the ulterior level. That is, the negotiator who settles for more has established goals and consciously shapes transactions to maximize the prospects of attaining those goals. Therefore, at the ulterior level the successful negotiator's Adult always guides his transactions. Communication often may be at the Adult-Adult level, especially if the respective negotiators have a professional demeanor. Frequently, however, to most effectively alter the other side's perceptions, the negotiator who settles for more resorts to overt communications that appear to originate in his Parent or Child ego state or that are directed at the other side's Parent or Child. For example, assume that negotiator Adam proposes inserting a cost-of-living index adjustment factor in establishing the rent to be paid by Betty but observes that Betty visibly stiffens at the suggestion, asserting in a firm voice and manner: "That's unheard of, nobody does business that way in this town!" In TA terms, an Adult stimulus has been rejected by a response from the other side's Critical Parent—a crossed transaction. To succeed with the proposal, Adam must find a way either to appeal to Betty's Critical Parent or get her to shift (turn on) to her Adult or her Child. Thus, Adam could respond by saying something like, "That's true, but this type of provision is becoming a standard practice in many parts of the country and I would like to discuss with you the advantages that people are finding in adopting this type of provision." Or, "I recognize that you know the real estate market and practices better than anyone in this town, but haven't you also been a leading business innovator in this community?" In the first instance, Adam is directing his overt transaction at Betty's Critical Parent in an effort to get Betty to shift to her Adult ego state. In the second illustration, Adam is responding to Betty's Critical Parent and trying to get Betty to shift to the Natural Child dimension of her personality.

G. Games and Other Time Structuring Behaviors

Berne first popularized the Transactional Analysis model through his book *Games People Play*. He hypothesized that all nonpsychotic persons use six basic patterns for structuring the time we spend with other people: Withdrawal, Rituals, Pastimes, Intimacy, Procedures, and Games. Games received title attention for the book because it is the time structure most often responsible for transactional difficulties.

Withdrawal is where someone is physically present in a transactional setting but does not participate—as, for example, by daydreaming. For the negotiator who settles for more, Withdrawal may give clues to a person's ego state, existential state, and script. It suggests that the transaction opportunity is not offering anything to meet that person's emotional needs. In strategic terms, Withdrawal increases the cost elements (AC and COIN) beyond normal expectations inasmuch as one cannot hope to communicate effectively with someone who, at a subconscious level, declines to participate in the transaction.

Rituals are wholly stylized transactions in which the outcome, among normal participants, is predictable. Rituals come from the Critical Parent and involve such conduct as nodding hello, making personal introductions, dressing appropriately for the setting, offering and providing hospitality, and the like. Rituals produce a high concentration of strokes and can be very complex and greatly valued in some cultures and subcultures. Although Rituals are not used for the formal exchange of information, they can provide important insight into a person's existential state and script—information that can influence perceptions of such things as emotional needs and personal reliability. For example, the opening greeting or closing salutations in a letter or opening and closing exchanges in conversation are Rituals that might reveal a person's sense of relative status ("Dear Mr. Jones," "Dear Tom," "Dear Tommy"); which ego state is in control ("Hi there Tom," "Tom, you're just the guy I was hoping to see," "How do you do, Mr. Jones"); and whether the person is pleased or displeased with what has taken place or with the prospects of what is about to take place. Existential state may also be revealed by the manner in which the Ritual is carried out (e.g., a firm versus a weak handshake, a mumbled versus a clearly spoken greeting, initiation of rituals versus responding only).

Information provided by Rituals is not necessarily reliable. Thus, the best confidence artists pay careful attention to adhering to the appropriate rituals. Inconsistency in Ritual behavior, on the other hand, is a good indicator either of unfamiliarity with the cultural or subcultural mores, or of amateurish efforts at deception.

Intimacy is as freewheeling a means of time structure as Ritual is stylized. Intimacy is defined as a candid, giving and taking relationship in which there is no exploitation. It comes from the Nurturing Parent and Natural Child dimensions of personality. Therefore, Intimacy is a hazardous structure in exchange or distributive bargaining. On the other hand, integrative bargaining, with its adjustment of common and compatible needs, can progress through Intimacy, especially if the parties have a good, long-term relationship. A prime example of negotiation taking place through Intimate transactions would be group decisions among members of a tranquil household.

Pastimes, as a structure for managing time through a series of transactions, have the repetitive quality of Rituals but are neither as stylized nor as predictable. Bull sessions, gossip, and cocktail party conversations are typical occasions for Pastimes. Pastimes provide the skilled negotiator with an opportunity to offer strokes and learn about the other side. In the course of face-to-face negotiations, such opportunites arise during the various formal and informal breaks.

A number of Pastime formats are common in American culture. One is called "General Motors." It involves comparing knowledge and experiences about a particular subject such as cars, ball teams, stocks, and vacation resorts. Another is called "Baseball Scores." It involves exchanging information about recent events such as the performance of a team, the stock market, an election, and reactions to new movies. "Do you know" is a different sort of Pastime. It requires the participants to seek out mutual acquaintances and information about common background experiences or affiliations.

Normally, some negotiating time is spent in Pastimes. Depending on one's astuteness, this can merely serve to exchange social strokes and structure time, or it can be a means for gaining valuable bargaining information and assessing the other side's ego state, existential state, and negotiating experience level.

Procedures constitute a fifth time-structuring pattern. Procedures, as the term is used in TA, are transactions oriented toward external realities. That is, a Procedure is a means of accomplishing a result that is unrelated to the actors' scripts. So long as the activity is overtly goal directed, the transaction is a Procedure whether or not it is carried out efficiently. Accordingly, work normally falls within this category. Recreational activities, too, can be Procedures.

However, a Procedure becomes contaminated if the actors' scripts alter their conduct. If the Procedure was well designed, such contamination will reduce efficiency. Thus, in the presence of contamination, the goal is less likely to be achieved or its achievement will require greater effort than otherwise would be necessary. Take, for example, the situation in which a proposed lease is being reviewed by attorneys, respectively representing the landlord and tenant, to ensure that no legal problems are raised by the negotiated provisions. If both have studied the document and researched any potential problems, they should be able to confer and promptly present their clients either with their approval or with recommended modifications. However, if one of the lawyers follows the script "I'm the Smartest Guy on the Block," the contamination of the Procedure, with the resultant reduction of efficiency, is too obvious to require elaboration. Moreover, if the Procedure is contaminated by both lawyers' scripts, their transaction may be transformed into a Pastime. Hence, if both follow the previously indicated script, instead of untying any legal knots, they may end up expending their clients' billed time exchanging quotes from archaic treatises on the law of property.

Bargaining is the method by which parties resolve to contractually modify relationships or determine that such a modification is not mutually agreeable. Accordingly, bargaining should function as a Procedure. However, as with any Procedure, there is danger of contamination of the negotiating Procedure thus transforming the transaction into what TA theoreticians call a Game.

Games are defined by Transactional Analysis as a series of ulterior transactions in which there is a psychological payoff. Such payoffs are strokes that usually reinforce the initiating player's existential position and probably further the player's script. Games can be a healthy means for structuring the time people spend together socially exchanging strokes. Often, though, they are exploitative or mutually destructive.

A necessary element of a Game is for the initiator, through an ulterior transaction, to "con" or "hook" the other person or persons into playing. This is followed by a series of maneuvering transactions that lead to the initiator pulling his switch or revealing his gimmick which provides the initiator's payoff. Transactional Analysis theorists assert that because Games are linked to existential status and script, people follow specific personal repertoires as Game initiators and also, sometimes, as participants.

If a negotiating party's ulterior emotional needs are inconsistent with the external realities the negotiators are trying to resolve, the bargaining procedure is contaminated and can be subverted into a Game. In terms of the bargaining strength model, if a negotiation becomes a Game, one or both sides' emotional needs become the sole and controlling element in the interaction. This is not necessarily mutually destructive. If one side recognizes the Gaming nature of a negotiation, it is sometimes possible to exploit that characteristic of the transaction. And, on occasion, the emotional needs of both sides may be served to a degree that outweighs any functional interests at stake in the overt transaction.

One often discussed Game is "Now I've Got You, You S.O.B.," generally abbreviated as NIGYSOB. An illustration of this Game in a bargaining setting is historically recorded in events that took place in May 1960. At that time the United States and the Soviet Union were at a summit meeting at which the respective leaders were vying for international support as the credible, reliable world power responsible for ensuring world peace. An advantage held by the United States was that we were led by the internationally popular hero of World War II, Dwight D. Eisenhower. During the course of the meeting the Soviet Union shot down an American U-2 spy plane over Soviet territory. Soviet Premier Nikita Khrushchev announced that an American spy plane had violated Soviet air space and had been destroyed. President Eisenhower took the bait and denied that the plane was spying. He insisted that it was a weather observation plane that had strayed. Khrushchev then revealed his gimmick. The American pilot, Gary Powers, had been captured and confessed, and parts of the plane's camera equipment had been recovered. President Eisenhower, with much embarassment, then admitted to the true nature of the plane's mission. Khrushchev, having won his round of NIGYSOB, then indignantly walked out of the summit conference. Without making any disarmament concessions, which the Soviets likely perceived as threatening their military security, he was able to "show" the world that the cold war was the product of American, not Soviet, duplicity. Had the American policy planners realized what Khrushchev was up to when he made the initial announcement, they could have avoided the Game by refusing to take the hook. That is, the President could have acknowledged the nature of the plane's mission, dissociated himself from and apologized for the stupidity of the timing of the particular flight, explained that the mutual sense of insecurity and suspicion that gave rise to such flights underscored the importance of a successful summit, and even pledged that there would be no further flights of this sort. (The latter would not have been much of a sacrifice. Since the Soviets had demonstrated their ability to shoot down the ultra high flying U-2, there was little purpose in continuing these missions.) Avoiding the Game may not have saved the summit, but it would have prevented Premier Khrushchev from walking away with the pot.

Although the above illustrated Soviet play of NIGYSOB was almost certainly a conscious maneuver by Soviet foreign policy strategists, negotiators often fall into Game patterns without being aware of the nature of their behavior and the probable consequences.

A Game related to NIGYSOB is "Last Straw." It is a Game in which the initiator "tolerates" a certain mode of behavior over a period of repeated transactions but suddenly treats a repetition of that conduct as intolerable and imposes a punishment calculated to deal with all of the past "wrongs" as well as with the most recent repetition. Last Straw is often played by parents who are erratic in disciplining their children and is a Game that can destroy marriages. Last Straw is encountered, as well, in bargaining. The trick in dealing with someone who has a propensity to play this Game is to impose a statute of limitations. Insist that the other side make any complaints about your conduct when the particular mode of conduct first arises. Make it clear that toleration of the mode of conduct legitimizes it by custom and usage. Of course, such insistence might cause a dedicated player of "Last Straw" to terminate the bargaining relationship.

Not every Game encountered in negotiations needs to be turned off. The philanthropist's Game, "Happy to Help," sometimes is initiated by someone doing penance for past wrongs or who is seeking to establish high social status. In those instances the Game initiator's ulterior transactions come from his Critical Parent. At other times this Game is initiated by someone who is competing to prove who is the nicest guy in town. In such instances it is a Game in which the ulterior transaction comes from the initiator's Nurturing Parent. In either event, it offers a welcome opportunity to be an obliging respondent. Indeed, when bargaining from weakness, one tactic is to try to get the other side to play "Happy to Help." If the other side is willing to play the Game, this provides a new emotional dimension to the other side's needs that the weaker party is able to satisfy. Therefore, in terms of the bargaining strength model, the respondent's bargaining strength is increased because his opportunity to meet the other's needs (OMON) has increased.

It is as important for the skilled negotiator to detect when he is initiating Games as it is for him to recognize when he is being made a respondent to a Game. Questions that have been suggested for determining whether one is involved in a Game include:

- Am I getting my stroke needs met outside of this activity?
- Am I volunteering unrequested information?
- Am I repeating information?
- Am I failing to learn the needed information or ascertain the available solutions?

- Is there an excess of emoting behavior?
- Do others look to me for permission to speak?
- Am I looking to others for permission to speak?
- Am I devoting an excessive amount of energy to the trans-action?

Perhaps the ultimate question is whether one finds oneself com-pulsively participating in exchanges that do not contribute to resolv-ing the external issues that gave rise to the desire or willingness to negotiate. That is, is your Adult in control of your behavior?

H. Conclusion

Transactional Analysis, as a tactical tool available to a nego-tiator, provides a model for controlling our own behavior and for better understanding and influencing the behavior of others. The TA model enables a person to protect his ability to accomplish an assigned task without being contaminated by personal idiosyncra-sies and emotional needs. It also facilitates selecting the most effec-tive method of altering another person's perceptions.

In the next chapters, where specific bargaining techniques are examined individually, frequent reference is made to the TA model as a means of better understanding the nature and use of particular tactics.

Selected References for Chapter 4

E. Berne, *What Do You Say After You Say Hello?* (Grove Press, 1972).

E. Berne, *Games People Play* (Grove Press, 1964).

E. Berne, *The Structure and Dynamics of Organizations and Groups* (Grove Press, 1963).

N. Haimowitz & M. Haimowitz, *Human Development — Selected Readings* (Harp-er & Row, 1973).

A. Harris & T. Harris, *Staying OK* (Harper & Row, 1985).

T. Harris, *I'm Ok — You're OK* (Harper & Row, 1967).

S. Woollams & M. Brown, *The Total Handbook of Transactional Analysis* (Pren-tice Hall, 1979).

O. Altorfer, "Group Dynamics: Dealing with Agitation in Industry Groups," 7 *Transactional Analysis Journal* 168 (1977).

F. Frank, "Adapted Child and Critical Parent," 4 *Transactional Analysis Journal* 8 (1974).

S. Gillert, "The Psychotherapist as Persecutor," 7 *Transactional Analysis Journal* 153 (1977).

R. Hughes, "Is the Little Professor Right?" 8 *Transactional Analysis Journal* 120 (1978).

J. McKenna, "Stroking Profile," 4 *Transactional Analysis Journal* 20 (1974).

K. Mellor, "Redefining," 5 *Transactional Analysis Journal* 303 (1975).

Chapter 5

Tactics for Modifying Perceptions: Obtaining and Weighing Information

A. Gather Accurate Information

The pervasive role that perception plays in determining bargaining strength has been portrayed in the bargaining strength paradigms discussed in Chapters 2 and 3. There we learned that bargaining strength is increased by the appropriate modification of perceptions respecting the bargaining elements. The reader will recall that bargaining strategy involves the choice of which elements a negotiator should select as the targets for the modification of perceptions while bargaining tactics involve the methods for accomplishing those modifications.

Some perceptions are rooted in a person's value system—the Critical Parent ego state, to use TA terminology. As previously noted, these rarely budge. Fortunately, most people rely on the Adult aspect of their personality to form a good share of their perceptions. Such perceptions are the product of applying reason to information. Therefore, in most negotiations information is a source of shaping and reshaping perceptions.

A general guideline for those who seek to settle for more is that the negotiator who dominates the discussion is probably not dominating the negotiations. It is difficult to dominate a discussion and at the same time learn what must be learned from the other side. Because establishing realistic perceptions necessitates having access to accurate and comprehensive data, information gathering and evaluation is an important negotiating tactic. It is important, too, because by understanding what information the other side relies on in forming its perceptions, one can better determine what additional or corrective information may succeed in modifying the other's perceptions. Therefore, information gathering, whether volunteered by the other side in the course of bargaining discussions, or from other sources, is the tactical starting point in settling for more.

1. Carefully Select the Investigator

The other side is not always forthcoming with information and often does not possess key information needed by a bargainer to form accurate perceptions or to help inform the other side's perceptions. Therefore, bargaining often entails preparatory efforts that involve information gathering.

Many pitfalls hinder the effort to obtain reliable, accurate information. Sometimes the initial stumbling block is the selection of the person to do the investigating. Obviously, that person should not be encumbered by preconceived notions of what will be found and should be intelligent, knowledgeable about the subject, thorough, and careful. Less obvious is the need to select someone with adequate status to elicit accurate, complete responses. Research indicates that investigators who have high status in the eyes of the people who are providing information receive more complete and more accurate reports than do others who pose the same questions or requests regarding the same events.

2. Verify Information Accuracy

Information may be gathered from many sources, including the other side. Whatever the source, when possible it is always prudent to attempt to verify its accuracy. Even bargainers who deal cautiously with information received from the other side too readily assume the accuracy of information gathered from impartial sources or gleaned from their own records.

Intentional distortion of information is, of course, one potential problem for a negotiator. Often, however, inaccuracy is the unintentional product of error made in observing, copying, analyzing, calculating, listening, or reading.

One indicator of inaccuracy is inconsistency. Thus, a way to catch an unpracticed liar is to ask the same question at different times. Similarly, a method for discovering deficiencies in a survey, data analysis, or an experiment, is to replicate the investigatory procedure to see if the results come out the same way.

It must be remembered, though, that while inconsistency is a good test of inaccuracy, and while consistency does offer some basis for relying on the resulting information, consistency does not offer an acid test of accuracy. Mistakes, especially conceptual errors, can be repeated. Hence, while the tabulations prepared by a careful inventory clerk who thinks that 2 + 2 = 5 may be consistent, they are inaccurate.

a. Audit

Auditing involves checking to determine if errors have been made and why they were made. There is a broad range of auditing techniques.

A very practical safeguard against the problem of inaccuracy is to use the auditing method of replication; that is, have more than one person repeat the data gathering or recording—if possible using different methods. For example, a common negotiator task is to calculate the financial implications of bargaining proposals. A single negotiator calculating the figures but once courts disaster. Running the figures a second time as a check, or running them once and checking a tape of those calculations, provides a margin of safety. Having a partner separately run the figures using a different calculating device provides an even greater safety margin.

Not all data need to be 100 percent accurate. For example, in preparing to negotiate a supply contract calling for daily deliveries it is necessary for the supplier to know what production levels are feasible. This, in turn, may necessitate knowing how many size 5 screws are available in inventory. The supplier's inventory records should provide this information. However, unless recently audited, those records may not be sufficiently reliable. On the other hand, the methods for checking data accuracy discussed in the previous paragraph, through replication of the measuring or calculating method, involve what is called a 100 percent audit—that is, the entire inventory must be recounted. A 100 percent audit is a slow and expensive method of ensuring accuracy. In our hypothetical problem of knowing how many size 5 screws are available, a 100 percent audit might be too time consuming and expensive for the supplier's purpose. An alternative technique, random sampling, provides a less expensive means of auditing accuracy based on a statistical projection of the probable margin of error. Accordingly, in our hypothetical situation, being assured of the inventory count of size 5 screws within a 2 percent margin of error likely would satisfy the negotiator's information needs. Randomly selecting boxes, counting them and matching their count against the inventory records may, therefore, provide a satisfactory means of randomly sampling the inventory to ascertain the degree of accuracy or inaccuracy of the records.

There are a number of related techniques for making such estimates of accuracy. For example, the accuracy of a recorded count can be tested by using a method for attaining a reasonable estimate. Thus, in the hypothetical illustration involving size 5 screws, if the inventoried screws are in barrels, taking the weight of the barrels and doing a count of the number of screws in a pound, should produce a sufficiently reliable estimate of the number of screws in inventory to reveal a significant error in the inventory records.

Gathering and recording data often is a tedious process that invites error. Hence, as suggested by the above illustration, a cautious negotiator must exercise skepticism respecting information stored in files unless there is a basis for knowing that accuracy verification safeguards were taken before the information was stored. Assessing accuracy also requires determining the skill, knowledge, and reliability of those who produced or previously handled the information.

Another method of verifying the accuracy of data is to compare and cross-check common data from different sources or compare the summaries thereof. Well designed accounting systems, with their use of balance sheets, probably provide the best example of the art of such devices for verifying accuracy. Accordingly, accountants are excellent consultants when designing systems to ensure and test data accuracy.

b. Discover Deception

Intentional deception comes in two forms—concealment and lying. In the first instance the potential source of information avoids revealing it; in the second instance the informant conveys false information. In at least one way, lying poses a greater problem than concealment since lying may give the recipient a false sense of knowledge. Not surprisingly, the law generally deals harshly with lies but often excuses concealment. For example, the doctrine that the buyer cannot assume that a seller will volunteer information detracting from the value of its goods, a doctrine capsulized in the motto "buyer beware," is a long established principle of commercial transactions. Generally, the law makes exceptions to it only in matters affecting health or safety, or where the deficiency is not readily discoverable through the buyer's own diligent efforts, or where the seller owes special responsibilities to, or holds special advantages over, the buyer. As is further explored below, under the discussion of the tactical use of questions, the lawyer's art of cross-examination offers a weapon against concealment.

When information is obtained from the other side, a technique for increasing the assurance of accuracy is to expressly condition the transaction on the correctness of the stated facts. The "buyer beware" doctrine does not apply to material misrepresentations (lies). Generally, such misrepresentations are a basis for setting aside contractual undertakings. Thus, if the other side certifies a document setting forth the content of those representations, the probable accuracy of the data is increased because the other side has greater reason to expect that it will have to pay for any inaccuracies in that information. This last statement, of course, assumes that the other side is aware of the applicable legal standard and available legal remedies, and has some expectation of legal enforcement of its obligations if it violates them.

Getting the other side to publicly state the facts upon which you rely often provides the same sort of increased assurance of the reliability of those facts, because public statements may provoke corrective statements from alternative information sources. Also, such statements provide a source of evidence that can be used against the other side in litigation. This, of course, deters a party from publicly making false recitations. In addition, having to make a public statement further dissuades the other side from engaging in intentional misrepresentation because it poses the prospect of public embarassment if the statement is later shown to be inaccurate.

Another method of gauging the accuracy of information is to assess the veracity of the source. Personal experiences with the source of information and the source's reputation for veracity obviously provide some basis for assessing reliability.

When information is transmitted directly to the negotiator, nonverbal aspects of the communication sometimes provide additional guidance for weighing the communicator's veracity. The term "nonverbal communication" refers to clues that accompany the words used to express a statement. These clues often confirm or contradict the content of the statement. This can occur in written as well as oral communications. Take, for example, a letter that reads: "Our engineering department, which has great experience in these matters, carefully and fully analyzed your product. They report some problems. Therefore, we are unwilling to offer as much as you have asked." Under such circumstances, doesn't the lack of details regarding the nature of the alleged "problems" provide a clue that in fact the engineering department found no deficiencies?

Under the topic of Transactional Analysis we have seen how verbal filtering, discounting, and similar patterns of characterization or explanation provide clues that the communicator's words do not accurately reflect his thoughts or feelings. A similar clue is the so-called Freudian slip—the word or phrase which on the surface is a verbal error but which reveals the true intentions or knowledge of the speaker far better than the "corrected" statement.

Verbal anxiety is the equivalent of nervous fidgeting. It is a profusion of irrelevant or superfluous comments accompanying a statement. Often, verbal anxiety provides another clue that the speaker understands the truth to be something other than the objective meaning of the recited words. Accordingly, experiments by Zuckerman, DePaulo, and Rosenthal[1] indicate that deceptive messages often are accompanied by increased communication of irrelevant information.

In recent years, students of communications have identified a broad array of physiological clues that can help detect misleading or false statements. Experimental studies reveal relationships between deception and such things as eye contact, rate and tonal quality of speech, body posture, the contraction or relaxation of particular facial muscles, and the like. Based on such observations, various "lie detector" devices and services have been marketed, generally with exaggerated and misleading claims of reliability. Nevertheless, because accuracy verification is so important to the negotiator, some attention needs to be paid to the concepts that underlie the use of physiological clues for detecting deception.

Reliance upon physiological clues for detecting deception is based on the assumption that everyone has had numerous experiences in which truth telling and lying had an emotionally favorable or unfavorable result. These experiences condition us to subconsciously anticipate similar effects when we repeat the same sort of behavior. For a variety of reasons, favorable and unfavorable emotional response normally is accompanied by observable physiolog-

---

[1] Reported in P. Blanck, R. Buck & R. Rosenthal, *Nonverbal Communication in the Clinical Context* (Pennsylvania State Univ. Press, 1986), p. 26.

ical changes such as muscle relaxation or tension, altered rate of breathing, blood rushing to or away from the skin surface, and the like. Therefore, it is assumed that the anticipated emotionally favorable or unfavorable effects caused by truth telling or lying are revealed by observable physiological changes that accompany the actual emotional response.

Relying on physiological clues of deceit has its ancient antecedents. It is said, for example, that in earlier centuries the Chinese required witnesses to chew and then spit out dry rice before testifying. It was assumed that deceit causes the mouth to go dry with the result that those who were about to lie would have difficulty spitting out the rice.

Some emotionally triggered physiological changes have clear functional purposes; others probably had such purposes at earlier stages of our evolution—though some are indeed puzzling. For example, gritting one's teeth when angry probably served as a means of sending a rush of blood to the jaw muscles to prepare them for combat at a time when teeth were an important weapon in our species' combat arsenal. Blood draining from one's face when fearful is the result of the need for an increased blood supply by the large muscles that will be used if a decision is made to take flight. The explanation for other reactions, such as blushing in response to a compliment, may be much more elusive, though in an article in *Science*,[2] Professor R.B. Zajonc observed that many aspects of emotional expression are connected with the impact of blood flow on brain and neurological temperatures. The temperature changes can have an effect upon biochemical control mechanisms to do such things as mobilize energy, reduce pain, and the like.

Many aspects of nonverbal expression probably arise from symbolic analogies that form a basis for our means of expression. For example, if we bite into something overly bitter or sour (characteristics that sometimes accompany inedible substances) we respond with a facial expression that facilitates ejecting the substance from our mouth and cleansing our tongue and lips. Similar facial expressions accompany our rejection of undesired ideas. As Professor Zajonc points out, "language is replete with sensation-emotion metaphors" such as terms of endearment that compare the loved person to a desired food treat ("sugar," "honey," "sweetie").

---

[2]R. Zajonc, "Emotion and Facial Efference: A Theory Reclaimed," *Science* (April 5, 1985), p. 15.

Although it is valid for behavioral theory to rely upon "norms" of response in designing, testing, and using behavioral models, it is important for the negotiator to recognize that in any individual situation there is the possibility that the subject deviates from the norm. As a result, in any individual situation there is a possibility, often a strong possibility, of misinterpreting that person's response. Illustrative of this fact are the very interesting correlations found between eye pupil dilation and such things as deceit and liking. For example, investigations by Dr. Eckhard Hess found that *generally* men respond more positively to photos of women with large eye pupils while women generally respond more positively to photos of women with small eye pupils.[3] Suggesting that this is a learned response is the fact that another study showed that, as do women, self-styled homosexual men prefer photos of women with small eye pupils. (Presumably, the latter similarity would not occur if the difference is a sex-linked biological variable.) Hess also found that, generally, a subject's pupils enlarge when confronted with something or someone desirable but contract when faced with an undesirable person or object. Yet, none of these variations were consistent among all subjects. In each instance responses to the same stimulus varied; the observed correlations were based upon norms, not absolutes. In addition, different emotional states (surprise, agreement, interest) can trigger the same eye pupil response. Therefore, there is a gamble involved any time one relies upon such nonverbal behavior to make veracity assessments.

Moreover, as is explained by Professor Paul Ekman in his intriguing book *Telling Lies*,[4] because the interpretation of nonverbal communication is based upon the assumption that physiological clues reveal the subject's true feelings, reliance upon such clues for deception detection must weigh the fact that deception does not have a uniform impact upon all deceivers nor upon the same deceiver under all circumstances. Therefore, if a particular act of deception is perceived by the deceiver as being morally or socially acceptable, it is not likely to produce the sort of shame, guilt, or stress that may readily be detected through the nonverbal clues of the physiological responses that accompany such feelings. On the other hand, apprehension of being caught in an act of deception, or the apprehension of being falsely accused of decep-

---

[3]E. Hess, "The Role of Pupil Size in Communication," *Scientific American* (November 1975), p. 110.

[4]P. Ekman, *Telling Lies: Clues to Deceit in the Marketplace, Politics, and Marriage* (Norton, 1985).

tion, might trigger those very same clues whether or not the deceiver has a strong sense of shame or guilt. Thus, the emotional signals that are assumed to accompany the guilt of telling a lie may sometimes be revealed because of the liar's apprehension of being caught rather than as a result of feelings of guilt. However, there is the very serious danger that the same signals reveal not a deceiver, but rather an honest statement by a person who fears being falsely accused or by one who is outraged at having his veracity questioned.

Another problem that complicates the art of detecting deception is that not all lies produce a sense of guilt. In some instances the successful lie means winning a game that depends upon deception. Professor Ekman points out that in such situations deception brings feelings not of guilt or shame to the perpetrator, but rather what he calls "duping delight." In these instances, therefore, the physiological cues of the deceiver's true emotions will be quite different from those of the liar who has an underlying sense of shame, guilt, or stress.

In relying upon nonverbal communication to access accuracy, it is important to remember that while a deceitful communication almost certainly provides inaccurate information, veracity does not assure accuracy. That is, as honest and sincere as an informant may be, the communication will not be accurate if the source is misinformed or confused. Indeed, in some negotiating situations the principal intentionally keeps the bargaining representative uninformed or misinformed in expectation that the representative's statements will thereby make a more persuasive impression. Professor Ekman's book provides some fascinating historical examples of this practice.

Keeping in mind that clues indicating deception may have been stimulated by causes that are wholly consistent with being truthful, let us now examine some physiological clues that, when cautiously used, may assist in assessing veracity.

Anyone who has spent a great deal of time watching videotapes of simulated negotiations can recount observed instances of deceit-revealing gestures such as hands passing over the speaker's mouth as if symbolically wiping away a misleading or false statement. Videotapes of simulated negotiations also show that a bargainer's gestures often reveal other types of unspoken feelings such as a suspicious or very cautious bargainer holding his arms in a closed, defensive position like a boxer fending off a fast barrage of body punches; open armed, forward leaning gestures showing interest in the other's statements or revealing a strong desire to get the other's acceptance of the particular proposal; or a gesture of arms folded while leaning back from the bargaining table revealing disinterest or resistence to what is being said. A difficulty with relying on these sorts of cues is that, like vague words, they can too easily be subject to manipulation. Another difficulty is that they are easily misunderstood. For example, such conduct is often nothing more than a habitual grooming gesture or fidgeting that results from concentration or the tension of being engaged in important work. Such gestures or fidgeting need not have any relationship to the communicator's veracity.

In recent times, promoters of reliance upon physiological clues to verify veracity and detect deception have created a multimillion dollar business through use of the polygraph measuring device. The polygraph method is based on the theory that lying is stressful and that the stress accompanying lying reveals itself through such physiological cues as altered strength and rate of respiration, altered blood pressure and heart beat, and increased perspiration. Although each of these changes can sometimes be visually observed in the form of such things as a red face, heavy breathing, beads of sweat on the forehead, or moist hands, the polygraph provides sensitive mechanical and electronic means of measuring and recording such changes. Some polygraph equipment even measures changes in voice volume and texture and eye pupil dilation and movement.

Laboratory investigation confirms a relationship between each of the above physiological changes and changes brought about by the stress of engaging in deceit. However, as previously noted, each of these clues also correlates with stimuli other than engaging in deceit. For example, just as telling a lie might be stressful, so might a subject's fear that the testor will fail to recognize the truthfulness of the subject's answer to a crucial question. Moreover, laboratory investigation shows that there are variations in emotional and physiological responses. Neutral investigators (those not in the business of conducting such tests for fees or selling the equipment) find a very significant margin of error even for the best trained polygraph operators using the most reliable examination techniques. More important, there are considerable variations in the skill and care possessed and exercised by those engaged in the business of conducting polygraph examinations. Many are not well trained and even among the well trained, many use less than optimal techniques. As a result, the industry has been characterized as being filled with incompetents and charlatans, and many jurisdictions now prohibit their use in a broad range of situations.

The commercial success of polygraph apparatus has generated competition in the form of alternative deceit detection devices— devices so small that they can be secretly carried into the conference room. If the polygraph, with its scientific foundation and its multifaceted methods of measuring physiological change, is vulnerable to misinterpretation and misuse, consider how much greater caution must be exercised when cruder instruments are offered to the negotiator as truth detecting tools to be hidden in a briefcase. One such machine claims to measure olfactory byproducts of the liar's guilt-induced biological response, and another claims to discover lies by means of voice quality analysis. The latter concept has some experimental support inasmuch as laboratory studies show correlations between raised voice pitch and the emotional states that often accompany the liar's sense of guilt or fear of discovery. However, raised voice pitch is not a universal physiological cue of these emotions and raised voice pitch also accompanies other emotions that may not have any relationship to deceitful behavior. Accordingly, impartial analysis of the effectiveness of these devices has concluded that they are virtually worthless.

In the past few decades, electronic sensors and photographic equipment have enabled scientists to study in minute detail the visual clues of gestures and facial expressions in an effort to better understand nonverbal communication. Dr. Albert Mehrabian[5] and his colleagues concluded from their studies that in terms of the impact of what is communicated, a listener's interpretation of a speaker's emotional intent typically relies 55 percent on facial expression, 38 percent on voice characteristics, and only 7 percent on the verbal content of the message. That, of course, does not mean that these nonverbal cues carry the same weight in accurately transmitting the speaker's true feelings. Each of these nonverbal cue sources is capable of being masked, at least to some degree. Thus, the value of different sources of nonverbal cues in revealing deception is more closely related to how well particular types of cues can be masked and the extent to which speakers normally resort to such masking.

Most people are well aware of the predominant nonverbal communication role played by facial expression. So apparent is this form of nonverbal communication that those who developed the ancient Greek and Classic Chinese and Japanese theaters used masks to give incontravertible personality traits to their characters. The same device has been used by those who have developed

---

[5]A. Mehrabian, *Nonverbal Communication* (A. de Gruyter, 1972).

theatrical protocols in many other cultures. Similarly, the universally acknowledged importance of facial cues is reflected in the stereotype modes of physical expression used in the British and American melodrama and silent screen traditions. In this regard, it is interesting to note that Professor Paul Ekman reports that one general finding of his studies is that while gestures are culturally influenced, facial expression is universal. (Here, too, though, his investigations showed a lack of complete agreement in the way various facial expressions are interpreted by people.) Indeed, recent studies show that even very young children are able to identify some basic emotions from facial expression with a degree of accuracy comparable to that of adults. And, other recent studies show that neither educational achievement nor sex significantly influence ability to identify facial expressions.[6]

Dr. Ekman's interest in understanding nonverbal communication led him to discover a number of physiologiocal clues of deceit, including what he characterizes as microexpression clues. His book *Telling Lies* is especially useful for the negotiator because, unlike the polygraph, his method can be employed without the consent or awareness of the person being assessed. On the other hand, Dr. Ekman warns that "behavioral clues to deceit . . . don't have to happen." That is, as with other techniques of behavioral science, his are based on statistical norms, not certainties. Lying and truth telling can be present despite contrary nonverbal clues. Nevertheless, the commercial potential of Ekman's methods have not gone unexploited by others. And, as with the polygraph technique, the exploiters often lack scruples. Based upon what he had seen prior to publishing *Telling Lies*, Ekman reports that in the materials used to train "experts" in spotting the microexpression clues of deception, about half of the information was wrong.

Ekman's book provides insight into gesture and voice clues of deceit as well as some particularly interesting observations respecting facial clues. Because about 70 percent of the people he has studied experience raised voice pitch when upset, Dr. Ekman also calls attention to the value of using this characteristic as an indicator of *possible* deceit. Thus, when a person's voice pitch rises under circumstances in which other voice pitch raising emotional factors

---

[6]P. Ekman, "Face Muscles Talk Every Language," *Psychology Today* (September 1975), p. 35; P. Ekman, note 4, above; C. Stifter & N. Fox, "Preschool Children's Ability to Identify and Label Emotions," 11 *Journal of Nonverbal Behavior* 43 (1987); G. Kirouac & F. Dore, "Accuracy of Judgment of Facial Expression of Emotions as a Function of Sex and Level of Education," 9 *Journal of Nonverbal Behavior* 3 (1985).

(such as anger or fear) are not present, it is likely that the person is upset about something else—such as the stress of engaging in deceit. Dr. Ekman also notes that emotionally packed words normally are accompanied by culturally dictated gestures. The lack of such accompanying gestures may well be a sign that the words mean less than they say. For example, in American culture, we expect an expression of anger to be accompanied by a clenched or partially clenched fist. Accordingly, a statement of anger made by someone whose hands are placed against each other palm to palm (a prayer gesture) is less likely indicate anger than a statement by someone whose clenched fist bangs on the table while expressing his or her anger.

Professor Ekman offers additional guidance in dealing with body gestures by pointing out that while most gestures are vague, some carry very specific messages. The latter type of gesture is culturally dictated sign language such as the up and down head nod meaning "yes" (in a few cultures that head nod means "no"). Other examples of such sign language in American culture include the approval symbol of the circled thumb and forefinger and the disapproval symbol of the extended middle finger (symbols that, similarly, communicate very different meanings in some other cultures). Ekman has observed that with surprising frequency such potentially truth revealing gestures are made unconsciously by people engaged in speaking deceitfully, though usually the gestures are only partially executed. Thus, observing a partially executed gesture that is inconsistent with the speaker's words likely carries greater accuracy than the verbal statement.

Probably the most interesting aspect of the work of Professor Ekman and his colleagues is the identification of a few emotion-revealing involuntary facial muscle movements and the occurrence of "microexpressions" through which a subject reveals his or her true feelings by very brief facial expressions that normally go unnoticed. In the latter case, the microexpression, the subject's face takes on a readily recognized expression that accurately communicates the subject's true feelings. However, the expression is so quickly overtaken by the subject's conscious control of voluntary facial muscles that the change goes undetected by all but the most careful observers. However, Ekman's studies have shown that the skill of detecting such microexpression changes can be acquired through a simple, flash card type training process. Moreover, some people may observe and react to microexpressions, but at a subconscious level.

Not all facial muscles are voluntary. Ekman discovered that as result of this, most people are unable to mask a few facial muscle clues that reveal their true feelings. One observable set of involuntary face muscle responses he has identified is brought on by sadness, grief, distress, and, perhaps, guilt. It is manifested by the raising of the inner eyebrows (above the nasal area) so that they angulate upward pointing to each other. At the same time, a triangular outline appears above the inner eyelids with the result that there is a diamond shaped outline from the top of the inner eyelids to the top of the inner portion of the eyebrows. (His book *Telling Lies* provides illustrations.) Another involutary facial gesture, that is, one that most people cannot mask, results from fear or worry. The involuntary portion of this gesture involves the lifting and pulling together of the eyebrows and the tensing of the lower eyelid so that its border becomes more pronounced. While the presence of the first-described involuntary facial expression may of itself indicate deceit, the significance of the second one is that its absence suggests deceit if it does not accompany verbal assertions of fear and worry—the emotional states that normally trigger this involuntary facial expression.

Research reported by Ekman also indicates that asymmetric expressions of joy and sadness (a smile or frown that is more pronounced on one side of the face than on the other), is an indication that the facial expression is artificial. But, as with other aspects of nonverbal communication, this characterisitic is no more than a "clue," it is not proof. Moreover, asymmetry of facial expressions sometimes result from nerve or muscle disorders or imbalances.

Ekman further finds that truly felt feelings normally are revealed through facial expressions that last but a few seconds, usually not more than five seconds—ten seconds at the outsidé. Therefore, expressions held for a more extended interval likely are masks of attempted deception. In addition, honest facial expressions normally precede or are initiated together with words that express the purported feeling. Thus, facial expressions and gestures that are initiated after the commencement of the word flow are likely to be false.

As previously noted, but perhaps not amply emphasized, many people have ideosyncratic patterns of nonverbal and verbal behavior. It is the variation from a person's normal pattern of communication, not the particular characteristic, that offers the more reliable clue that the person is burdened with feelings that are inconsistent with the overt message being conveyed. However,

Ekman contends that symbolic gestures that are inconsistent with the stated message, and microexpressions, provide clues that are independent of a person's normal pattern of communicating. The latter types of clues, therefore, are particularly useful to an observer who is unfamiliar with the person whose veracity is being evaluated. Another clue source of this latter category is the "slip of the tongue" in the course of a flurry of words uttered in anger or fear.

At best, skilled observation and assessment of nonverbal communication enables the evaluator to make an "informed guess" as to whether a person is practicing deception. Of course, the negotiator who hopes to settle for more is better off making an informed guess than hazarding the random assessment of gut reactions. Dr. Ekman offers a checklist of 38 questions a "lie checker" should address in gauging the degree of confidence with which one can assess whether a person is engaged in deception. Because an effective negotiator seeks accurate information as the foundation for forming perceptions, the negotiator must weigh whether an informant is credible. This, of course, is especially important when the source of information is the other party to the bargaining. The list that follows capsulizes the essence of Ekman's list for weighing whether one has a good or poor prospect of being able to reliably assess an informant's veracity. Accordingly, a negotiator can place greater confidence in his ability to accurately determine the speaker's veracity if:

1. The suspected deceit is in the form of a stated lie rather than concealment.
2. The speaker is inexperienced at engaging in the suspected type of deception.
3. The speaker likely possesses correct information.
4. It is unlikely that the speaker has had a chance to rehearse the suspected deception.
5. The speaker has a sense of responsibility toward the listener.
6. It is unlikely that the speaker feels justified in deceiving the listener or in engaging in the suspected deception.
7. The speaker stands to gain something significant from successful deception.
8. The speaker stands to be significantly punished if the deception is detected.
9. The speaker has a track record of inept deceptiveness.
10. The speaker probably will feel a sense of accomplishment from successful deception.

11. The speaker has a poor memory.
12. The listener is familiar with the speaker's personal and cultural values and personal mannerisms.
13. The listener generally is skeptical and untrusting.
14. The listener is in a position to pose questions to test whether the speaker has information that would not be possessed by an innocent person.
15. The listener is a calm, careful observer.

3. Use Independent Research

Often negotiators can gather needed information from libraries, trade associations, government publications, and consultation with experts. The advantage of such sources is that the data archived by them almost always has been gathered and reported for purposes unrelated to the transaction at hand. Accordingly, while this fact alone does not guarantee data accuracy, at least it is unlikely that it has been intentionally distorted for purposes of serving the other side's efforts to shape the initiator's perceptions in the current bargaining transaction.

Using independent research to obtain information does not carry the same importance with respect to all elements of bargaining strength. For example, independent research is not likely to shed much additional light, if any, upon the negotiator's Accrued Costs. In addition, the utility of independent research as a means of obtaining bargaining information will vary depending on the nature and extent of the negotiator's prior experience with similar transactions. Thus, the negotiator who embarks on a particular type of transaction for the first time has much greater need to obtain information from outside resources than does the bargainer who regularly deals in such transactions. The latter, of course, can rely upon the cumulative data obtained from experience for information needed to make strategic and tactical decisions. Therefore, one tactic for the negotiator who is new to a particular category of transaction is to consult with an impartial expert whose experience provides a substitute source of information. That is, one in effect buys or borrows the benefits of the expert's experience.

A related technique is to seek information from trade sources such as the staff of trade associations and from the standard publications of the trade. These, too, in effect provide at least a partial substitute source for the information normally gained by the schooling of experience.

Even when dealing with experts and "independent" sources, a skilled negotiator practices a modicum of skepticism. Government agencies, experts, trade associations, and the like, often have their own agendas and biases that can distort the neutrality with which information is collected, analyzed, and presented. These biases can take very subtle forms. For example, in the next chapter we observe how the manner in which a survey question is posed can alter the resulting data.

Despite the phone company's promotional efforts to "let your fingers do the walking," too often we overlook the telephone's value as an inexpensive research tool. Frequently a telephone can provide access to places we may not be permitted to physically enter, or allow us to promptly reach persons who have needed expertise, or facilitate avoiding disclosing the true purpose of our effort to obtain information. The personal computer has added a new vehicle for gaining such access through the message sending and receiving device called computer mail and through a device known as a computer bulletin board, that serves as a computer network's version of a newsletter.

Depending on the data needed, local congressional offices and government administrative agencies, such as the Small Business Administration, Bureau of the Census, Bureau of Labor Statistics, Departments of Agriculture, Interior, and Commerce, State Department consular offices, and the like, frequently provide valuable, reliable information at little or no cost. As is further discussed in Part III of the book, computer technology offers a variety of ways to enhance independent research, including subscription access to data banks—electronic libraries with vast compilations of information stored in a manner that permits rapid discovery, retrieval, and updating.

4. Learn the Power of Silence

Cultures differ in their tolerance for social silence. Some cultures are very comfortable with it. Merely being in the company of another person carries its strokes. In such cultures, constant efforts to converse may be considered impolite. Other cultures have little tolerance for social silence. People in close contact with each other are expected to give frequent verbal strokes. In such cultures, failure to offer such conversation may be considered impolite. Notable differences in the role of social silence can be found among subcultures within the United States. Thus, the stereotypical New Yorker may be cautious about extending a friendly greeting to someone he does not know well but may maintain a steady conversational flow once in social contact with that same person. In contrast, the stereotypical rural Southerner may be quick in offering a friendly greeting but may do little to initiate or maintain a conversational flow once in social contact with that same person.

Awareness of a person's tolerance for social silence can serve a dual role in bargaining. One purpose is that it is an indicator of whether that person has a similar or different cultural background. Those who share a common cultural background are more likely to regard one another as the sort of person they "understand." Because we have more confidence in our ability to predict that which we understand, we can more easily form a favorable opinion regarding the reliability and veracity of someone whose background we perceive to be similar to our own. One consequence of this is that, in terms of the elements of bargaining strength, people who perceive that they have a shared background can more easily form a perception that the other has a high Probability of Performance.

However, as we have seen in the previous example of differences in tolerance for social silence in American rural and urban areas, often people who share general cultural characteristics place excessive attention upon such differences and fail to recognize the degree to which they indeed do "understand" each other. On the other hand, in the previously noted case of the New Yorker and the rural Southerner, our mass media and our society's high degree of geographic mobility produce considerable awareness of such behavioral differences. In contrast, people tend to be less prepared for the extent of such cultural differences likely to be encountered when crossing national boundaries. Therefore, those engaged in cross-national negotiations often find it very useful not only to retain someone for linguistic translation but also to select someone who has sufficient dual cultural awareness to serve as a go-between or advisor in dealing with differences in cultural values and social norms that too easily can result in misunderstandings.

While misperceptions respecting the meaning of social silence can distort understanding, there is another reason for assessing the other side's tolerance of social silence—social silence has potential power in eliciting information. Those of us whose cultural backgrounds are characterized by little tolerance for social silence tend to feel stroke deprived when involved with a person who does not say very much. The normal response is to attempt to elicit the expected conversational strokes by taking increased initiative to maintain the flow of words. In a bargaining setting, too often this can result in giving away too much information, giving it away too soon, or giving it away without receiving an exchange of needed data. Therefore, a negotiator who has a low tolerance for silence must remember that it is all right to not talk, that it is acceptable to wait silently for the other person to initiate further conversation. And, as an offensive technique to gather information, and even to obtain concessions, skilled negotiators play upon the other side's stroking needs by quietly listening—particularly when the other side has little tolerance for such social silence.

In summary, settling for more often requires taking guidance from two observations of folk wisdom. First, the eyes and ears are closer to the brain than is the mouth. Hence, our brains can do more with what we see and hear than with what we say. Second, because we have been given two ears and two eyes but one mouth, we should accept nature's mandate by doing twice as much listening and observing as talking.

5. Ask Questions—The Hallmark of Skilled Bargaining

The dictionary defines question as "a sentence in an interrogative form, addressed to someone in order to elicit information." One who has mastered the art of negotiating is more likely to define question as the most versatile and powerful tool in the negotiator's arsenal. In addition to providing a means for obtaining information, questions often offer an effective way to prepare the other side to receive, as well as give, information, and offer a means for altering which ego state is in control of the other side.

There are four basic types of questions. One form of question is the rhetorical question. A rhetorical question is not designed to elicit information from someone else. Rather, it serves as a device to introduce the information or contentions that the "questioner" wishes to present. In other words, the person who poses a rhetorical question intends to answer that question. Why ask a rhetorical question? Because it alerts the other side that it is about to receive a particular category of information and indicates the significance of that information. In this way, a successful rhetorical question is directed at the listener's Adult ego state. The Adult, it will be recalled, deals with information and analysis. Because a rhetorical question calls upon the listener to process the information that the "questioner" is about to convey, it is designed to turn on the listener's Adult. (In case the reader overlooked the illustration, the question posed in this paragraph is a rhetorical question.)

A second form of question is the "pregnant" or leading question. Such a question is posed in a manner that indicates the correct answer. As with the rhetorical question, it is designed not to elicit information or contentions from the listener but rather to obtain the listener's affirmation of the information or contentions suggested by the questioner. In much the same way as it can be said that a rhetorical question is directed at the listener's Adult, can it be said that the pregnant question is directed at the listener's Adaptive Child or Nurturing Parent? The goal of the successful pregnant question, of course, is to get the listener to recite, and in effect identify with and adopt as his own, the information or contentions suggested by the question. (In case the reader overlooked the illustration, the question posed in this paragraph was a pregnant question.)

A third form of question is the open-ended question. In asking such a question, the questioner is truly eliciting information. Such questions are exploratory; they are best utilized when the questioner is seeking new information or ideas and is uncertain as to the likely content of the answer. In TA terms, a successful open-ended question addresses the other side's Adult or Natural Child. Of course, rather than merely provide information or offer tentative ideas, a listener might choose to give an answer from his Critical Parent. That is, the response cuts off exploration by taking a fixed position.

Finally, the fourth form of question is the closed or directive question. Here, too, the questioner truly elicits information or contentions from the other side. However, unlike the open-ended question situation, the person who poses a directive question has a firm expectation respecting the nature of the answer. The purpose of a directive question is to extract specific details not previously revealed to the questioner or to obtain the listener's confirmation or rejection of the questioner's expectations. Accordingly, it is the sort of question most often asked by able trial lawyers on cross-examination.

Occasionally a statement that greatly exaggerates what are likely to be the facts can serve as a substitute for a directive question. To illustrate, an assertion such as "You inspected these parts and must know that the failure rate is over 45 percent!" if it greatly exaggerates the probable failure rate, often will elicit an accurate report of the manufacturer's actual inspection findings, whereas a request for that information might be greeted by evasion or silence. The exaggerated statement carries an implied direct question— can you prove me wrong?—a challenge that listeners often find irresistible.

In the course of bargaining, the negotiator who settles for more uses all four types of questions. He uses both open-ended and directive questions to learn from the other side. Open-ended questions are asked to get an overview of the other side's position and to explore what areas of information might be obtained from the other side. Directive questions are asked in order to pin down specific details and confirm that the questioner correctly understands the information offered and the positions taken by the other side. Normally, the skilled bargainer, like the skilled lawyer taking a deposition, begins with open-ended questions to get the broad picture and then uses directive questions to ascertain the details and to confirm his understanding of previously presented information. But, just as the skilled bargainer uses both open-ended and directive questions to learn from the other side, he also uses rhetorical and pregnant questions to help shape what aspect of the other side's personality will be reacting to the negotiator's bargaining efforts.

6. Exploit Rituals and Pastimes

While examining the topic of gathering accurate information, it is worth referring back to the previous chapter's Transactional Analysis discussion of Rituals and Pastimes. Rituals, it will be recalled, are stylized transactions such as shaking hands and reciting a customary greeting, introducing people to each other in a stylized manner dictated by rules of etiquette, or waiting until everyone has been seated before beginning to eat. And, Pastimes, it will be recalled, are time filling verbal stroking transactions such as recalling the circumstances of a previous encounter, exchanging information regarding common acquaintances, or recounting a recently heard joke.

Both forms of time structuring, Rituals and Pastimes, are encountered repeatedly in any prolonged negotiation and offer indirect opportunities to gather information about the personalities, backgrounds, experience level, scripts, and prejudices of both sides. People tend to be less guarded in what they say when engaged in Rituals and Pastimes than when engaged in a Procedure. Accordingly, the skilled negotiator's Adult maintains control of the situation, both as listener-observer and as speaker, even when engaging in these largely Critical-Parent-oriented time structuring activities.

7. Avoid the Dangers of Selective Observation

When bargaining perceptions turn upon hearing or seeing, a negotiator must exercise particular caution because everyone is susceptible to filtering, selecting, distorting, and inattentiveness in making and remembering observations.

In her book *Eyewitness Testimony*,[7] Professor Elizabeth Loftus presents a considerable body of research findings demonstrating the dangers of unreliable selective and distorted observations. Among the findings she discusses is the tendency of people to see and hear what they expect to observe as opposed to what they actually observe. One dramatic example she offers is an experiment in which subjects were shown a sketch of a subway car interior in which some passengers were seated and two were standing. One of the standing passengers is a conservatively dressed young black man who is making a gesture of inquiry while facing a shorter white man who is standing close to him and is pointing his finger making a gesture of emphasis with one hand while holding a straight edge razor close to his body with the other hand. The subject was directed to describe the picture to a second person who in turn repeated the description to a third and this process continued until the sixth or seventh person in the line of communication described the picture to the experimenter. Over half of the final reports in more than forty sets of repetitions of this experiment had the black man holding the razor and, while there is no indication of violence in the actual picture, a number of the final reports described the black man as engaged in threatening conduct. Dr. Loftus reports other studies in which subjects transform the location of drug stores in a photo from the middle of a block to the corner—the more familiar location for such a shop.

Reports of observations are susceptible to memory failures as well. The passage of time between an event and the requested recollection results in very substantial slippage of accuracy. Moreover, the passage of time increases the possibility that memory will be influenced by the contamination of other sources of information

---

[7]E. Loftus, *Eyewitness Testimony* (Harvard Univ. Press, 1980).

concerning the observation or concerning similar situations. This is confirmed in experiments reported by Loftus, whose research demonstrates that if observations are not reported until there has been an opportunity for memory to fade, misleading information received just before the report is solicited often distorts the subject's recollection.

Because of the problems in relying on reported observations, a negotiator should try to discover the circumstances in which the observations were made, the time lapse between the observation and the recollection, and the prospects of distortion resulting from observer bias or exposure to competing information. All of these factors must be weighed before the bargainer determines how much reliance to place on the reported observations.

Moreover, when the other side presents information that we know is inaccurate, we must be cautious about concluding that it is intentionally trying to mislead or misinform us. Negotiations and underlying relationships often dissolve as a result of the emotional reaction to what someone perceives to be an intentional effort at distortion. Yet, the above exploration of the pitfalls awaiting the person who tries to gather accurate information should remind us that the other side's misstatements are not necessarily the result of bad motive or incompetence; it might be nothing more than data that got bruised or damaged as a result of the normal hazards of information gathering, filtration, and transmission.

B. Adjust Data Analysis for the Variable of Time

When we were children we expected to grow up in a world that closely resembled the one we were then experiencing. As we age we become more aware of the verity that time is a variable that affects all aspects of life. Einstein revolutionized the theories of physics by demonstrating the need to take account of time as a factor that interacts with the other dimensions of the physical world. When assessing needs, alternatives, and costs, the negotiator, too, must heed the dimension of time.

1. The Present and Future Value of Money

Money is a system that enables us to equate the comparative value different people place upon property and services so as to facilitate indirect exchanges. These exchanges transfer valued objects and services among large numbers of people and at different times and places. Because the monetary measure of the value of different things changes over time, and because negotiations often involve transactions that continue over extended periods, accurate analysis of monetary value requires us to take account of the time dimension.

This section examines some of the more significant aspects of the problem of analyzing monetary information in relation to the impact of time. Such analysis is necessary in order to understand accurately the bargaining elements we have identified as the Offer to Meet the Other's Needs (OMON), the Best Alternative to the Proposed Agreement (BAPA), and the Cost of Impending Negotiation (COIN).

Your promise to pay me $10,000 next year is worth less to me than a payment of that amount today because (a) if I had the money now, I could lend it at interest—therefore, the delayed payment deprives me of the opportunity to earn a year's interest on the money; (b) I risk the possibility that you will no longer be able to pay the money a year from now; (c) the $10,000 may buy less in a year than it buys today. The composite impact of these three factors represents the difference between the present and future value of money. Because of the difference between those values, to analyze the monetary impact of a proposed transaction, the future values should be converted into present value equivalents. To illustrate, if a one year demand deposit with a federally insured bank yields 8 percent interest compounded daily, I am losing the ability to earn that interest if the negotiated transaction will require me to make expenditures for which I will not receive payment for a year. A banker would explain that the present value of the future payment must be "discounted" to reflect the lost opportunity to earn money from that delayed payment. Moreover, if the delayed payment is not secured by property of very significant value, the amount of discount deducted to determine the present value of the delayed payment should be increased to reflect the risk of nonpayment. Accordingly, there are elements of judgment involved in selecting the rate of discount appropriate to the risks, lost opportunities, and expected inflationary or deflationary changes.

Various tools are available to the negotiator who is estimating the present monetary value of a transaction. Thus, published interest rates for instruments of indebtedness (such as demand deposits, treasury notes, mortgages, and bonds) involving various levels of risk and durations of inaccessability to the funds, provide reasonable guidance for selecting the discount rate most appropriate to the types of risks involved in the transaction being evaluated. Once a judgment has been made regarding the appropriate discount rate, charts and easy-to-use computer programs can be purchased that permit quick calculation of present values as long as the future payment is made at one time or in accordance with a regular payment schedule. (Calculations are a bit more cumbersome if payments follow an irregular schedule.) Once the calculations have been completed, the bargainer can make strategic and tactical decisions with increased assurance that his financial perceptions have been adjusted to reflect reality more accurately.

An alternative to calculating the present value of a transaction is to shape it in a way that is designed to eliminate the differences between present and future values. Hence, the lost earning ability of money invested in the transaction can be included as a cost of doing business when assessing whether the other side's offer meets the bargainer's needs. In addition, the gamble respecting the possibility of the other side's failure of performance often can be reduced or eliminated through the purchase of the type of insurance (such as indemnity, fidelity, replacement, liability, health, or life) that is appropriate to cover the category of feared risk. Or, substitutes for performance can be ensured through various types of security devices—a tactical technique that is discussed in Chapter 6. Finally, future price changes can be taken into account by providing for price adjustments to be made based upon indexes, such as the consumer price index or wholesale price index, that are designed to reflect general changes in monetary values.

2. The Expected Durability of People and Things

Another form of time-based uncertainty in analyzing the information that guides bargaining decisions is the life expectancy of people, things, and relationships. A class of statistical specialists, called actuaries, make a science of estimating how long people will live, will be members of the work force, will be free from serious illness, and the like. When the determination of whether a transaction will meet its expectations turns on the availability or well-being of individuals, proper analysis of the underlying information deserves reference to actuarial tables or consultation with actuarial specialists. Of course, actuarial uncertainties often can be removed from a transaction by providing for the purchase of insurance which is to be paid to the benefit of the party who bears the risks of such uncertainties.

An example of influencing bargaining perceptions by removing the factual analysis problems arising out of the uncertainties of life expectancy is an approach to resolving personal injury claims known as the "structured settlement." The traditional method of adjusting such claims is to negotiate a lump sum payment. This leaves the claimant with the uncertainties of having to prudently manage the settlement funds so as to assure a desired level of income to meet long-term living and medical care expenses for the duration of disability. The structured settlement removes those uncertainties by substituting the certainty of receiving insured periodic payments and related insured benefits. It also substitutes for the abstract benefit of a stated sum of money, a program of specific, described benefits and payments tailored to meet the claimant's concrete daily, weekly, and monthly living needs. For example, a structured settlement offer might consist of an initial cash payment to cover past lost wages, medical expenses, and attorney's fees; a medical benefits insurance policy to cover future medical care needs; insured rehabilitation treatment; insured periodic disability and survivor's income payments; and a college tuition policy for dependent children. In this way, the structured settlement facilitates the claimant's ability to visualize how his particular needs will be met. Because the defendant is purchasing annuity and insurance policies to be paid over an extended period of time, the premium cost of a sufficiently attractive settlement is often considerably less for the defendant than would be the cost of a lump sum settlement offer which the claimant finds to be comparably attractive.

Uncertainties regarding life expectancy can also arise respecting the durability of objects. Often cumulative experience or testing data provide a basis for reducing these uncertainties and, therefore, these data are essential to a proper analysis of the information that guides bargaining decisions involving such objects. In such instances, accurate assessment of real values should include depreciation or replacement reserves to account for the anticipated decline in the value of the object. The assessment of real value must also take into account the possibilities of loss or destruction. Here, too, there are substitutes for such evaluative information. Thus, an alternative way to reduce the uncertainties respecting the durability of an object is to offer or obtain guarantees of the hoped-for qualities or arrange to purchase insurance against the possible risks.

3. Impact of Federal, State, and Local Taxes

Most transactions involving transfers of money, things, services, or responsibilities carry tax consequences. Because the tax burdens attached to a transaction often are substantial, a negotiator cannot know whether he is settling for more without ascertaining the extent of those consequences. Moreover, the tax consequences of a transaction can often be altered by changing the terms of the arrangement. Thus, the impact of those extractions must be weighed to determine the true net monetary value of alternative proposals.

Another reason for the skilled bargainer to weigh the tax consequences of a transaction is that tax planning can provide a means of discovering and satisfying common or compatible needs. Or, to put it in previously defined terms, the tax aspects of a transaction often provide a means of transforming what would otherwise be a purely exchange type of negotiation into an integrative bargaining situation.

Because of the complexities and frequent change of tax laws, it is not possible to offer any simple guidelines for reducing the tax burdens that might accrue from a negotiated transaction. Hence, only one piece of tactical advice can be offered respecting this aspect of bargaining: if the financial stakes of a transaction are substantial, it is generally worthwhile to consult with a tax expert to determine how variations in the transaction might produce a reduced tax burden.

Chapter 6

Tactics for Modifying Perceptions: Information Exchange

A. The Functions of Information Exchange

Information exchange serves two strategic purposes. First, by giving new information we provide the other side with a basis for reevaluating, and thereby altering, its perception of its needs, costs, assessments, and alternatives. Second, by receiving new information we can reassess our own perceptions so as to increase the likelihood that they accurately reflect reality.

B. Information Exchange Tactics

1. Avoid Deaf Ears

Offering information to the other side cannot achieve its function of altering perceptions if it falls upon deaf ears. Therefore, an important tactical consideration is to ensure that the other side is prepared to receive and weigh offered information.

Transactional Analysis provides guidance for determining when someone is likely to be receptive to information and when information exchange efforts are likely to be wasted. The side of the personality that seeks and weighs information is the Adult ego state. Accordingly, an Adult-to-Adult transaction offers assurance that the other side is ready to receive the offered information. In contrast, information conveyed in a way that appears to come from the initiator's Critical Parent and is directed at the listener's Adaptive Child will not be well received if some other ego state is presently in control of the listener. This, of course, is the common dilemma of parental efforts to guide the conduct of teenage children. It can be a dilemma, as well, in negotiations among complete strangers. Thus, information that is offered in a doctrinaire manner, or with an apparent attitude of superiority, is likely to be totally rejected, or received with cautious skepticism, by a listener who is in an Adult, Natural Child, or Little Professor ego state. If the listener himself is in a Critical Parent ego state (not unusual for a teenager), the effort at information exchange is likely to deteriorate into uproar because two conflicting doctrinaire approaches are competing for domination.

Three simple devices for avoiding deaf ears are: (1) use dramatic or graphic methods of presentation, (2) ask questions early in the presentation to prompt the other side's attentiveness, and (3) ask questions toward the end of the presentation to confirm that the message was heard and understood.

2. Use Biofeedback

In most negotiations, one aspect of information exchange consists of giving the other side a sense of your personality that is consistent with your bargaining strategy. This tactic enhances your ability to increase the other side's assessment of your Probability of Performance, and supports your efforts to get them to reconsider their Predictive Accuracy. Another aspect of information exchange in most negotiations is the need to ensure that the respective ego states are appropriate to the type of personal interaction sought by the bargainer.

Our examination of TA and of the tactical value of questions have suggested ways to influence one's own and the other side's ego state. Biofeedback offers an additional method of influencing your own mood and the mood of the other side, both as a means of conveying a sense of your personality and as a tactic to facilitate the exchange of other information.

The previous discussion on detecting deception explored the extent to which a person's true emotions often are revealed through physiological clues. There is growing evidence that emotions not only generate physiological reactions but that the converse is also true—emotions are influenced by physiological activity.

Actors, athletes, and salespeople long have recognized that by imitating the facial expressions and body movements associated with an emotional state, they can generate a genuine internal sense of that emotion. Thus, skilled salespeople train themselves to put on a friendly smile before the potential customer comes to the door, answers the phone, or reaches the desk or counter. That the purpose of doing this goes beyond meeting the potential customer's likely social expectations is most obvious in the case of the telephone solicitor. Rather, putting on an appropriate "face" for the expected transaction "psychs up" the salesperson to speak and act in a relaxed, friendly manner—a manner that will convey self-confidence and confidence in the product or service. Athletes and actors similarly get psyched up by feigning the physiological clues of the emotional state they want to feel until the feedback generates the genuine feelings.

In the same way, a negotiator who seeks to settle for more can use this form of biofeedback to be able to more convincingly project the desired image and establish the best mood for effective communication. Moreover, occasionally there are opportunities to use this form of biofeedback to help change the ego state that is in control of the other side. For example, getting someone to participate in acting out a ritual of politeness or deference to a senior person ("Do me a favor, my boss is a stickler for politeness, when he comes in, please stand until he is seated") may influence the actor to respond to that person from his Adaptive Child. Similarly, getting parties to participate in a cooperative or coordinated procedure, such as eating a meal in which dishes and condiments are passed back and forth, can help them return to an Adult-Adult transaction.

3. Seek, Assess, and Adhere to the Truth

Distorting the truth by lying or withholding important information can be used successfully by a negotiator who seeks to maximize his gains. However, those gains are likely to be short-lived. If the other side can be expected to place substantial reliance upon the information about which the lie was told or the truth was withheld, the law normally gives the other side a right to rescind the agreement. Often, it will also give the victim of the distortion a right to recover any damages suffered as a result of reasonable reliance upon the distortion. In addition, if the distortion was malicious or willful or was designed to accomplish a fraud or violate a fiduciary responsibility, it may result in very substantial punitive damages being added to the legal remedy.

In some situations a negotiator's distortions of the truth constitute a violation of criminal law. For example, a party can be criminally prosecuted for willfully making a false statement in doing business with the government or making false claims for government benefits. The law often also imposes criminal penalties in situations in which a person willfully lies in dealing with a person or entity to whom or to which he owes fiduciary responsibilities. For example, in some situations, people such as brokers and professionals can be criminally prosecuted for lying to customers, clients, or patients or, similarly, can be held criminally liable for withholding information that the law requires them to disclose.

Lies carry additional potentially adverse consequences for the liar. If the liar is a licensed broker or professional, the lies can give rise to costly disciplinary proceedings. Moreover, once others begin to perceive of the negotiator as a liar, that negotiator's future ability to alter perceptions through the exchange of information is greatly diminished. Similarly, those who lose confidence in a negotiator's truthfulness are likely to lose confidence, as well, in that negotiator's Probability of Performance, thus further weakening the negotiator's bargaining strength. Additionally, the backfire of being caught deceiving the other side can damage the bargainer's general reputation and weaken bargaining strength in future transactions with others as well. Finally, the victim of a lie has a right to feel indignant; the liar lie has affronted the victim's dignity because the implication of the lie is that the victim is too stupid, too careless, or too inept a judge of character to discover the deception. The resulting indignation often is accompanied by a desire for vengeance—a very powerful means of satisfying our status drive that will not be satisfied until the victim has seen the wrongdoer paid back in spades.

Having said all of this, it must be noted that in negotiations there is one category of deception that generally is not treated as lying because the parties do not expect total candor respecting such matters. That category is the bargainer's or principal's state of mind with regard to such matters as bargaining intentions, priorities, goals, emotional state and responses, and assessments of what the party considers to be "fair or reasonable." For example, the American Bar Association's Code of Professional Responsibility, and its more recent Model Rules of Professional Responsibility, both state that in representing a client, a lawyer shall not knowingly make a false statement of law or fact. However, an official comment to the Model Rules notes that in negotiations parties conventionally do not treat as a statement of fact such things as the price or value placed on the subject of the transaction or a party's intentions. The distinction between such statements and statements of fact is that while facts are fixed, a person's state of mind is likely to change from moment to moment. Accordingly, we accept representations concerning such matters with the knowledge that they are not immutable, that they are fluid and, indeed, their susceptibility to change is the very focus of the negotiator's persuasive efforts.

Of course, if the negotiator is dealing in a situation of special trust or dominance, the sort of situations in which courts hold parties to fiduciary standards (as when dealing with minors, incompetents, patients, clients, students, parishioners, and the like), even representations concerning the bargainer's state of mind are expected to be made in total honesty. In such situations, courts and professional disciplinary bodies treat any deviation from complete candor as a violation of the expected standard of conduct.

4. What Information to Convey; What to Avoid Revealing

As previously noted, the bargaining strength model presented in Chapter 2 offers a framework for determining whether particular information should be offered to the other side or whether it should be withheld if possible. To make such an assessment, the negotiator must decide how the information will affect the other side's perceptions with respect to each element of bargaining strength (OMON, POP, AC, DA, BAPA, COIN, PA). By referring to the bargaining strength model, the negotiator can then determine whether the information will influence those perceptions in a manner that increases or decreases bargaining power.

To take an easy example, suppose an iron work contractor who has been asked for a proposal for remodeling a staircase so that it will conform to federal safety requirements is asked what prior experience he has had with such work. The contractor increases the weight of the potential customer's perception of the contractor's offer to meet the customer's needs (Offer to Meet the Other's Needs—OMON) if he can cite specific completed jobs of a similar nature. However, if he mentions a job on which he knows that the customer was upset over a delay in getting the work done, the iron work contractor risks reducing his bargaining power because an inquiry of that customer might cause the present prospect to lower his perception of the contractor's reliability (Probability of Performance—POP), a change that will reduce the contractor's bargaining strength.

In deciding whether to withhold information, a negotiator must not only weigh its impact upon his bargaining strength but additionally must determine whether he has a legal obligation of disclosure. Withholding information in situations in which there is a legal obligation of disclosure constitutes deception and poses the risks of legal liability discussed in the previous subsection. To illustrate, in the above example there would be no legal obligation to call attention to the work done for a customer who had complained about delays. But let us assume that the iron contractor knows that the potential customer faces fines if the work is not completed within sixty days and that the contractor's current commitments will prevent him from completing such a job for at least four months. In that situation, if the contractor fails to disclose his inability to get the work done promptly, local law may well hold the contractor liable for damages resulting from delay even if the contract is silent respecting the time period for completing the job.

When the Best Alternative to the Proposed Agreement involves litigation, or where the negotiator is facing a potential criminal action, deciding what information to convey must also take into account the legal rules of evidence. Questions of liability or guilt often are close judgment calls on the facts, the law, or both. Similarly, it is often difficult to predict whether the other side will be able to gather and present the necessary evidence to persuasively prove its position. Nevertheless, to more fully explore the prospects of working out a negotiated settlement, a party sometimes is willing to acknowledge, assume, or share information that it would not readily concede in the courtroom.

The modern approach to legal evidence takes into account the benefits of resolving potential litigation through negotiated settlements. Accordingly, the modern approach is to reject efforts to introduce into evidence statements made during the course of settlement negotiations. But some jurisdictions have not adopted the modern approach and allow the introduction of testimony, as admissions against interest, respecting statements made during settlement discussions. At common law, such testimony can be used, among other things, as the basis for proving liability.

Furthermore, even under the modern approach, exceptions are recognized that permit use in litigation of testimony respecting what was said in settlement negotiations where the purpose of the testimony is to show a witness' bias, disprove an allegation of undue delay in seeking a trial, or to prove an effort to obstruct justice. Accordingly, when negotiating a dispute that may become a subject of litigation, especially if the litigation might be controlled by common law rules, a party should take special precautions before presenting information for the sake of better bargaining communication. This can be done in a variety of ways, such as posing the information as an assumption for the sake of discussion or by expressly disclaiming any such admissions. The safest course is to prepare a written disclaimer of admission or, better still, negotiate an agreement that statements made during bargaining will not be used in litigation.

In criminal proceedings, offering reparation to an injured party often carries a great deal of weight in persuading a court to accept a lenient plea bargain or in persuading a judge or jury to go light on sentencing. However, in a few jurisdictions reparation and offers of reparation are risky because at trial the prosecutor is allowed to introduce such offers or acts into evidence as an admission of guilt.

5. Carefully Select the Media for Information Exchange

The thesis that "the medium is the message" has become an important operating principle in our world of expanded methods of communication. The choice of whether to communicate in person, in a formal or informal setting, by telephone, letter, pamphlet, charts, videotapes, computer screen, or other means, obviously imposes limits on such things as the duration of the communications opportunity, the prospects for mutual inquiry and challenge concerning the presented data and ideas, the level of available specificity, the opportunity for dramatic emphasis, and the like. In addition, it should be noted that the site or sites at which the participants are located when they communicate can control what media are available for communication. Moreover, the time and place of communication are themselves dimensions of the media of communication that affect the scope and nature of the opportunity and resources available for exchange of data and ideas.

In selecting the media for information exchange, attention should be given to the above noted limits that are controlled by that choice since they have a considerable influence upon how thoroughly and persuasively the parties will be able to exchange data and explore ideas. Attention should also be given to the impact these variables might have upon the interpersonal dimensions of the transaction. Chapter 4, which discusses Transactional Analysis, offers a method for weighing the likely consequences in terms of the interpersonal dynamics of the transaction that may be influenced by the choice of media.

One illustration of the impact of media choice on bargaining dynamics is the effect it has upon the available degree of physical closeness or distance. A room with a large conference table tends to keep people far apart; a lunch or dinner table brings them closer. A telephone and a computer screen both link people who are physically apart but the telephone does so with greater intimacy because the sound of the voices are pressed into each other's ear. For example, when people are angered in a telephone conversation they often hold the instrument away from their heads whereas they generally press it to their ear when enjoying the conversation. To some degree this may be a function of the voice volume being used, but does that provide the full explanation? Speaker phones, on the other hand, detract from the telephone conversation's unique form of intimacy.

Behavioral scientists who study communication have noted that the physical distance between communicators has an impact upon their perceptions and that the amount of distance that will modify perceptions varies from culture to culture. Each society has its own protocols concerning the range of distance that should separate people engaged in normal social or business transactions. Violation of those protocols creates a sense of discomfort. It suggests a modification of the relationship and this, in turn, can alter behavior.

For example, in one study Professor David Buller had students solicit other students to sign a petition.[1] The physical arrangement allowed the student who was to be solicited to select the distance between him or herself and the solicitor. Buller found that solicitors were more successful in obtaining signatures in those instances when the solicitor moved closer to the subject than the distance initially selected by the subject.

Physical contact is another element of the media of communication that appears to carry messages that affect behavior. Thus, another study found that a touch on the shoulder accompanying a request obtains a higher frequency of compliance than the same request made without a touch.[2] Of course, the findings may be specific to the cultural group involved. Since such studies normally

---

[1]D. Buller, "Communication Apprehension and Reactions to Proxemic Violations," 11 *Journal of Nonverbal Behavior* 13 (1987).

[2]M. Patterson, J. Powell & M. Lenihan, "Touch Compliance and Interpersonal Affect," 10 *Journal of Nonverbal Behavior* 41 (1986).

use college students as the subjects, very possibly, people in other age groups may respond differently.

The choice of media also affects the availability of spontaneity or the probability of a studied reaction to the communication. Face-to-face conversation clearly provides the best opportunity for spontaneity while written communications involving delayed transfers of messages facilitate a studied reaction. This, of course, can alter the content of what is stated in the response. Additionally, the more spontaneous the response, the more likely it is to reveal the emotional as well as the intellectual reaction of the other side. Of course, in many situations, a bargainer may want to insulate himself, or the process of reasoned deliberation, from spontaneous emotional reactions—in which case the medium for communication can be selected to maximize the prospects of the other's ability to provide a studied response.

Another aspect of the interpersonal dynamics of the transaction that deserves particular emphasis at this point is the selection of the person who will be the source of communication. This variable has received some attention under the topic of Transactional Analysis and will receive additional attention in a later chapter. However, at this time, it is appropriate to emphasize that in addition to the parties or their representatives being available sources for communicating data and ideas, negotiators often can look to neutral or only marginally interested third parties to serve in this capacity. In its most formal structure, this technique is called mediation or conciliation (in the United States the terms are interchangeable). At its least formal level, any or even all of the participants may not be conscious of the fact that the third party is playing a mediator's role.

Although the level of mediator intrusiveness can vary from casual to domineering, the central characteristic is that the mediator participates in the exchange of information and ideas without having a direct interest in the outcome. It is this aspect that is particularly significant for this portion of our discussion because, as a result of the mediator's apparent neutrality, the negotiating parties tend to be less defensive, less cynical, and less cautious in evaluating and responding to data or ideas suggested by the mediator. Thus, the same information or proposals are likely to be treated as having greater reliability, credibility, and merit if introduced by the third party than if propounded by the other side. Therefore, information exchange often has greater impact upon altering perceptions if its apparent source is a neutral third party. In addition, when such exchanges appear to originate in the mediator, the perception of the other side's Probability of Performance will likely increase because the representations that form the basis for settlement have been witnessed by such a neutral. As previously noted in the discussion of bargaining strategy, the availability of an impartial witness to the discussions enhances the perception of the Probability of Performance (POP) since having such a credible source for confirming the party's fidelity or infidelity to the undertaking may aid in obtaining formal or informal sanctions in the event the settlement is later violated.

6. Confirm Information, Understanding, and Positions

All of us have had the experience of misunderstanding what others have tried to tell us and of being misunderstood. Obviously, we cannot influence another's perceptions in the intended manner if the information we seek to convey is misunderstood. By the same token, we cannot accurately reassess our own perceptions based on additional information if we fail to correctly understand what is being conveyed. Accordingly, if we are to master the skills of bargaining, an essential tactic is to always attempt to confirm the other side's understanding of what we are trying to communicate to them and, similarly, to always attempt to confirm the accuracy of our understanding of what others are attempting to tell us. Moreover, when negotiations are stretched over an extended period, this same precept dictates that we periodically attempt to reconfirm understandings respecting critical information so as to safeguard against the hazards of poor memories, the distortions of wishful thinking, and the interference of undetected intervening information from alternative sources.

The least formal way to confirm mutual understanding of what has been discussed is to ask questions about the other side's understanding or to recite one's own understanding and request confirmation. When negotiations are extended over a period of days or weeks, a letter or memorandum sent to the other side summarizing one's understanding of what has transpired to date, including the basic information presented by both sides, provides a more formal method of avoiding misunderstandings, particularly if the other side is invited to call attention to any errors in the statement. And, at a still higher level of formality, a memorandum of understanding specifying the information exchanged and the positions taken can be prepared for both sides' signatures.

7. Avoid Distorted Information Processing

Studies demonstrate that in a number of ways, how information is received or perceived results in its being used, unused, underused, overused, or misused. One such distortion factor is the ease with which particular information can be recalled. For example, it has been shown that people generally overestimate the frequency of well-publicized events, such as shootings or homicides, while they underestimate the frequency of poorly publicized events. Thus, studies show that people typically judge homicide to be a more frequent cause of death than a disease such as diabetes even though, in fact, the disease takes many more lives.[3]

Similarly, vivid, detailed reports of events have a more dominant impact than abstract ones. Thus, research reveals that a single recounted personal experience with the performance of a particular make of car generally has greater influence upon consumer choices than composite comparative performance data from impartial sources such as *Consumer Reports*.[4] This may well explain the advertising industry's preference for anecdotal television ads.

Because ease of recall alters the prospect of whether the decision maker will rely on particular data, presenting the data in a visually as well as verbally succinct manner often appears to add to its influence. This, too, is a lesson not lost on the advertising industry nor upon political campaign managers. Moreover, it is a technique whose value should not be underestimated just because the information is directed at a relatively sophisticated audience. For example, in his investigations of the conduct of lawyer negotiators, Prof. Roger Haydock was persuaded that graphic and multimedia presentations are effective with lawyers despite the assertions by some that professionals are immune to the allure of such techniques.[5]

Similarly, well-organized data presentation makes a stronger and more lasting impact than does haphazard information exposure. Thus, studies show that if there are favorable comparisons to be communicated, it is best to present the comparative data at the same time in a compact form rather than offer it sequentially with

---

[3]D. Kahneman, P. Slovic & A. Tversky, *Judgment Under Uncertainty: Heuristics and Biases* (Cambridge Univ. Press, 1982). They characterize this source of data distortion as being based on the "availability" of information.

[4]R. Hogarth, *Judgment and Choice*, 2d ed. (Wiley, 1987). This type of data distortion falls into the category of selective perception.

[5]R. Haydock, *Negotiation Practice* (Wiley Law Pubs., 1984).

gaps of time or space separating the fragments of information. Similarly, experiments have demonstrated that the clear, well organized presentation of data is often successful in masking omissions of critical information.

Because ease of recall influences the prospects of whether data will play a decisional role, the negotiator who wants to settle for more should present favorable data in simple, carefully organized, vivid terms. Further, when possible the presentation should use visual as well as verbal media. Equally important, in forming one's own perceptions a skilled bargainer must be alert to the danger of being unduly influenced by well-publicized data or by information presented in a clear, vivid and conveniently organized manner.

How we understand information is often a reflection of the extent to which our attention is drawn to particular aspects of that information. Accordingly, experiments have shown that our perceptions of the role played by ourselves or others in an event is influenced by the extent to which environmental factors, such as relative status, appearance, or seating arrangements, call attention to particular participants. Generally, we attribute a greater causal role to those to whom our attention has been drawn. For example, experiments show that people attribute greater importance to the conversational role played by participants whom they can directly observe than to the role played by participants whom they can less easily observe.[6] Experiments have also demonstrated that people who are seated closer together report a greater sense of intimacy with each other than do those who are engaged in the same activity but not seated as close.[7]

Another way people commonly distort information is by giving excessive weight to the absolute number of events while neglecting comparative data. For example, many people will be favorably impressed by the stockbroker who offers to give them the names of ten customers who doubled their portfolios during the past year while following his advice. However, an accurate appraisal of the broker's performance is not possible until one learns how many others followed the broker's advice and what happened to their investments. Too often, though, information respecting the number of unsuccessful efforts is not readily observable nor offered.

---

[6]R. Jones, "Perceiving Other People" in *In the Eye of the Beholder: Contemporary Issues in Stereotyping*, A. Miller, ed. (Praeger Pubs., 1982) p. 41. Also, I. Vine, "Territoriality and the Spatial Regulation of Interaction" in *Organization of Behavior in Face-to-Face Interaction*, A. Kendon, R. Harris & M. Key, eds. (Mouton, 1975), p. 357.

[7]R. Gifford & B. O'Connor, "Nonverbal Intimacy," 10 *Journal of Nonverbal Behavior* 207 (1986).

Nevertheless, where such comparative data are essential to an accurate understanding, it merits a direct inquiry or investigation.

In their book *Judgment Under Uncertainty*,[8] Kahneman, Slovic and Tversky call attention, as well, to a rather different sort of information processing error—the tendency to overlook information implicit in nonoccurrences. Although we commonly seek cause-effect relationships in a known sequence of events, too often we overlook the significance of the nonoccurrence of an event in an expected sequence. For example, suppose a union has had a twenty-year collective bargaining relationship with Blunder Corporation and that its collective agreement with the company is being rene-gotiated. Suppose, too, that for the past ten years, at the initial bargaining meeting, Blunder's Chief Executive Officer has pro-claimed that the company is on the verge of financial ruin and has demanded the elimination of the seniority system, a rollback in wages, a reduction in the medical care plan, and similar employee concessions. However, no such presentation is made at the first round of the current contract negotiations and in record time a settlement is reached that the union's bargaining committee con-siders quite satisfactory. The bargaining committee members con-gratulate each other and announce the good news to the mem-bership. Is it a time for celebration? Perhaps so. The company may have embarked upon a more conciliatory approach to its labor relations. On the other hand, the modification in the company's bargaining stance may also be the result of reduced concern respecting the contractual terms because a secret decision has been made to close, move, or sell the operation. Nonoccurrence is an indication of alternative, as yet undetected, variables that have intervened in the expected sequence of occurrences. Thus, nonoccurrence of expected events is a signal calling for further inquiry or more careful analysis before making any bargaining decisions.

Further complicating the process of information processing is the tendency to downplay conflicting information—information that does not offer a consistent profile. This has been identified as the "king has no clothes" phenomenon. Such information is inconve-nient; it poses uncertainty and experimental psychologists find that people generally avoid uncertainty by discounting evidence of it.

For the negotiator this means not being discouraged by the presence of data that conflicts with the perception that you are

---

[8]D. Kahneman, P. Slovic & A. Tversky, note 3, above.

trying to prompt the other side to adopt. Suggesting a favorable "most likely" hypothesis to the other side aids the other to discount uncertainties. On the other hand, the skilled negotiator must, of course, avoid becoming the victim of this category of data processing distortion by recognizing that the only certainties in life (death and taxation) are unpleasant and that, therefore, uncertainty is to be expected and explored. If a negotiator adopts perceptions of the weight to be given to the various bargaining elements without examining conflicting data, there is considerable danger that those perceptions will mislead and will detract from optimal bargaining performance.

One way we reduce the burdens of data processing is to model the information. We try to think of analogous data or situations and try to be guided by our prior experiences, or the recounted experiences of others, in dealing with those analogies. However, in the process of seeking analogies, we are apt to overlook critical distinctions. Thus, an illustration of the risk of information processing by resort to generalizations is that encountered when social, business, and political decisions are guided by ethnic stereotyping. A negotiator who makes the same sort of information processing error, who relies upon generalizations as data reference points without examining whether the information in question is categorically different, is reducing the prospects of settling for more.

Another source of data processing distortion is the tendency to treat changing situations as though they are static. An illustration offered by Dr. Robin Hogarth in the book *Judgment and Choice*[9] is the situation in which a manager reprimands a worker for poor performance and attributes the worker's subsequent improvement to the impact of that reprimand. What the manager tends to overlook is that human performance is not static. It is better at some points and worse at others. Therefore, performance at the extremes is likely to be followed by performance that moves in the direction of the mean level. Accordingly, the worker's performance may well have improved even without the reprimand. Thus, what the manager assumes is a cause-effect relationship (poor performance followed by reprimand equals improved performance) may be an unrelated sequence of events.

The above example illustrates the predictive error of overreliance on past experience. That error results in part from the tendency to treat changing situations as though they are static. Among

[9]R. Hogarth, *Judgment and Choice* (Wiley, 1980).

other problems for the negotiator, such overreliance on past experience tends to cause people to assume that a bargaining style that succeeded in the past will continue to meet the negotiator's needs. In Chapter 3 we saw why particular bargaining styles are more suitable for some bargaining situations than for others. Rather than attempt to restage a prior successful experience, the negotiator who settles for more separately analyzes each bargaining setting to determine the approach to be taken.

Another problem resulting from excessive reliance on past experience as a source for predicting the future is the tendency to overlook incomplete data. Here Hogarth gives the example of evaluating a personnel director's skill at picking from among job candidates by assessing the quality of the performance of those hired. Such an evaluation is incomplete because it overlooks the relative potential performance of candidates who were rejected by the personnel director and who, therefore, are not in the pool whose performance is being evaluated. Had they been selected for the jobs, it is possible that their performance would have exceeded that of those selected. Thus, even though the personnel director is judged successful on the ground that selected workers have proved to be competent, it is possible that a more effective work force would have been selected had someone else made the hiring decisions. Of course, typically the comparative data needed to make such a performance assessment will be more difficult to obtain than information available respecting internal operations. Nevertheless, the effective negotiator will try to discover those benchmarks that most accurately reflect measurement based upon the goals of the bargaining effort.

In processing information, people often ignore basic principles of statistical probability, including people who have taken several courses in statistical science. One common error of this sort is according excessive weight to data that constitute too small a sample of the entire data set that the sample is supposed to represent. An extreme example of this is what has been described as "egocentric attribution bias," a fancy term for operating on the assumption that our own judgment of a situation is widely shared by our peers, our social group, our compatriots.

Another common error, known as the "gambler's fallacy," is to assume that in a sequence of randomly determined events, a result that has occurred with greater than expected frequency is less likely to occur upon the next opportunity. For example, after a balanced coin has come up heads six tosses in a row, most people are better prepared to bet on tails for the seventh toss than they were on the first toss. Yet the statistical probability of the result remains unchanged.

Statistically unsound analysis is particularly prevalent when people try to predict compound events. Kahneman, Slovic and Tversky provide the following example.[10] Assume that Bill is described as follows: "He is 34 years old, intelligent, unimaginative, compulsive, and generally lifeless. In school he was strong in mathematics but weak in social studies and humanities." Rank order the following statements by their degree of probability using "1" as the most probable and "8" as the least probable.

Bill is an accountant.
Bill plays jazz for a hobby.
Bill is a reporter.
Bill surfs for a hobby.
Bill is an accountant who plays jazz for a hobby.
Bill is a physician who plays poker for a hobby.
Bill is an architect.
Bill climbs mountains for a hobby.

What the researchers found is that most subjects give the number 1 probability ranking to Bill being an accountant and the lowest average probability ranking to Bill playing jazz for a hobby. However, the average probability ranking given by the subjects for the statement that Bill is an accountant who plays jazz for a hobby is second only to the probability ranking for the statement that Bill is an accountant. The results are quite similar for groups of raters who have no statistical background and for those who have taken advanced courses in statistics and probability. Yet, a basic rule of statistical science is that the more specific the attributes of the item one is trying to predict, the less probable it is that one can successfully make the prediction. In this situation, a statistician will explain that the probability that Bill is both an accountant and plays jazz cannot exceed the probability that he plays jazz because to belong to the category of an accountant who plays jazz one must first belong to the category of those who play jazz. That is, occurrence A cannot be less probable than occurrence A + B. The logic of this conclusion is readily perceived by most people when the principle is illustrated to them. Nevertheless, it appears that most of us make intuitive judgments (as contrasted with judgments based

---

[10]Note 3, above.

upon statistical logic) that violate the probability rule, perhaps because we find reassurance in the situation that is defined with greater specificity.

One negotiations application of the statistical principle we just observed is in assessing the Probability of Performance (POP) element of bargaining strength. As the number of detailed requirements imposed in an agreement increases, the Probability of Performance decreases. Similarly, as the number of detailed requirements increase, the number of Best Alternatives to the Proposed Agreement is likely to decrease. Often, however, the requirements of the contract for which a negotiator is bargaining have been set by people who are under pressures to meet a deadline. Superfluous details may be included in the requirements as a result of cutting and pasting from prior lists of specifications. Hence, the negotiator who seeks to settle for more must make every effort to understand which "requirements" are essential and which are superfluous.

A negotiator who understands that there is a special seductive quality to the prediction that is offered in the form of a detailed scenario of events (the more detailed, of course, the less statistically probable is its predictive strength) can use this knowledge to more effectively alter the other parties' perceptions. However, sophisticated negotiators must realize that they, too, are ready victims of the allure of what Drs. Kahneman, Slovic, and Tversky describe as the "illusory sense of insight that such constructions often provide."

8. Evade Revealing Damaging Information

It can be difficult to avoid providing the other side with information that weakens one's bargaining strength if the other side inquires about the data. Sometimes a simple refusal to share the information, on the basis of its confidentiality or its purported irrelevancy, will suffice. Often, though, overtly withholding potentially damaging information simply persuades the other side to assume the worst, thereby maximizing the potential reduction of one's own bargaining strength.

Assuming that there is no legal obligation to share the information being elicited, an alternative response is to pretend not to have heard or to find a way to divert attention to another subject and conveniently forget that the question was ever asked. The diversion can take all sorts of forms—"urgent" phone calls one suddenly remembers must be made, a pressing need to use the restroom, a sudden recollection of a humorous anecdote, and the like. Still another evasive tactic is to pretend to have misunderstood the inquiry and to react to the misunderstood communication rather than to the actual question. A variation to that category of evasive action is to provide an overly general response, one that avoids providing the damaging specifics. Alternatively, an overly narrow and precise answer can be given—one that avoids revealing the full range of information being sought. Still another evasive technique is to restate the question, so as to remove the threatening focus, and answer the restated question.

Because people so often are careless listeners, such evasiveness frequently succeeds because the questioner assumes that the answer was adequate. Similarly, unskilled inquisitors tend to pay more attention to framing the next question than to evaluating the adequacy of the answers. But, even when a questioner realizes that the answer did not provide all of the desired information, or did not provide it with satisfactory precision, the questioner is often reluctant to press for more details out of politeness, laziness, or frustration with not finding an effective way to pose the query.

Chapter 7

Tactics for Modifying Perceptions: Setting the Agenda and Framing Issues and Choices

A. Agenda Control

1. Agenda Content

A negotiated settlement is more likely to meet a party's needs if those needs are included in the agenda for discussion and decision. Therefore, a key tactical device in bargaining is to explore and define the agenda. In doing this, the negotiator must, of course, be sure that his own needs fall within the confines of that agenda.

Some negotiators make the error of ending their agenda control efforts upon being satisfied that their own needs will be addressed. However, our bargaining strength diagrams demonstrate that achieving maximum bargaining power calls for increasing the other side's perception that its needs are met by the initiator's offer. To do this, the initiator must know what those needs are and have an opportunity to influence the other side's perception of how those needs are being met. Accordingly, settling for more includes seeking a complete agenda of discussion and decisions, an agenda that takes into consideration both sides' needs.

2. Agenda Sequence

Although an agenda need not fix the order of discussion and decision making, often it will influence that procedural sequence. In Chapter 3 we examined how the sequence in which issues of different levels of difficulty are considered can be an important dimension of bargaining style and how some bargaining styles are more effective for some negotiating situations than for others.

Therefore, the proposed order for listing agenda items should be guided by the negotiator's strategic choices respecting the bargaining style to adopt for the particular transaction.

3. Offering Alternatives

An agenda defines the sphere for decision making. In a lawyer's language, it sets the issues. It does not, however, define what choices are available for resolving those issues. Often, a negotiating proposal can be structured so as to offer the other side choices among alternative acceptable resolutions.

Recent research by behavioral scientists has demonstrated that people are healthier, happier, more effective, and feel less stress when they are given choices and the ability to select the outcome from among those available choices. Because people are more likely to carry out decisions that they felt good about making (that is, their Probability of Performance is increased), it makes sense to present bargaining choices, where possible, in a way that enables the other side to feel happier with those choices. For this reason, it is a good bargaining tactic to seek ways to offer the other side an opportunity to choose from among alternative, acceptable resolutions of the bargaining issues.

In offering alternatives, the negotiator should remember that differences in the number of offered choices can affect the choice that is made. When there are two or three possibilities, it is relatively easy for the decision maker to manage the information that must be weighed in order to thoroughly assess the costs and benefits of each alternative. However, as the number of alternatives increases, analysis becomes more complex and difficult. Accordingly, the greater the number of choices, the more likely it is that assessment will focus upon comparing a limited number of the total attributes—those that are most prominent (though not necessarily most important)—in determining the net value of the choice.

4. Stating the Issues

Experienced lawyers understand that the manner in which the issues to be decided are stated—referred to as "framing the issues"— significantly influences judicial and jury decisions. In recent years the insight of experienced attorneys on the need to give careful attention to how one frames an issue is being borne out by the work of behavioral scientists, who are discovering mounting evidence that the manner in which choices are communicated influences selections that are made. These researchers have noted that in making choices, even the most sophisticated people often fail to apply rules of statistical probability and fail to carefully analyze information so as to make the decision most appropriate to the relative costs and benefits of the available choices. Instead, frequently the decision-making process is shaped by the complexity of the decisional problem, the manner in which information is presented, the availability and type of reference points, whether the decisional mode is selection or bidding, and whether the options involve attractive or unattractive outcomes.

To illustrate, in one study, groups of physicians, chronically ill patients, and students were asked which of two methods of lung cancer treatment they would choose—surgery or radiology therapy. One set of subjects was presented with the choice in terms of the relative survival rates using the alternative forms of treatment. For surgery the rates are lower for the short term but greater for long-term survival. The other set was presented with the choice in terms of the relative probability of dying. Of those presented with the problem as expressed in terms of survival, 84 percent preferred surgery; of those presented with the problem as expressed in terms of dying, 56 percent preferred surgery. Moreover, the results were similar among all three groups of subjects.[1]

While the above illustration supports the proposition that choice is significantly influenced by the manner in which an issue is framed, it also demonstrates another important point. Given the same information and the same decisional problem, framed the same way, people did differ in the choice made. Regardless of how the choice was posed, some elected surgery while others elected radiology therapy. To some extent this may result from differing levels of attentiveness to the information that was provided or the question that was asked. For example, if 100 bookkeepers are asked to add 5 + 4 + 6 + 3, a few are likely to come up with the wrong answer, not because they disagree with the rest but because they misread the problem or their thinking was distracted. But inattentiveness aside, when dealing with the type of decisional problem described by the cancer treatment example, some disagreement probably results from differing value systems or beliefs (for example, some may have religious objections to surgery), different tolerances toward

---

[1]D. Kahneman, P. Slovic & A. Tversky, *Judgment Under Uncertainty: Heuristics and Biases* (Cambridge Univ. Press, 1982).

risk, or different life goals. Although the experiment was conducted with three sets of subjects having distinguishing characteristics, the selected categories did not necessarily identify such variables as differing value systems, life goals, or risk toleration that might lead to different decisions regarding a problem of this sort.

Moreover, it is possible that although the question was framed in the same manner, people made different choices because of differences in their decisional styles. This last possibility is explored in the discussion of bargaining teams presented in Chapter 10.

a. Values Implicit in the Statement

A well-framed issue suggests the set of values that most supports the result being sought. For example, in dealing with the constitutional protections afforded defendants in criminal cases, prosecutors frame the statement of the issues as involving rules that protect the guilty. In contrast, defense lawyers frame the same issues as involving rules that protect the innocent.

When negotiating, a well framed issue should reflect not only the values implicit in the parties' respective needs, but also the parties' attitude toward the bargaining process itself. For example, some people consider willingness to compromise a virtue, others consider it a form of weakness. Hence, depending on the other party's attitude toward bargaining, one can pose the questions to be resolved in negotiations in terms of the other side's participation in a compromise (what you are giving, what we are giving; what you are getting, what we are getting) or pose the same series of choices solely in terms of what the other side is achieving (what you are getting, what we are giving up).

b. The Power of Indirect Verbal Suggestion

Much of what is involved in shaping how people respond to choices is undoubtedly a facet of the power of suggestion. Most of us have seen dramatic displays of that power when people are placed under hypnosis. However, subtle verbal suggestion often seems as powerful as hypnosis. For example, in one experiment subjects who were requested to estimate a person's height by being asked "how tall" the person was gave substantially taller average estimates than did subjects requested to make the same estimate by being asked "how small" he was. Professor Elizabeth Loftus asked participants in a market research survey the number of products they had tried; when asked whether they had tried 1, 2, or 3 of a group of headache products, the average answer was 3.3 of the products, whereas the average answer was 5.2 when she asked a similar group whether they had tried 1, 5, or 10 of the same group of products.

The power of indirect verbal suggestion is further revealed in another study by Dr. Loftus and her colleagues in which, a week after seeing a film of an auto accident, subjects were asked if they had seen broken glass at the accident scene.[2] An introductory question for one group was "about how fast were the cars going when they smashed into each other?" while the introductory question for the other group was "about how fast were the cars going when they hit each other?" In fact there was no broken glass. Nevertheless, 14 percent of those asked the question about the cars that "hit" each other and 32 percent of those asked the question about the cars that "smashed" reported seeing broken glass. In a similar study in which subjects were asked to estimate the speed of cars in a filmed accident, average estimates were highest when the question was posed in terms of the cars having "smashed," a bit lower when asked about the speed when they "collided," and lower still when questioned in terms of the cars having "bumped." Still lower estimates were made when asked about the speeds when the cars "hit" and the lowest estimates were given by those asked about the speed when the vehicles "contacted" each other.

Noteworthy in the above illustrations, first of all, is that the content of the question suggested a nonexistent fact that was adopted by a consequential number of the observers. Perhaps more significant, of course, is the fact that the more dramatic the verbal form of indirect suggestion, the greater was the impact. Is it any wonder that understated ads often win awards for artistic merit but have short broadcasting lives?

c. Difference in Response to Loss Risks and Gain Risks

There are two ways to make money on the stock market: selling long and selling short. Why is it that a substantial portion of adult Americans play the market with the expectation of making a profit from selling long but relatively few invest as short sale traders? Although one sells short for the purpose of making a profit, the

---

[2]E. Loftus, *Eyewitness Testimony* (Harvard Univ. Press, 1980).

gamble succeeds only if the stock's price declines. Thus, our success is tied to a symbol of loss. Perhaps, most of us have a special aversion to seeing losses and it is this aversion that accounts for the preference for looking for stocks that are expected to rise rather than for those that are expected to fall.

In fact, behavioral science research reveals that most people, at least most people in the western cultures that have been studied, associate less pleasure with winning a particular amount than displeasure with losing the same amount.[3] As a result, most people are more willing to take gambles to minimize prospective loss and are less willing to take gambles to increase prospective gains.

Clearly, the greater aversion to prospective loss suggests that negotiators should do more to emphasize to the other side any risks of loss incurred by not accepting a proposal and be less concerned with emphasizing the gains to be achieved by acceptance. That is, in terms of the bargaining strength model, information suggesting negative values of the other's best alternative to the proposed agreement (a reduction of the weight to be given by the other side to its BAPA) will more effectively alter the other's perceptions than will information suggesting increased value in the offer to meet the other's needs (the moving party's OMON). In other words, an effort that calls attention to the risked loss should have a greater perception-altering impact than an equivalent one that calls attention to risked gain. Of course, this suggestion must be weighed in light of the earlier strategic analysis in which it was noted that emphasizing the negative increases stress levels with the resulting increased prospect that the other side will resort to the fight or flight response. However, the danger posed by increased stress can be reduced by also taking note of the prospective gains. Thus, as previously observed in discussing the honey and vinegar strategy, the best negotiators normally use tactics that call attention to elements on both sides of the bargaining strength paradigm.

A general proposition supported by research into the decision-making characteristics of small groups is that they "tend to make decisions that are more extreme than, but in the same direction as, the initial tendencies manifested in the population from which the groups are drawn." A study by McGuire, Kiesler and Siegel[4] indicates that this holds true when a small group confers, face to

---

[3]D. Kahneman & A. Tversky, "The Psychology of Preferences," *Scientific American* (January 1982), p. 160.

[4]T. McGuire, S. Kiesler & J. Siegel, "Group and Computer-Mediated Discussion Effects in Risk Decision Making," 52 *Journal of Personality & Social Psychology* 917 (1987).

face, regarding the action it should take when presented with choices among different risks of gain and different risks of loss. They found that, consistent with the more general proposition, just as people individually are more prone to take risks to avoid loss than to achieve the same gain, when groups make decisions there is an even greater willingness to take risks to avoid the same prospective loss. Similarly, when groups make decisions concerning a prospective gain, they are even less willing than are individuals to take risks to achieve that gain. Interestingly, at the end of group deliberation, the individual judgments of group members move further in these same respective directions but not to the same degree of intensity as the group decision. These findings, too, suggest tactical lessons for the negotiator who wants to settle for more.

Negotiation often is carried out by a small group or is carried out in consultation with a small group of decision makers. Although the influence of group dynamics toward intensifying individual decisional tendencies may provide psychological reinforcement for all of the participants, it detracts from the goal of gaining the benefit of each person's soundest judgment. To get that judgment, it is better to minimize any distortion generated by the group dynamics— the herd effect. One likely way to reduce the intensity of that distortion is to have the group members write out their final judgment rather than reach an open group decision. A related technique is to have the group members silently put their judgment in writing both before and after the group discussion so as to facilitate detecting whether judgments are being unduly influenced by the group's dynamics.

On the other hand, when it is the other side that is making the choices among gain or loss risks, the skilled negotiator will want to encourage open group decision making if the goal is to increase the respective risk-averse tendency regarding gain choices, and risk-taking tendency regarding loss-avoidance choices. And, of course, the skilled negotiator will want to encourage secret voting when seeking to avoid the intensity-reinforcing character of group decision making.

Another characteristic of general reactions to risk deserves attention. Studies show that people make less risky choices when under time pressure to make those choices. Similarly, when assessing their options while under time pressure, people spend more time observing negative information than they do when making decisions under relatively relaxed conditions. This indicates that by imposing or deferring deadlines, it should be possible to influence the other side's perceptions in favor of selecting, respectively, less risky or more risky alternatives.

d. The Impact of Benchmarks on Risk Choices

The difference in the way people respond to gain risks as compared with loss risks is still another way the decisional conduct of most people violates rules of statistical probability. An additional violation of those rules results from the way most people are influenced in such judgments by the context in which the risk issue is posed. For example, suppose you are having a garage sale and before the sale a junk dealer has told you how much he will pay for any unsold items. Among these items is an old color television for which he will pay $100 and a stereo system for which he will pay $1,000. In fact, you sell the television for $200 and the stereo system for $1,100. Do you get the same level of satisfaction from your respective gains? For most people, the gain from $100 to $200 provides a sense of greater achievement than does the gain from $1,000 to $1,100. Yet, in each case the amount of gain is the same. Apparently, the difference in our response is due to the fact that we use benchmarks in valuing our gains and losses, and for most people these benchmarks are provided by the context in which the problem arises.

To further illustrate, imagine you are in a store examining a programmable calculator that you need. It is $130 at that store but a friend comes along and shows you a newspaper ad informing you that it is on sale for $120 at a store across town. Will you make the trip? Alternatively, assume the same facts but it is a simple calculator priced $20 at the store where you are but $10 across town. Will you make the trip? Your answer, of course, will be influenced by the time it takes to get across town and probably by your income level. That is, if the distance is very far and the income level is high, your answer is apt to be no to both questions. However, surely it is no surprise to learn that researchers find that more than twice as many people say they will go across town when the question is posed in terms of a $10 savings from $20 to $10 than say they will do so when asked in terms of $130 to $120. Apparently, in making such a choice, most people look not at the absolute impact of a $10 savings but rather assess that savings in relation to the amount of money being spent. Therefore, when $130 is being expended, what is gauged is the inconvenience of going across town to achieve less than a 10 percent savings, while when $20 is being expended, the inconvenience is gauged in relation to a potential 50 percent savings.

The tendency that people have to gauge the value of a choice in terms of the way it is described to them demonstrates the tactical need to assess how to "package" a proposal so as to provide the desired benchmarks or mental account allocations for comparison. This, of course, is what is involved when the salesman tells you that including the deluxe stereo option with the $18,000 new car only changes the monthly payment from $506 to $514 or when the rental agent quotes the cost per square foot per month for the retailing space. It is also what is involved in the earlier illustration respecting the choices people make when asked whether they would opt for surgery or radiology therapy—the choice was influenced by whether the risk is posed in terms of survival or terms of dying.

Of course, negotiators must be careful not to provoke the indignation of the other side by being too obvious in the way they present proposals. However, with that caution in mind, one who has mastered the negotiator's art will weigh the likely impact that such packaging alternatives will have upon the comparisons that will be made by the other party.

e. Choice Changes Relative to the Degree of Risk

Professors Kahneman, Tversky[5] and others have additionally shown that typical reactions to situations requiring a choice from among alternative risks defy the rules of probability in another interesting way. Although statistically the value of a 2 percent risk reduction or increase is the same whether the overall degree of risk is high or minimal, most people put enhanced value on those changes that are near the extremes of either total certainty or pure uncertainty. For example, the value that most people place on reducing the probability of a loss from 2 percent to zero is considerably greater than is the value they place on reducing the probability of loss from 40 percent to 38 percent, even though in both situations there is the same 2 percent gain. Thus, when dealing with choices that approach very low statistical probabilities, people tend to be willing to expend more to further reduce the probability than they are willing to expend to accomplish the same benefit

---

[5]D. Kahneman & A. Tversky, note 3, above, at p. 160.

when dealing with changes in probabilities that are not proximate to total removal of the risk.

There are yet other examples of the tendency to ignore statistical rules of probability in ways that should be particularly tantalizing to negotiators seeking to settle for more. To explore these further dimensions, assume you are presented with an opportunity involving a 50-50 chance of gaining $100 and an alternative opportunity involving an absolute certainty of gaining a smaller amount. How large would that smaller amount have to be to make that certainty just as attractive as the 50-50 chance of gaining $100? The experimenters have found that a very common selection for the balanced choice is $35 for the alternative that is a certainty. Statistically, of course, the point of equivalency in fact is $50. Thus, those who answer $35 in effect prefer to pay up to a $15 premium to avoid taking a gamble. This, of course, reveals the strength of the preference most people have to avoid risk.

The experimenters have further found that if the stakes are increased tenfold or twentyfold, the answers are changed proportionately. In addition, they find that if the same question is posed in terms of a risk, for example, a 50-50 chance of losing $100 and a certainty of losing a particular sum, a common choice is that people would equate a certain loss of $40 to a 50-50 chance of losing $100. One way of looking at this is that, as previously noted, it indicates that people are more prepared to gamble in hopes of avoiding a certainty of loss than to gamble when they have an opportunity to assure a certainty of gain. As a result, when faced with a chance of gambling on losing or gaining, most people avoid the gamble if it is equal; given an equal chance of gaining or losing, they accept the gamble only if the potential gain is considerably greater than the potential loss. Thus, instead of abiding by the weight of statistical probabilities, most people place greater weight on the risks of loss.

Of course, not everyone has the same attitude toward risk. Some people are less risk averse, some are more risk averse. In either case, though, the risk choices such people are prone to make are still likely to vary from those indicated by a strict application of the statistical laws of probability.

Obviously, the skilled negotiator's understanding of typical risk perception distortion can be used as a tool in influencing the other side's perceptions respecting the elements of bargaining strength. However, the negotiator who settles for more is also one who has insulated himself from being a victim of these same risk perception distortions. The soundest way to do this is to employ the methods of statistical analysis whenever cost-benefit or other risk-taking problems are present. In Chapter 9 we will examine how, as a defensive measure, computers can help us protect ourselves from these judgment errors in making risk-based decisions.

B. Calling Upon Precedent and Other Norms

Perceptions largely are formed by making comparisons. A stone is large or small relative to the size of another stone or relative to stones in general. The luxuries purchased by the wealth of princes in medieval Central Europe may have been the envy of their vassals but largely pale in comparison with the luxuries enjoyed today by the average American worker (color television, central heating and air conditioning, instant music, automobiles, frozen delicacies, and the like). Accordingly, the comparisons that shape our perceptions often depend on what we have experienced and what others report or do. This holds true particularly with respect to value judgments such as determining what is "fair," "generous," "successful," "satisfactory," and the like. Such benchmarks can be of a personal nature—our private expectations. Often, though, we rely upon the general experiences and conduct of others to help us understand what expectations should guide our judgments. Those socially recognized or public norms thereby provide an index for making the comparisons that help us to shape our perceptions.

1. Official and Unofficial Norms

Many norms are sufficiently important to social and economic stability that they are adopted as the official standards by which government regulates behavior. These provide the benchmarks for reciting the "thou shalts" and "thou shalt nots" that we call law. Not all such standards are spelled out in the form of a statute or regulation. Many are established by judicial pronouncements of the common law in the course of issuing case decisions. Others are spelled out by courts and administrative agencies in the course of interpreting the meaning of statutes and regulations as applied to actual situations that come before the tribunal for decision. Because we expect some consistency from government, we anticipate that analogous situations will be treated similarly. Accordingly, we look to the norms applied in the past—*precedent*—to predict the standards that government will enforce in the future.

Government is not the only source of power that coerces conformity to standards. Social and economic alliances, too, have ways to generate conformity with established norms. These norms are unofficial precedents, while those enforced by government are official precedents. In many cultures and subcultures, as well as within social structures such as communities, families, social circles, professions, partnerships, political alliances, and the like, unofficial norms play a far more important role than official ones in regulating the group's prevalent conduct. And in some situations, the law even looks to and enforces unofficial norms as the governing standards for resolving disputes within relationships that are normally guided by such unofficial norms.

2. Norms and the Perception of Needs

When we understand what norms shape a person's expectations, we are better able to predict whether a proposal will meet that person's perceptions of his needs. People use norms to gauge their needs because norms provide benchmarks for assessing subjective qualities such as fairness. They are also a basis for determining whether an undertaking is "prudent," "sound," or "reasonable." The underlying assumption is that experience is an excellent teacher and, therefore, the patterns of behavior that have emerged from collective experience should constitute sound, prudent, reasonable modes of conduct.

An interesting illustration of this last point is the relationship between price and perceptions of quality. If I offer to sell you two diamonds that appear to be the same size but price one at $1,450 and the other at $2,375, and you have no expertise for assessing diamonds, which do you assume is the higher quality, more valuable, stone? If Dr. Able charges $995 to perform bypass surgery and Dr. Baker charges $2,500 to perform the same surgical procedure, which do you assume is the better qualified surgeon? If one bottle of wine costs $6.89 and another cost $18.35, which do you assume will taste better? Why do we make such assumptions? Certainly we have all suffered the experience of paying more but getting less. Yet do we not continue to make the assumption that price indicates quality because more frequently we have found that there is a correlation between quality and price? Also, we continue to correlate price with quality (value) because we assume that there are enough people who have a better knowledge or skill than we do for assessing the quality of the particular item or service so that the market impact of their unwillingness to pay more for less will improve the likelihood that price will reflect quality. Thus, we rely on relative price levels as a norm that provides an index to communal appraisals of relative quality. As a result, if Able perceives that he needs expert legal advice but does not possess the knowledge or skill to assess whether a particular source of service has the desired quality, Able is not likely to perceive that Baker's law firm can meet his need if he learns that Baker's fees are among the lowest in town.

3. Precedent as a Basis for Assessing the BAPA

In the early 1970s, in an article in the *Harvard Law Review*, Professor Melvin A. Eisenberg called attention to the different dimensions of precedent and the roles that official and unofficial precedent play in negotiating.[6] Some of the insights he offered are integrated into earlier portions of this book. Now it is time to explore, and expand upon, other facets of Eisenberg's discussion of the role of norms in bargaining.

In the United States, litigation is the ultimate step for the enforcement of most official norms. Because official norms are not always clear and because litigation can be very time consuming and expensive, the parties' perceptions of the strength or weakness of each side's ability to turn to litigation as the Best Alternative to a Proposed Agreement is usually based on a lawyer's expert evaluation of the likely outcome of a courtroom struggle. This involves deciding what legal standards will be applied, what facts will be found based on the evidence, and what conclusions will be reached based on those facts and governing standards. Often this requires weighing not only what a judge is likely to decide but also how a jury is likely to respond. As a result, the lawyer's confidence in his or her ability to accurately predict the litigated outcome, and the client's confidence in the lawyer's predictive ability, play a critical role in determining bargaining strength. Of course, if that assessment is to fully inform the client of what is in store, it must take account not only of the prospective outcome but also of the costs of achieving it—including the stress that inevitably accompanies litigation and the time lost by the client from alternative activities.

Once a lawyer's evaluation of litigation prospects has been obtained, it usually cannot be modified without persuading the

---

[6]M. Eisenberg, "Private Ordering Through Negotiation Dispute-Settlement and Rule-making," 89 *Harvard Law Review* 637 (1976).

advising counsel to reassess the basis for the original advice. Thus, one way to alter the other side's bargaining strength is to reduce the level of confidence placed in counsel's initial legal analysis. It is possible that this can be accomplished by presenting to the other side's attorney a summary of the competing legal arguments and supporting precedent. However, this is a most difficult and delicate task because that lawyer's professional competence is implicitly challenged. Thus, there is a substantial likelihood that the lawyer will resist altering the assessment of the close calls and will find ways to distinguish the precedent upon which you would have him rely. Often, however, it is possible to avoid this problem by presenting, at the outset, a summary of both the legal precedent that will shape the results of a litigated BAPA and the reasoning leading to the perception you would prefer the other side to have of that BAPA. There is no guarantee that the other side's lawyer will come to the same conclusions, but at least there has been an opportunity to influence counsel's perception at a point at which that assessment is not prejudiced by the need to defend his professional reputation.

When litigation is the best, or only, alternative to a proposed agreement, the BAPA element ceases to be a bargaining strength variable if the other side's lawyer has a rigid perception of the prospects of success at the courthouse. Often, though, the other side's BAPA will reemerge on the eve of trial as a bargaining strength variable. The imminent prospect of having one's predictive falli- bility tested is often quite sobering and prepares a party to recon- sider the weight of its BAPA (the outcome of the impending court- room contest). As a result, a high percentage of lawsuits are settled on the courthouse steps. Similarly, they are often settled in the judge's chambers because at a pretrial conference the judge's impartial appraisal of the probable impending verdict induces the parties to reassess the BAPA.

In recent years courts and bar associations in many parts of the United States, in an effort to reduce the number of cases awaiting trial, have introduced procedures designed to provide impartial expert appraisals of the likely outcome of the pending litigation well in advance of the trial date. The expected, and expe- rienced, effect is similar to the judge's role in discussing settlement possibilities at a pretrial conference. The opportunity is created for reshaping perceptions of legal precedents and norms of jury behav- ior so that the weight of the Best Alternative to the Proposed Agreement regains flexibility as one of the bargaining strength elements that determines whether the conditions are conducive to settlement.

4. The Precedent-Making Impact of Settlements

Precedent influences negotiations not only by providing a reference point for assessing the acceptability of the proposal, but also by often modifying the norms that influence future negotiations. In other words, while settlement of the current transaction can be influenced by existing norms, precedent—if the settlement varies from those norms—creates a new norm to guide the resolution of future transactions. Obviously, this is particularly important where the parties have a long-term relationship involving similar transactions or where the settlement agreement is likely to become known to others involved in similar transactions with at least one of the parties.

The potential precedent-making impact of a settlement sometimes poses a barrier to agreement on an otherwise acceptable offer. The party resisting agreement may fear that others with whom it has similar dealings will cite the settlement as a basis for comparable treatment. One method of avoiding this problem is to agree to keep the terms of the settlement confidential. Often this solution is not available because the nature of the agreement precludes keeping its terms secret or because there is no confidence that confidentiality will be successfully maintained.

Sometimes the precedent-making impact of a settlement can be avoided by expressly denying that the settlement has any value as precedent. For example, often this is done in settling grievances arising under collective bargaining agreements. In fact, despite the explicit disclaimer, a frequently repeated pattern of such settlements likely will function as a new norm that generates expectations respecting the resolution of future grievances. Nevertheless, even in the face of such a pattern of like settlements, the explicit undertaking that the settlements have no value as precedent continues to have an impact on the parties because the disclaimer portion of the settlement agreement effectively prevents it from attaining the status of a legally enforceable norm.

Another method of reducing resistance to a proposal, when there is fear of a precedent-setting effect, is to note the ways in which the matter under discussion is a unique and exceptional situation. Such characteristics provide a means of distinguishing the issue under consideration from anticipated future cases and, thereby, presents the basis for rejecting future attempts to cite it as precedent.

5. Precedent and the Parent Ego State

In using norms as a basis for attempting to modify perceptions, it is useful to remember that from the perspective of Transactional Analysis, a person who is functioning in his Critical Parent ego state makes different use of precedent than when functioning in his Adult ego state.

The Critical Parent ego state relies heavily upon norms. Norms are a source of the absolutes that constitute the basis for Critical Parent reactions. Of course, these norms can be drawn from many sources such as law, social custom, religious conviction, personal values, and habits. Once it adopts a normative standard, the Critical Parent ego state does not easily alter what it accepts as the norm. Therefore, if the other person's Critical Parent ego state is in control and he must make a decision for which he has not yet adopted a standard to guide his conduct, you should have an excellent prospect of influencing that decision if there is a precedent you can cite that supports the result you desire. Similarly, if the other person's Critical Parent ego state is in control and he must make a decision for which he *has* adopted a standard to guide his conduct, you should have an excellent prospect of influencing that decision if there is a precedent you can cite in your favor that is consistent with his adopted values. However, if his value set already covers the subject matter, it is very unlikely that reference to conflicting precedents will have any impact other than to prompt an angered rejection. On the other hand, if the standard that is guiding the Critical Parent ego state's response can be identified, it may be possible to successfully suggest why a different standard held by, or acceptable to, that person is more appropriately applicable to the particular issue or information.

The Adult ego state uses precedent differently. It treats it not as the basis for judgment, but rather as a potential guideline for analysis. To the Adult ego state, norms provide a useful shortcut for gauging risks and for predicting the conduct of others. Therefore, if conflicting norms are presented to a person whose Adult ego state is in control, the response will be to weigh which norm is most consistent with other sources of data or which is more likely to control the behavior of those whose future conduct is being weighed. Thus, if the Adult ego state is in control, one is unlikely to provoke uproar merely by calling attention to or relying upon precedents that differ from those previously cited by the other side.

C. Empathize and Mobilize the "Halo" Effect

To influence the other side's perceptions of the various elements of bargaining strength, it is necessary to understand those perceptions. We are better able to do this if we attempt to view the situation from the other's perspective. While there is no simple method of achieving such a state of empathy—of placing oneself in the other's shoes—it requires recognizing the distinctions between our own values and goals and the other person's values and goals. That is, if we are to succeed in better understanding the other side's position by resorting to the technique of empathy, we must be particularly aware of the danger of projection—subconsciously attributing our own values and goals to the other side.

The previously examined Transactional Analysis models offer some guidance in achieving empathy that helps us to identify both our own and the other side's basic personality attributes. Having identified the other's personality characteristics, we can guard against projecting ourselves into the other person's situation by weighing whether someone having such characteristics is likely to have the attributed goals and values. The TA models also alert us to the fact that empathy is characteristic of some ego states but not of others. Thus, we are unlikely to empathize when responding to another person from the perspective of our Critical Parent ego state. In contrast, empathy is likely to be forthcoming if analyzing another's situation from the perspective of the Nurturing Parent, Adaptive Child, or Adult ego states. Thus, it is the "I understand," "how can I help," "me too," "let's see if we can work this out" type of language that holds the best promise of producing a sense of empathy.

Empathy enhances the negotiator's effectiveness not only because it is a source for better understanding the other side's perceptions, but also because it provides a technique for altering those perceptions. This latter aspect of empathy aims at taking advantage of what is sometimes called the "halo effect." The term "halo effect" refers to the favorable, sympathetic approach people take to evaluating those things which they identify as being related to themselves or as being related to people or events that are viewed favorably by the evaluator. It is reflected in the "any friend of your's is a friend of mine" attitude. It is a form of stroking in that it reassures the other side that it is in familiar surroundings.

Empathy in this latter sense can be achieved by demonstrating that you share such things as attitudes, values, associations, conduct, and even vocabulary. Psychologists sometimes refer to this as "congruence." The tactical method of congruence is to discover and call attention to the shared acquaintances, experiences, backgrounds, values, and the like, so as to induce the other to assume that we will regard all matters from the same perspective.

The Pastime transactions that usually precede bargaining transactions and that are likely to occur intermittently as the parties take a break from the pressures of those procedures, provide an excellent opportunity to discover or introduce the sort of information and engage in the type of behavior that will promote a sense of mutual identity. It is an opportunity to learn about common background, friends, memberships, experiences, and the like. This form of empathy can also be generated by avoiding being contentious and, more positively, by expressing concurrence about matters upon which there appears to be no disagreement. Additionally, it is promoted by adopting the other side's terminology and pronunciation of words over your own (unless there is an important substantive need to use particular language), by using as much of the other side's ideas as is possible, and by giving the other side opportunities to take the initiative, such as by letting the other side provide leadership in determining when to move to the next step on the agenda.

An advantage of using the techniques of congruence is that it is likely to improve the other side's perception of your Probability of Performance, promote their trust in the reliability of the information you offer, and cause them to give full consideration to your suggestions. On the other hand, the tactic of generating a halo effect has its hazards. As with most tactics, there is danger of overdoing the technique. The goal is to sympathize, not patronize. Should a lack of subtlety, an excess of empathetic strokes, take one over that line, the other side is likely to respond indignantly to your obvious attempt at emotional manipulation.

D. Do Not Embarrass or Humiliate

The converse of the techniques of gaining empathy is to embarrass or humiliate the other side. Whereas convergence reinforces a person's perception of having a recognized, respected status, embarrassment and humiliation displace a person from such a position. Often this is referred to as a "loss of face" because it causes the victim to "disappear" socially.

Not surprisingly, the stress of being subjected to embarrassment or humiliation often leads to flight. For the negotiator this means that doing or saying something to the other side that is perceived as embarrassing is likely to result in disengagement from the transaction. Alternatively, the person will take whatever steps are necessary to regain the lost status. Hence, "don't get mad, get even" is the battle cry for one seeking to avenge being subjected to such treatment. Thus, a negotiator who resorts to humiliating or embarrassing the other side can anticipate either that no further offer will be made to meet his needs or that if it is made, it is unlikely to be fulfilled. Accordingly, if the other person has been subjected to loss of face, it is unlikely that he or she will have a high Probability of Performance. Therefore, if you have inadvertently embarrassed the other side, either you must take your own steps to reestablish that person's sense of recognized status, or you would be well advised to disengage from any further transactions.

E. Seek and Create Prominent Points and Formulas

The prior discussion about distorted processing of information noted the tendency to give excessive attention to that which is highlighted. In making decisions, people generally favor selecting from among what can be described as the prominent points. Prominent points are those numbers, formulas, words, and phrases that stand out among the alternative numbers, formulas, words, or phrases being discussed. Their prominence may result from their relative physical location or the order of presentation. It may also result from the use of a graphic method of highlighting or from pithy wording.

1. Prominent Points

We can only speculate as to why people favor selecting from among prominent points. In many instances the strength of prominent points may be that they have qualities that are readily recalled during the selection process. In other instances, such as in the case of round numbers, it may be that they are easier to work with arithmetically. For example, if I make an offer of $5,685 and your last proposal was at $6,200, there is a better chance that we will settle for $6,000 than for $5,942.50, unless, perhaps, we agree to "split the difference." Splitting the difference is a formula that carries no special logical force. Nevertheless, much of the bidding in pure exchange bargaining is guided by one or both sides' expectation that the final step to agreement will be acceptance of that formula. Likely it is used frequently because, like round numbers, it offers convenience. In the case of the round number, the convenience is arithmetic; in the case of the split-the-difference formula, the convenience is prompt finality achieved by using the simple and easy process of dividing by 2. This creates a prominent point in the sense that it lies midway between the parties' positions.

An interesting variant of the role of prominent points is that persistent deviation from them often causes confusion and frustration. Suppose, your proposal is to settle at $6,500 and I counteroffer with $3,831.26. You then agree to come down to $6,250 and my counteroffer is $4,106.88. Surely at this point you will be asking yourself "Why these weird figures?" Perhaps you will ask this of me, as well. There may be a reasonable explanation. I may be making my offers based upon a foreign currency and then converting round numbers from that currency into dollars; or I may be working with a formula based on the price of securities that will have to be sold to pay the agreed price. However, if I fail to provide a reasonable explanation, is it not likely that you will decide to avoid doing business with me? There is a good prospect that my eccentric method of bidding will suggest that my behavior is generally unpredictable. In terms of the bargaining strength model, my inexplicable insistence upon the use of inconvenient numbers may adversely affect your perception of my Probability of Performance.

Precedent can constitute a prominent point that guides negotiators to a settlement. Among other things, well-establised norms provide terms that are readily identified and remembered during the decisional process. Therefore, in making a proposal that is supported by precedent, it is generally a good idea to call attention to that status.

2. Formulas

Flipping a coin or a similar random method of choice from among "final" proposals is another common method of reaching a bargaining decision. It differs from splitting the difference only in that it involves a level of gambling risk—a characteristic that some negotiators, because of their attitude toward risk taking, have difficulty resisting and others have difficulty accepting.

Formulas for decision often have another virtue; they offer the potential of outlining the categories of needs and alternatives and, thereby, help direct attention to the required fact finding aspects

of reaching a negotiated resolution. To illustrate, one way to negotiate a divorce settlement is to go through a series of monetary
offers and counteroffers involving the various combinations of possibilities concerning child support payments, division of property,
and the like. An alternative is to separate the quantifiable and
nonquantifiable items and discuss formulas for achieving a reasonable balance for quantifiable items and a method of alternative
selection, random selection, or third-party selection, respecting
the nonquantifiable items. Such discussions tend to be less emotionally intense and can lead to the discovery of ways to maximize
the achievement of goals through such things as weighing the relative present value of money to the parties and the respective tax
impact of the alternatives.

Where property or such things as domains of authority are to
be divided, a procedural formula for decision is available that does
offer a special virtue. The procedure is for one side to select the
lines of division and for the other to select which portion it will
take for itself. (For example, you cut the pie in thirds and we will
select the first and second pieces and you will take the remaining
one.) The virtue of this approach, of course, is that the party draw-
ing the lines realizes that the only way it can maximize its own
gain is to establish portions of equal value.

Formulas can also be created by coming to agreement upon
criteria (e.g., market rate of return for the type of investment).
Settlement is then arrived at when agreement is reached respecting
the values to be given to the variables. If the parties can agree on
the formula, often it is possible to arrive at the terms of settlement
by turning to disinterested experts, such as brokers, accountants,
government officials, architects, or engineers, to determine the
correct numbers to be plugged into the formula.

3. Form Agreements

The terms for a settlement can often be found within a prior
agreement between the parties. Such agreements combine the
characteristics of prominent points and formulas. If previous
arrangements were agreed to after extensive negotiations, there is
usually no reason to reexamine every alternative provision. Acceptance of the prior agreement as the basic model provides a series
of prominent points that can quickly be adopted or modified. This
not only helps reduce the costs of bargaining but also aids in focus-

ing attention on potential formulas for resolving the differences that require reconsideration.

When parties follow well-established patterns of agreement in commercial transactions, it is common for the industry to develop "form agreements." These are preprinted documents in which the standard provisions of agreement—the norms—are set forth and a few blanks are inserted for the parties' names and a limited number of other variables. Form agreements provide the efficiency of relying on normative provisions and use of them often facilitates settlement at a minimum cost of negotiating. However, they must be treated with caution. Often they are poorly drafted documents containing many ambiguities, gaps, internal conflicts, and unnecessary vagueness. Often, too, they have been prepared by those representing one side of the typical transaction and do not represent an arm's-length balance of protections for all parties. Therefore, the negotiator who settles for more recognizes that there is nothing sacred about a form agreement, unless imposed by statute or regulation. Lines can be crossed out, inserts can be added, or the entire approach can be scrapped. Seeking variation from a well-established form agreement, however, will normally meet considerable resistance based either on reluctance to abandon the one-sided cast of the form or on suspicion that the changes contain hidden traps. One reason is that form agreements often become integrated into the Critical Parent ego state of those who use them with great frequency. Therefore, before balking at using such standard documents, the negotiator who has mastered the skills of bargaining weighs whether the deficiencies of the form justify undertaking the burdens of overcoming the probable resistance to change.

The problems faced when seeking modification or abandonment of form contracts suggests another tactical consideration— the desired degree of formality in presenting a proposal. Part of the resistance to tampering with the language of a printed form agreement likely stems from the common preference for neat, clean documents. A somewhat related aspect of that resistance probably stems from the use of printing as a symbol of importance and permanence. And, perhaps, too, the resistance is based in part on a sense of the relative cost of using different media and a reluctance to destroy the value of relatively costly preparation. Interestingly, this perception persists even though, typically, the form document in fact is less expensive to prepare than the specially created typed equivalent. It persists, too, despite the fact that, in this day of laser printers and desktop publishing, the document that appears to have been printed may have been prepared at no more cost and may have no more inherent permanence than the typed sheet containing strikeovers and whiteouts.

Nevertheless, in our society there is a hierarchy of formalism, with the accompanying resistance to tampering, based upon the method of recording and presenting a proposal. In that hierarchy, handwriting generally is treated as less important than typing, and typing is treated as less important than printing. An example of this hierarchy is the rule followed in many jurisdictions that rejects handwritten wills. (Of course, that rule also reflects the fact that lawyers are unlikely to have participated in the preparation of such a document.) This hierarchy of formality in document preparation serves as a symbol of how willingly the presenter of the proposal will entertain modifications. Therefore, presenting the other side with what appears to be a finished, formal product can be used as a means of discouraging tampering with the provisions. The more formal the document, the greater is the implicit message that this proposal is the final, take-it-or-leave-it position of the party presenting the document. Accordingly, the negotiator who settles for more realizes that presenting a proposal in a highly formal format, such as a printed document, dated and signed by the presenter, heightens the risk of no deal but also increases the prospect that if a settlement is reached, it will be on the proposed terms.

F. Use Commitment

When engaged in the "feeling out" process of exchange bargaining, negotiators often attempt to alter the other's perceptions by declaring a "final" or "bottom line" position. In terms of the bargaining strength model, this is an effort to persuade the other that its OMON is insufficient or that the other must choose between the proposed OMON and the other's BAPA because the moving party will not sweeten the proposed OMON any further. This is a powerful bargaining tactic (that is, it effectively alters the other's perceptions) *if* the other side believes that declaration. However, such statements generally are treated with skepticism since experience teaches us that, in an effort to settle for more, parties frequently pronounce their "final" position well short of the point from which they, in fact, will go no further. In other words, assertions such as "this is the best I can do" or "you've got me at my rock bottom position" often are nothing more than bluff.

If the moving party is to succeed in settling for more by asserting that the proposal is the "final" position, it is necessary to persuade the other side that this representation is not a bluff. One way to do this is to gain a reputation for not bluffing and to be sure that the other side has access to people who can confirm that reputation. Gaining such a reputation, of course, can only come from extended experience in dealing with the same group of people and consistently adhering to the rule of not backing off from an assertion of a final position (unless the backing down is accompanied by a very convincing excuse).

An alternative to relying on a well established reputation for not bluffing is to make a persuasive commitment to the stated position. The purpose of commitment is to demonstrate that the statement is not a bluff.

There are various ways to make an effective negotiating commitment. All, however, involve an investment either in commencing resort to the committing party's Best Alternative to the Proposed Agreement, or in cutting off or reducing its avenue of retreat from the committed position. For example, if the negotiations are being conducted over lunch, stating that the last offer was the bottom line accompanied by asking the waiter for the check is a form of commitment. It initiates the process of abandoning the present bargaining process, presumably in favor of some alternative, and thereby reduces the likelihood that there will be any further proposals. Similar methods of demonstrating commitment are to arrive at the meeting with packed bags or, with the other side present, to phone the airline, or ask the other side to contact the airline, to confirm your return trip reservations.

Commitment can also be demonstrated by openly investing in the preparation for the BAPA. Illustrative of this technique is the collective bargaining situation in which the employer starts building up an exceptional inventory or notifies customers of the need to do so. On the union side, taking a strike vote or announcing the size of a strike fund is designed to do the same thing. Similarly, openly meeting with the other side's competitors to initiate negotiations for an alternative transaction is yet another, rather persuasive, way to show commitment to a bargaining position.

Another form of commitment is to formalize the bargaining proposal in a signed writing or to make a public declaration of the bargaining position. Although American culture may not place as much emphasis as some other cultures on not losing face, that concept does carry considerable force in our society. We are reluctant to back off from a concrete or generally pronounced position because it suggests weakness, indecisiveness, or unreliability— traits that our culture regards as undesirable.

Commitment can be attained through legal devices as well. For example, a party can purchase an option to ensure the availability of the Best Alternative to the Proposed Agreement or can accept a bid from a third party conditioned upon a contract not being reached within a stated period in the current negotiations. In some situations the commitment can be made firm by transferring to an escrow agent or broker, for a limited period, the authority to close the transaction upon the proposed terms. Of course, in all these instances, the commitment is effective only if the other side is informed about the action.

Finally, commitment is most persuasive when it appears to come from the committing party's Critical Parent; the Critical Parent is the most stubborn dimension of human personality—it rarely moves.

G. Facilitate Decommitment

Many potential negotiated transactions are lost because bluff becomes nonbluff or because a party prematurely makes a commitment to a bargaining position. Bluff is transformed into nonbluff when a party overplays its efforts to persuasively present as "final" a bargaining proposal that is really intended to be an interim position. A similar dilemma is presented when a party commits itself to a bargaining position without having fully analyzed its needs or alternatives.

A negotiator who settles for more is sensitive to the power of commitment and is prepared to make every effort to aid the other side in backing away from its use of the commitment technique. One method of facilitating decommitment is to have a convenient lapse of memory, to pretend that you were unaware that a commitment was made. A lapse of time or an intervening event, even a short recess, between the act or statement that constituted the other side's commitment and the parties' next encounter, makes it easier to pretend that the commitment never took place.

Perhaps the most dramatic illustration of the tactic of facilitating decommitment occurred in the fall of 1962 when the United

States, upon discovering that the Soviet Union was building nuclear missile launch sites and introducing missiles into Cuba, revealed this threat to peace at the United Nations, imposed a naval quarantine upon further weapons shipments, and prepared to eliminate the sites by means of tactical bombing. Simultaneously, messages were sent to Nikita Khrushchev, the Soviet leader, seeking an agreement to remove the weapons systems in exchange for a public pledge from the United States not to invade Cuba. On Friday, October 26th, a conciliatory message was cabled by Khrushchev to President John F. Kennedy. However, the next morning, before Kennedy had a chance to respond to the Soviet leader, broadcasts monitored from Moscow included the text of a new letter sent by Khrushchev, this one far less conciliatory. Some advising the president reacted with consternation and declared that there was no longer an alternative to an American military response. The president, however, saw the need for further deliberation. That afternoon, Attorney General Robert Kennedy proposed that the latest, less desirable Soviet response be ignored and that the president answer the first letter. The president adopted this tactic and the next morning Khrushchev's reply was received. The reply accepted the approach suggested in Kennedy's letter—the approach that was consistent with the Soviet leader's initial, more conciliatory position and that ignored the escalated posture taken in the later, ignored communication.

Another technique for facilitating the other side's decommitment is to introduce into the negotiations new people, new information, new dimensions to the transaction, or a new formula for reaching agreement. New people representing the side that wants to encourage the other party's decommitment can more credibly pretend to be unaware of the commitment and thereby enable the committed party to back away from its position without losing face. New information, new dimensions, or a new formula for reaching agreement provide the committed party with a way to rationalize its decommitment on the grounds that its commitment applied to the bargaining situation as it had previously been presented, a situation that was very different from that with which the parties are now dealing.

Still another way to facilitate decommitment is to introduce a mediator into the bargaining transaction. As with new dimensions and new facts, the intervention of a mediator changes the negotiating situation. The committed party can reconsider its position out of "respect" or "consideration" for the mediator. Instead of losing face by implicitly acknowledging error or weakness in decommitting, the party can rationalize the decommitment solely as a personal favor or gesture of good will toward the mediator.

H. Provide Verification and Assurance of Performance

The bargaining strength model demonstrates that bargaining power can be significantly altered by changing a party's perception of the other side's Probability of Performance. The four categories of steps that can be taken to alter the perception of POP are summarized in the acronym VISE:

V erification
I ndemnification
S elf-annihilation
E fficient enforcement

1. Verification of Performance

One reason parties have uncertainties about the other side's Probability of Performance is that there are often barriers to determining whether the other side is carrying out its promises. For example, if the engine of my car is running roughly and I am told that I need a new carburetor, I may be hesitant to allow an unknown mechanic to do the work. I may feel that unless I stand over him while the work is done, he will do more work than is needed or will charge me for more than was done. To increase my perception of his Probability of Performance, the mechanic may mention that he will give me the old carburetor when the repair is completed. If I am only mildly suspicious, this may suffice to alter my perception of his Probability of Performance. But, if I am very skeptical, I may suspect that he has a supply of old carburetors to hand out or that while he will in fact replace the carburetor, the replacement will be a rebuilt or that an adjustment of the old carburetor would accomplish the same thing at a much lower cost.

There are many ways to verify performance. All involve some costs of time, effort, or payment for services. Often, though, the increased bargaining strength gained by verification far outweighs the costs. Among the more standard means of verification are self-inspection or inspection, testing or audit by an independent third party such as a laboratory, consultant, architect, CPA, or government inspection agency.

Separation of integrated functions can also provide a means of performance verification. For example, if the recording artist separately pays one company to manufacture the video disk jackets, a second one to duplicate the disks, a third one to pack and ship them, and a fourth one to promote and sell them, he can have a high degree of confidence in the sales count provided by the promoter. The disk jacket manufacturer, the duplicating studio, and the packing and shipping company are unlikely to understate the volume of work for which they want to be paid. Thus, the artist can verify the sales volume by examining the volume of activity reported by the other entities. Of course, if all act in collusion to defraud the recording artist, they can profit from their own separate joint venture. To protect against such collusion, the artist may want to retain the contractual right to occasionally spot inspect the inventory and books of each entity for further verification of performance.

2. Indemnification

Indemnification increases the perception of the other side's Probability of Performance by providing, from a reliable source, a guarantee that if performance is not forthcoming, there will be a full substitution of the monetary value of that lost performance. That is, one way or another, the indemnified party will get the benefit of the agreement. Hence, a negotiator who settles for more seeks to improve the other side's perception of his Probability of Performance by offering a method of indemnification—if the cost of the means of indemnification is more than offset by the gains expected from the resulting increase in bargaining strength.

A number of standardized legal devices are available to ensure indemnification for failure of performance. These include performance bonds, life and property insurance, warranties, and various sorts of security agreements such as mortgages, pledged collateral, escrow agreements, guarantors, endorsers, and the like.

The negotiator who settles for more often seeks indemnification assurance from the other side as an aspect of meeting his own needs. When seeking assurance of indemnification from the other side, the experienced negotiator recognizes that for indemnification to be complete, it should include the costs of exercising the right of indemnification—such as the need to incur attorney's fees and other collection costs, and the lost profits and interest.

3. Self-Annihilation

Most people do not want to injure themselves. Therefore, one method of improving the perception of Probability of Performance is to link nonperformance with the promisor's own injury. Forfeiture provisions provide one means of doing this. That is, we have greater assurance that the promisor will indeed make every effort to perform because he loses all he has ventured on the transaction if the promise is not fulfilled.

In many situations an undertaking that subjects the promisor to public exposure for failure of performance provides an effective source of self-annihilation. Thus, the other side's perception of the Probability of Performance often is enhanced if the promisor agrees to publicly declare his undertaking. Of course, the more reason the promisor has to value his public reputation or to avoid public embarrassment, the more effective such a public declaration should be in altering the other side's perception of the promisor's Probability of Performance.

It is not always necessary to make a public declaration of intentions for the device of self-annihilation through embarrassment to be available as a means of altering perceptions of Probability of Performance. Often, merely committing an undertaking to a signed agreement provides sufficient potential for later public disclosure of nonperformance, a similar prospect of self-annihilation.

4. Efficient Enforcement

When parties negotiate an agreement, normally they do not intend to purchase a lawsuit; rather, they intend to obtain the bargained-for performance in the form of property to be transferred, services to be rendered, or differences to be resolved. The availability of legal enforcement of the settlement, therefore, is not the performance being sought; it is a substitute for performance. The prospect of such enforcement, however, reduces the temptation to ignore the bargained-for obligations. Therefore, the easier it is for a party to enforce the settlement and the more certain it is that such enforcement will be available, the less motivation the other side has to not perform. Hence, perception of the Probability of Performance should be enhanced if the other side recognizes that the agreement is capable of efficient enforcement.

Most, but not all, settlements can be enforced through legal action. The availability of a judicial remedy for breach of the settlement, therefore, provides a means of improving the perception of the Probability of Performance. However, judicial enforcement can be a very expensive and slow process. Moreover, when the legal issues become more complex, the process is likely to become even more cumbersome. If the underlying transaction involved people or activities in different legal jurisdictions, a complicating issue can be the determination of which jurisdiction's laws and rules should control the lawsuit. This particular potential source of complications can sometimes be eliminated by contractually specifying which jurisdiction's law will control any litigation.

Not all settlements, however, are legally enforceable. Some are unenforceable because they do not conform with legal prerequisites for judicial recognition of the particular type of settlement. To be recognized for purposes of judicial enforcement, some types of contracts, such as those transferring longer term leaseholds or ownership interests in realty, must be in the form of a signed document. Similar requirements, under the statute of frauds, often are imposed for contracts requiring more than a year to be performed or involving more than a specified amount of value. An additional formality sometimes required as a prerequisite of enforceability is that the signature be witnessed or be witnessed by someone holding a particular type of public office or license (such as a court clerk or notary) or even be witnessed through a specially ritualized procedure (as in a contract of marriage). Often, certain types of agreements are unenforceable unless recorded at a specific type of government office. These sorts of requirements differ from jurisdiction to jurisdiction and occasionally it is unclear which jurisdiction's requirements must be satisfied for the agreement to be enforceable.

The advice of legal counsel, therefore, is often critical in building confidence that the form of the agreement and the procedure by which it is executed are correct; this process will support a party's expectations that performance is probable because nonperformance can be remedied by the courts. As a result, when the other side appears to have a weak or uncertain perception of the Probability of Performance, the skilled negotiator often can favorably alter that perception by (a) encouraging the other side to obtain legal counsel; (b) providing the other side's attorney with reassuring statutory, regulatory and decisional references; (c) referring the other side to the supportive legal opinions expressed by respected neutral experts; (d) getting advisory opinions (if available) from informed government officials; or (e) calling attention to the participation in like transactions on the part of other parties whose cautious and prudent approach to such matters are well known.

There are other potential legal impediments to judicial enforcement of an agreement. The procedure and substance of some agreements are subject to various types of government regulations. Examples include information disclosure requirements in making various types of loans, usury law limits on interest rates, information disclosure requirements for corporate securities transactions, statutorily imposed warranties on the qualities of a product or service, minimum remuneration standards, zoning restrictions, and the like. Here, too, competent legal counsel is often essential to being assured that the promised performance will be backed by the power of the state.

In addition, consultation with an attorney respecting the availability of judicial enforcement for the proposed agreement can be important because the courts generally will not recognize an agreement if (a) the type of transaction is prohibited in the jurisdiction, (b) the agreement has not received legally required approval of a specified government official, or (c) certain participants are deemed incompetent to contract. Moreover, courts generally do not enforce agreements if they find that the terms are incomplete, too vague, or uncertain. They shy away from enforcing such agreements on the ground that there is no legal standard to be applied. Similarly, American courts are constitutionally barred from enforcing agreements that interfere with the exercise of constitutionally protected liberties, or which result in the judiciary becoming embroiled in a religious dispute, or require the bench to exercise what judges characterize as "political discretion."

In addition to improving perceptions of the Probability of Performance by recognizing and taking steps to avoid the legal pitfalls to enforceability of a proposed agreement, there are steps that can be taken to increase the likelihood that enforcement will be accomplished with a minimum of cost or delay and with a maximum remedy. This, too, increases the Probability of Performance because introducing such elements into the transaction gives the parties increased motivation to satisfy their obligations by performance rather than by making legal amends for nonperformance.

One aspect of the technique of providing for efficient enforcement of the settlement has already been discussed in the section on Indemnification. Most often a legal remedy is provided in the form of a monetary award. Experienced attorneys know that too often winning the lawsuit is but the beginning of the battle and sometimes proves to be an empty victory because the other side is "judgment proof"; that is, there are no assets against which the judgment can be collected. Even when such assets exist, executing against them can be costly and can take considerable time. The devices discussed above under Indemnification provide methods for improving the prospects that the judgment will be promptly paid. Some indemnity devices, such as pledged property, even provide ways to obtain the remedy without having to initiate the judicial process.

Should litigation become necessary to obtain a remedy, in some situations the process can be expedited if a "confession of judgment" provision has been included in the parties' agreement. When recognized by the courts, such provisions eliminate the need to prove the right to a judicial remedy. The court in effect converts the contractual provision into a judgment as though it had been the end product of litigation. However, this device is not available in all types of transactions.

Another means of expediting judicial enforcement of an agreement is to include in the contract an agreed statement of material facts, in clear, precise language. This can reduce the expenses and delays involved in presenting the case to the court. Similarly, the efficiency of the enforcement process is improved if the parties' agreement provides an explicit right of ready access to all material documentation respecting facts that might be in dispute.

A factor that often delays and sometimes bars enforcement proceedings, and almost always adds to their costs, is proving the amount of damages resulting from nonperformance. Often, this problem can be eliminated by including provisions detailing the method for measuring damages or establishing a specific schedule of damages (a "liquidated damages" provision).

Two important elements of damages that generally are not covered by standard judicial remedies in the United States are interest at an appropriate rate, and the costs of recovering the remedy, including the costs of counsel and related litigation expenses. As a result, delays in the enforcement process frequently work to the benefit of the nonperformer, and thereby reduce the impact of the prospect of legal recovery as a means of improving the Probability of Performance. In many situations this problem can be eliminated by contractually establishing the interest rate to be assessed upon the recovery and specifying the breaching party's liability for the specific categories of collection and enforcement costs.

Generally, enforcement efficiency can be improved by contractually providing for the arbitration of disputes arising out of the agreement. Arbitration can resolve some disputes that courts are not permitted to decide (e.g., which group is entitled to be treated as the successor to ownership of church property when there has been a schism). Often, too, courtroom litigation is an impractical method of enforcement because it is inaccessible (often a problem in international transactions) or is too slow, too public, too adversarial, or even too uninformed.

Arbitration is an alternative means of impartial resolution of differences. When recognized by law, as generally it is in the United States, arbitration decisions are judicially enforced as final, binding, and unreviewable. The arbitral process has several advantages over judicial proceedings, including greater speed than courtroom litigation and flexibility to select decision makers who possess the desired degree of expert knowledge or experience. In addition, because an arbitration proceeding is less formal than judicial processes, the greater flexibility of these proceedings allows for such things as the introduction of evidence in forms and ways that are not available in American courts.

The flexibility of arbitration is especially valuable in international business transactions. Even though the parties may be separated by thousands of miles, operate under conflicting legal systems, and speak different languages, arbitration can provide a practical method for enforcing the parties' obligations. Similarly, where the subject matter of the contractual dispute is likely to involve highly complex, confidential or secret information, arbitration offers the needed quality of privacy. Arbitration provisions can also lend assurance to the Probability of Performance where the parties have, or want to have, a long-term relationship. It is especially important in this situation that differences be resolved with a minimum of adversary tension. Arbitration provisions can also be of special use in cases where the highly technical subject matter of the dispute permits only a specially trained or experienced neutral to be able to intelligently resolve the parties' dispute.

I. Bypass the Agent

Agents (whether employees, lawyers, brokers, officers, or the like), not principals, conduct a large portion of all commercial and political negotiations. The agent normally assumes that the quality of his representation will be judged by the extent to which the result achieves the principal's goals. Yet frequently the principal and agent do not spend enough time or effort identifying those goals. Even when goals are initially identified, the agent may need to reexamine them because the principal can change them during the course of negotiations. Nevertheless, the course of negotiations is determined by the agent's perception of those goals regardless of whether that perception has kept pace with changes in the principal's intentions or whether that perception accurately reflects all dimensions of the principal's needs. And, as we explored under the topic of the Offer to Meet the Other's Needs, goals can involve emotional as well as physical and fiscal needs.

This potential contrast between the agent's perceptions and those of the principal poses two types of problems. First, it can result in a substantial investment of time, effort, and expenditures negotiating for a settlement that ultimately will not be ratified by the principal. This potential problem is illusory if the agent has the authority to bind the principal. Therefore, a negotiator should try to learn the extent of the agent's authority to act in the name of the principal. If it is determined that the principal's ratification is necessary, the negotiator who settles for more makes every effort to avoid building up high Accrued Costs of bargaining without receiving certain assurances that the agent is indeed in close communication with the principal and that the principal is being kept abreast of the bargaining table developments.

The other possible misperception on the part of the agent may be that the principal may in fact be seeking less than the agent realizes. This problem is particularly acute when there is a possibility of appealing to the Nurturing Parent dimension of the principal's personality. For example, the rental agent may feel that it is his duty to extract the going rent from the young couple embarking on their first venture into business whereas the building owner, if aware of the characteristics of the prospective new tenant, might recall a break he received early in his own career and be quite pleased to have the opportunity to help out the couple by leasing at a discounted rental rate.

There are a number of ways to bypass the agent in order to verify that the principal's perceptions are accurately represented at the bargaining table. However, procedural protocols sometimes impose ethical as well as cultural regulations on the manner and extent to which this can be done. For example, if requested to do so, a lawyer has an ethical obligation to transmit to his client a proposal presented by the other side. A lawyer is also ethically prohibited from dealing directly with a party who is known to be represented by another attorney unless that attorney has approved the direct contact.

In most commercial and political transactions the true principal is not an individual but a collection of people—the shareholders, the union members, the partners, the association members, the citizens. Therefore, to reach the true principal it is sometimes necessary to bypass not only the bargaining agent but also the person or group delegated the authority to act in the name of the principal. Most frequently, it is impractical, unmanageable, and undesirable to bypass the delegated decision makers and deal directly with the collective constituency that constitutes the true principal. On occasion, though, this becomes necessary because the views of those holding positions of decisional power are sometimes unaware of changes in their constituents' perceptions of what is appropriate and what is desirable. Accordingly, historically, reform groups of various sorts—including the civil rights movements, the consumer protection movement, the labor movement, and others—have made many of their initial, most dramatic inroads by using negotiating techniques that bypassed the delegated decision makers and concentrated on appealing to the conscience or sense of self-interest of the represented constituency.

J. Accentuate the Positive

Because perception is the central element of bargaining strength, it is a mistake to approach bargaining with the gloomy assumption that the other party has all the bargaining power. A negotiator whose strategic and tactical choices are guided by knowledge of the nature and structure of bargaining strength can bargain from weakness and still settle for more. As shown by the bargaining strength paradigms examined in Chapter 2, bargaining weakness, like bargaining strength, is a state of mind; it is the total impact of the parties' relative perceptions of the weights of their respective bargaining strength elements. If the controlling perceptions can be modified, weakness can be turned into strength.

A first step when negotiating from a position of *apparent* weakness is to reassess the other's needs—not just the other party's fiscal and physical needs, but more important, the negotiator's and principal's emotional needs. Does the other side have a script that places a high value on status, on entertainment, on uniqueness, on image, or the like? If so, increase your bargaining strength by modifying your conduct and proposals to meet those needs. Certainly, many skilled lobbyists succeed by playing up to the almost inevitably powerful egos of elected officials. Can't one just hear a confidant winning Lyndon Johnson's backing by telling him "John Kennedy couldn't have done this, but I'll bet LBJ can!"

Many illustrations of successful bargaining from weakness are provided in the history of the civil rights movement of the 1960s. Leaders such as Dr. Martin Luther King understood that southern communities that were trying to attract new investment or tourism wanted to project an image of being pleasant, progressive, growing communities. Dr. King and others discovered that this image was threatened by graphic mass media reports of marches, bus boycotts, lunch counter sit-ins, and similar actions in which a significant segment of the community protested having to live under a regime of indignities and lack of public services. The desired image was further marred by news reports showing snarling dogs, police clubs, and tear gas being used to harass peaceful citizens and their religious leaders. By staging civil rights demonstrations at times and places designed to get maximum attention, the civil rights movement was able to make its demands felt as well as heard. Thus, southern business and political leaders came to the realization that the civil rights movement had something important to offer in exchange for equal opportunity—restoration of the image of tranquil, harmonious communities. Therefore, although civil rights leaders were unable to elect their own political representatives or buy out the businesses that provided jobs, goods, and services, they were able to negotiate changes in the political, economic, and social structures of their cities and towns.

The civil rights movement of the 1960s offered another lesson for those who must bargain from apparent weakness—find and recruit allies. The person who negotiates from weakness can often find others who are similarly situated and who can be recruited to join or coordinate their negotiating efforts. There are numerous illustrations of the strengthening effect of organizing an alliance of similarly situated people or entities including unions of workers, associations of small business licensees or franchisees, taxpayer groups, neighborhood associations, and consumer buying clubs. Allies need not have common financial interests. Sometimes the only thing they have in common is the burden of coping with the same dominating party on the other side of the table. Other times they have shared or compatible emotional or ideological needs.

Whatever the force that brings them together, bargaining alliances increase bargaining strength for a variety of reasons. One is that they can create a realistic and attractive Best Alternative to the Proposed Agreement (BAPA)—such as by being able to attract an alternative source with which an alliance can negotiate a package deal as an alternative to working out a settlement with the previously dominant party. If the dominant party's BAPA is built upon the willingness of those with whom it deals to accept less in order to preserve the dominant party's patronage, an alliance among the subservient group can reduce that BAPA by eliminating their competition for that patronage. For example, if one model of a manufacturer's cars are selling well, and if it does not have to face a dealers' alliance, the manufacturer might condition deliveries on a dealer's also accepting an excessive number of a model that is selling poorly. The dealer's alliance, on the other hand, can insist upon dealership rules that require the manufacturer to deliver orders without linking those deliveries to other models.

In other situations, an alliance may strengthen the BAPA of all its members by generating opportunities that would not be available to them acting individually. An example of this would be the ability of the group to make bulk purchases and share the resulting savings.

Another avenue to successful bargaining from weakness is to appeal to the Nurturing Parent ego state of the other side's personality. Once again, we can find examples in the civil rights movement of the 1960s. Not every influential southern white supporter for change was motivated by concern for the community's commercial image and economic future. Some undoubtedly acted out of a genuine sense of *noblesse oblige*, a desire to use their positions of power responsibly to create a better life and society for the citizenry. What was necessary was to identify those in power who had the requisite sense of social responsibility and at the critical moments appeal to their conscience.

Chapter 8

Timing and Bidding

A. Timing

Our experiences with natural events have taught us to examine whether it is the "ripe time" to do something. A fruit eaten before the ripe time may taste excessively bitter or sharp and give us intestinal pain instead of digestive satisfaction; eaten after the ripe time it may have no taste and no nutrition. A fine wine uncorked too early lacks the subtleties and smoothness of its full potential; uncorked too late, it may have turned to vinegar.

In dealing with food, we seek clues to ripeness. Color, texture, touch, and aroma all help us judge whether it is too early, too late, or the optimal time. Measuring the precise passage of time from a particular starting point—when the wine was bottled, when the fish was caught—can also help us make such judgments. But with all of that, we still occasionally err.

Perception, too, is affected by time. People are not static in their feelings, attentiveness, convictions, knowledge, understanding, or any of the other dimensions of personality and personal response that contribute to forming and modifying perceptions. Because time alters all things, a negotiator must constantly weigh whether the time is ripe for whatever tactic the negotiator is considering. Although determining the ripe time to modify perceptions is especially elusive, a few clues can be identified.

1. Control the Sequence and Timing of Information Exchange

Experiments performed by behavioral scientists indicate that if a person is presented with two conflicting sets of information about the same subject, the information first presented has much greater influence upon the recipient's judgments than does information that is presented later. This is called the primacy effect and its impact tends to persist. The primacy effect has been found to operate with respect to forming opinions as well as to information retention. Because of the persistence of its impact, the primacy effect is referred to by some behavioral scientists as the anchoring bias.[1]

Studies of the primacy effect also confirm the proposition that first impressions about people persist despite later information that conflicts with the information that created the first impression.[2] Interestingly, the primacy effect applies as well to initial judgments we make about our own characteristics and abilities.[3]

However, there are situations in which the primacy effect's impact upon judgment and memory appears to be overcome by what is called the recency effect. This term refers to those situations in which information or arguments put forward later in a presentation sequence appear to carry greater perception-forming weight than information or arguments presented earlier in the sequence. A stronger argument that is second in a sequence of two presentations has greater influence over an extended period of time (30 days in the experiments).[4] Also, there is evidence that if the decision maker is prepared for the fact that additional information will be provided and that the decision maker will be required to explain the decision, the later presentation (the one that is most recent) has a stronger influence upon the decision.[5]

These lessons, of course, have potential value in guiding the negotiator's decision as to when and how to present information. If within a short period of time the bargainer must compete with alternative ways for the other side to meet its needs, it is important to obtain the opportunity to make the first presentation—to gain the added influence of the primacy effect. If that is not possible, the next best thing is, prior to the other side's contacts with the competition, to ask the other side to keep an open mind because

---

[1]R. Bostrom, *Persuasion* (Prentice Hall, 1983); T. Leahey & R. Harris, *Human Learning* (Prentice Hall, 1985).

[2]S. Belmore, "Determinants of Attention During Impression Formation," 13 *Journal of Experimental Psychology: Learning, Memory & Cognition* 480 (1987).

[3]P. Peake & D. Cervone, "Sequence Anchoring and Self-Efficacy," 7 *Social Cognition* 31 (1989).

[4]H. Cromwell, "The Persistency of the Effect on Audience Attitude of the First Versus the Second Argumentative Speech in a Series," 21 *Speech Monographs* 280 (1954).

[5]A. Furnham, "The Robustness of the Recency Effect," 113 *Journal of General Psychology* 351 (1986).

you will want to explore with them the relative value of your competing proposals. Finally, if there is an extended period between the decision maker's exposure to competing proposals and the decision, gaining the benefits of the recency effect by being last in line and making a persuasive presentation would appear to be the superior tactic.

2. Wait Until You Can Address the Desired Ego State

The Transactional Analysis model offers an excellent guide for deciding whether the time is ripe to engage in particular types of communications. The TA model teaches us that we should determine which ego state is being addressed by our intended communication and then wait until the other side is in the receptive ego state. For example, if we are attempting to modify the other's perceptions by presenting information, we want to address either the other's Adult or Adaptive Child ego state. In contrast, the time is not ripe for such a presentation if the other side is expressing indignation (and, hence, likely in a Critical Parent ego state) or laughing at a joke or anecdote (and, hence, likely in a Natural Child ego state).

Similarly, we learn from the TA model that a particularly favorable time to offer a bottom line proposal is when the other side indicates that its Adaptive Child ego state is in control. Indication of this would be plaintive statements or questions such as "Can't we come to some kind of terms?" or "I'm tired, let's get this over with," or "I can't take all this haggling."

Another timing lesson suggested by the Transactional Analysis model is to avoid interrupting when the other side is communicating from its Nurturing Parent ego state (e.g., "What we want to do for you is . . . " or "I understand your problem and . . . "). At such moments there is a good chance that the other will make a more generous offer to meet your needs than you had anticipated.

Generally, interrupting someone is considered impolite and, therefore, may offend. This is especially true when the other side is communicating from its Critical Parent ego state. Of course, there comes a point when the pronouncements and lectures being delivered by someone in their Critical Parent ego state become repetitious and seriously impair the efficiency of the negotiating process. At such moments it is necessary to redirect the transaction. One way this can be done is to interrupt in a way that acknowledges the other's feelings and values and then to pose a question calculated to turn on the Adult ego state so that negotiations can progress. For example: "Yes, Mr. Adams, we realize that you and your ancestors farmed this land for many generations and that you take just pride in its beauty. But, would not a sense of the special quality of this land be preserved if we incorporate your arbor and flower garden as a centerpiece of the landscaping for the shopping center we have planned?"

3. Avoid Premature Proposals

Participants in exchange bargaining (that is, where one side's gain is the other's loss) do not expect the first offer to be the final offer unless the other side has a well-established reputation as a practitioner of the best-offer-first negotiating style or unless best-offer-first bargaining is customary among the parties. Normally, leading with one's best offer in exchange bargaining must overcome the barrier of the other side's conviction that you undoubtedly have left room for additional concessions. Therefore, unless you are operating in the exceptional setting in which the parties expect the best offer first, it is counterproductive to make an offer intended for acceptance until there has been an exchange of at least a few progressively more attractive proposals.

In situations that both sides acknowledge as being integrative (that is, the parties have mutual or compatible interests), the same sort of skepticism respecting the first proposal should not be encountered as when engaged in exchange bargaining. However, integrative bargaining poses another problem with respect to the first proposal. Because the goal is to find the most satisfactory solution, the demerits as well as the merits of each proposal must be tested. Unless a proposal has no deficiencies, the discovery of its demerits will cause it to be set aside while alternatives are examined. In setting aside the proposal, it has been tarnished by its rejection—even if that rejection is only tentative. If no perfect solution is found, and seldom is one found after a process of thorough analysis, resurrection of the early proposal carries the burden of overcoming the blemish of its prior rejection. Therefore, many experienced negotiators find it is more productive to withhold their brightest solutions—especially those that are innovative—until the most obvious possibilities have been explored and rejected. Although this is not the most efficient use of the negotiator's time, it has the virtue of ensuring less biased assessment of what the negotiator judges to be the soundest resolution.

There are other factors that should also guide the timing of proposals—and most counsel patience. We have already discussed many of them in the context of examining the bargaining strength and transactional analysis models and particular tactical considerations in attempting to alter the other side's perceptions. These can be summarized as follows: A proposal should await until you have—

- gathered and confirmed desired information and provided the other side with information that might favorably alter your bargaining strength;
- attained familiarity with the other side's preferred use of language and jargon so as to enable you to utilize the halo effect;
- ensured that the other side has a favorable perception of your Probability of Performance and understands that you have an attractive Best Alternative to the Proposed Agreement;
- assessed the other side's emotional as well as fiscal and physical needs;
- established that the other side is in an ego state that is receptive to the type of proposal you intend to make;
- ascertained the extent to which the parties' needs are integrative or distributive in nature;
- provided an opportunity for the other side to make the proposal first;
- made sure that the other side is listening.

B. Bidding

Exchange bargaining (distributive bargaining) normally involves a series of offers and counteroffers that move progressively closer until either (a) settlement occurs upon reaching a mutually acceptable term, (b) the parties agree to use a formula to determine the settlement figure, or (c) they deadlock and resolve not to deal any further. We can refer to this aspect of negotiations as bidding inasmuch as it is similar to the fact-finding process of auction bidding. In other words, the parties are engaged in a sequence of communications designed to establish the best that each is prepared to offer.

The auction analogy suggests one basic rule regarding the bidding process of bargaining—avoid bidding against yourself.

Therefore, if you made the most recent proposal, normally you should refuse to alter that offer until the other side has modified its proposal. A skilled negotiator is particularly careful to adhere to this rule when a recess or a long discussion has interrupted the bidding sequence and, thereby, poses the risk of losing track of who made the last move. The rule that you should avoid making successive bids applies, of course, solely to exchange aspects of bargaining and has no place in purely integrative bargaining situations.

There are two exceptions to the exchange bargaining rule that one should not modify one's last proposal until the other side has modified its last position. The first is when significant new information is learned that requires the negotiator to modify his overall perception of the strength of his bargaining position; the second is when the time has come to make a last, final bargaining offer.

If the information reveals that the last-stated position was overly generous, it must be promptly withdrawn because, under most circumstances, an outstanding offer that is accepted prior to being withdrawn results in a legally enforceable contract. In such situations, it is important that the recantation be accompanied by a plausible explanation so as to retain credibility. Of course, when the two proposals are made in sequence in order to withdraw from an overly generous proposal, the situation does not violate the underlying proposition that you should not bid against yourself.

There is also justification for bidding against oneself (or revising a position) based on new information if the resulting reappraisal reveals that the last stated position was so unrealistic that it was an insufficient inducement to keep the other side at the bargaining table. In this instance it is useful to accompany the modified proposal with an explanation so as to make clear that you have not abandoned the normal expectation that this proposal and future proposals will either be accepted or be reciprocated with a counterproposal.

If there has been a clear sequence of alternating proposals, breaking the rule against bidding against oneself when stating a last, final offer is a sound tactic because the change of pace can serve to emphasize that the bidding process has come to an end. Therefore, if the other side is not very perceptive, it may be necessary to call attention to the fact that the last proposal was made out of sequence because you are going no further.

As previously described, the bidding stage of exchange bargaining is a fact-finding procedure. Each party seeks a better understanding of the value the other side places on the exchange. It is the sort of fact finding in which, at least in American culture, deception is not morally or legally condemned. As a result, a common method of attempting to deceive the other side in the bidding process is to take exaggerated early positions (sometimes called "highballing" or "lowballing"). This is the style that we have previously described as Hard Nut negotiation. As with the Hard Nut bargaining style in general, there is the danger that the tactic of exaggerated initial bargaining positions will cause the other side to seek out its Best Alternatives to the Proposed Agreement; that is, the other will respond by abandoning the transaction. This danger increases if the other side has a high level of knowledge respecting the likely limits of a reasonable settlement. Conversely, experiments have shown that if the other side has limited knowledge respecting the alternatives to the proposed settlement, very high or very low initial bargaining positions can significantly reshape perceptions respecting those alternatives and can result in a more beneficial settlement for the party that used the exaggerated opening bargaining position tactic.

One response that can be made by a negotiator who is faced with what appears to be an excessively high or low proposal is to counter with a comparably exaggerated bid. Usually the other side gets the message and the exchange of bids then quickly moves toward more realistic boundaries. Another approach is to calmly explain that because the proposal is too far removed from the likely sphere of settlement, there will be no responsive bid until the other side reconsiders its opening position and presents a realistic offer. The firmness of this latter approach can be very effective if the other side accepts it as an Adult-Adult communication. It will be even more effective if it is received as an Adult-Adaptive Child transaction. In the latter case it might cause the other side to make amends by quickly moving toward its bottom line position. However, should the response come from the other side's Critical Parent, there is danger that the firmness of this approach will cause the other side to abandon the transaction because of the responder's unwillingness to play the game "the right way." The danger of prematurely cutting off the transaction by refusing to deal with an unreasonable offer can be reduced by posing that bargaining position in an interrogatory rather than in a declarative manner. (E.g., "If you were in my shoes, would you be prepared to respond to that kind of offer?" or "Since your proposal appears to be far from realistic, is it possible that one of us is missing or has misunderstood some of the pertinent information? Is there something about the situation I don't know, or, perhaps, is there information I could clarify for you?") The interrogatory approach is, of course, designed to elicit a response from the other side's Adult ego state. Since it is the Critical Parent ego state that generates the indignation of refusing to deal with someone who "does not know how the game is played," the process often can be salvaged by a question that evokes an Adult-Adult response.

Part III

Procedural Tools

Chapter 9

Use of Computer Technology

A. The Computer—A Familiar Tool

Many people are intimidated by the word computer, despite the fact that in the past decade this instrument has become standard equipment for most businesses and for a substantial number of homes. While it is true that many aspects of computer technology require special training and abilities, to a large degree, computers have become user friendly, meaning that people of normal intelligence and education (often even people with below normal intelligence and education) have no difficulty learning to use them. In other instances, the complexity of the tasks to be performed requires assistance from specially trained people to ascertain the full potential or to customize the computing process to particular needs. In the past few years, that expertise has become readily available both in specialized staffs in large organizations and in a wide array of consulting firms.

The wizardry of computer technology is so impressive that many people expect computers to rapidly replace all facets of human endeavor—including negotiating. However, the latter prospect remains remote because, for all the magnificence of the technology, computers cannot engage in the mental process we call perception. And, as we have seen, bargaining power and the negotiated resolution of differences ultimately turns on the respective parties' perceptions.

Nevertheless, computer technology is becoming an important tool in negotiating. Its usefulness largely involves improvement in the accessibility of information and the ability to analyze and present this information efficiently and dramatically. In terms of the bargaining strength elements, computer technology helps the user find and present information that can serve as a basis for modifying the other side's perceptions, and verifying the soundness of one's own perceptions, without adding excessively to Accrued Costs or the Costs of Impending Negotiations.

The improvements to the negotiating process offered by computer technology principally involve four basic types of tasks that can be performed by most computer systems designed for home or business use. The next five sections describe and discuss these categories of tasks and their potential utility for the bargainer. The concluding section in this chapter presents some basic rules for avoiding the pitfalls of excessive reliance upon the seeming infallibility of computer technology. This last aspect is very important because, as with most technological methods that offer great improvements, misuse of computer technology has produced its share of disasters.

B. Spreadsheets

The spreadsheet is an accounting tool. It is a sheet of paper on which lines have been drawn to create separate columns on which numbers and other notations can be listed. A spreadsheet enables the user to conveniently arrange related information and easily perform arithmetic calculations to analyze that information. One need not be an accountant to use a spreadsheet. At the very least, most of us use them in dealing with checking accounts. Thus, examples of spreadsheets include the check register found in most checkbooks and the account reconciliation sheet that accompanies a bank's monthly checking account statement. Another example is the income tax return form provided to all of us by the U.S. Department of the Treasury.

Some spreadsheets, such as the check register, come already organized for us. If we are entering into a new transaction, we may need to create our own spreadsheet. Thus, most businesses must organize information respecting accounts receivable and payable, inventories, payrolls, and the like, in a manner that reflects the unique characteristics of the data, methods of data collection, and the desired analysis, in order to keep track of business activities, needs, and accomplishments.

Computer programs, known as spreadsheet programs, are designed to make it possible to use the format of a spreadsheet while using the computer's superior data storage and retrieval capabilities and capacity to perform ultra-high-speed calculations. Just as some printed spreadsheets are available already customized to meet particular user needs, so too some computer spreadsheet programs are available that have been customized for particular tasks. For example, a number of computer programs are available that store the information normally kept in a check register. These programs also perform the calculations needed to maintain a current report of the checking account balance and to reconcile the account owner's records with the monthly bank statement. Similarly, computer programs are available that have been designed to help the user fill out income tax returns.

Many negotiated transactions require collection of large amounts of information and analysis of many variables. This can be done by creating a spreadsheet to organize the information and then performing the needed calculations. As each proposal made during the course of negotiations alters the data, it is necessary to redo some or all of the calculations to reflect those changes. This is very tedious, time consuming, and burdened with the hazards of arithmetical errors. As the number of variables increase, performing such tasks by hand becomes geometrically less manageable. The computer spreadsheet program simplifies these tasks because it can be designed to automatically do all necessary calculations at extremely high speeds any time a change is made in any piece of data. In addition, such programs can be designed to handle such complex calculations as depreciation, amortization, and compounding of interest. Also, they can be supplemented with special types of data references such as the Consumer Price Index, mortality tables, past sales experience, parts inventories, and tax rates in various localities, that may play an important role in accurate financial or performance projections or analysis.

To illustrate, suppose Adam is negotiating for the purchase of a large quantity of three different sizes of bolts, nuts and washers that are capable of withstanding certain temperature and stress factors. Adam may have various preferences respecting the method of delivery and will be concerned, as well, with the terms of payment and responsibilities for insuring shipments. To determine the attractiveness or unattractiveness of any proposal, Adam must perform a cost-benefit analysis. That analysis requires attaching values to each of the variables, determining their relationships to each other, and making the required calculations. With each new proposal, one or more of the variables is likely to change. If Adam uses a computer spreadsheet program as a tool in preparing for bargaining, with each data change the spreadsheet program will automatically recalculate the information and his bottom line figure or figures will appear almost instantaneously.

The more widely used spreadsheet programs can perform basic algebraic as well as arithmetical processes. Therefore, they can be used to rapidly explore all the alternative combinations of variables potentially involved in resolving a negotiated transaction and, thereby, establish bargaining limits and optimal variations. For example, the program could be instructed to calculate the largest number of screws that can be shipped per day, given the normal rate of absenteeism, without having to pay overtime to production workers, and without having to purchase metal rods in quantities exceeding one carload a month. The flexibility and ease with which alternatives can be explored simplify the task of preparing for negotiations and remove the hazards of hit or miss techniques of mental or pencil-and-paper calculations when attempting to resolve transactions involving many variables. On occasion, the ability of spreadsheets to explore the "what ifs" of a situation has been jointly used by negotiating parties in resolving integrative aspects of their transaction.

Miniaturization of computers has made them highly portable. Accordingly, it is very practical for negotiators to take advantage of the convenience and reliability of computer spreadsheets even when engaged in face-to-face negotiations. Indeed, computers no larger than a handheld calculator are available which have built-in spreadsheet programs or programing capability if the transaction involves relatively small amounts of data and variables.

C. Data Management Programs

Some people can reliably remember large amounts of information, including statistical data, while some of us have difficulty remembering more than three telephone numbers at any one time. Typically, those in the latter category must rely upon recording important information and referring to those records when information is needed. Generally, the person who reliably remembers data can use it more efficiently than can one who has to record it because a large memory relies on the brain's ability to assort (put related data in the same place) and retrieve the remembered information quickly.

A number of techniques have been developed to aid people in an efficient search of recorded information. One simple method is to file related information on the same page or in the same folder and store the pages or folders in an ordered method, such as by subject or category, so that they can be identified quickly. File cabinets, catalogs, and telephone books are common examples of this technique. Another method is to maintain an index, based on categories, key words or numbers, which show the location of the stored data. Indexes, of course, often are used to help us find information in books, documents, and libraries. This method can be used in conjunction with a structured system of filing or can be used with a system of mere sequential storage of information. Another, but usually less efficient, system is to rely on key words or codes that have been highlighted in the stored documents and simply scan the documents until those words or codes are spotted. Each of these systems poses advantages and disadvantages with respect to the three central problems of data storage: (a) efficient use of space, (b) rapid information retrieval, and (c) access to all relevant information.

When information is stored using computer technology, it is helpful to use a program that has a structured method of storage and access to make information retrieval faster and more complete. Such programs carry names indicating that they are designed for data management.

Because of the fantastic speed and reliability with which data can be reviewed by means of a computer search, word scanning is used as a primary search technique much more frequently than when the scanning tool is the human eye. Efficiency is increased by using word combinations and subject categories or codes to narrow the data fields. These techniques are sufficiently similar in concept to those used for standard library and book research that they are easy to learn. More important, one does not have to be thoroughly familiar with the data management program's operational methods to be able to discern ways the available information might be manipulated to enhance analysis and usefulness.

These days much of the information a negotiator needs is already stored in computerized files. If the negotiator represents an enterprise, the negotiator's chore is to find out what data is available in its computers, how it was compiled and stored (so that reliability assessments can be made), who knows how to retrieve it, and in what forms it can be accessed. When data is needed for spreadsheet analysis, often it is possible to transfer it from the company's data storage equipment directly into the spreadsheet program and thereby avoid the risk of accidentally altering information in the process of feeding it into the spreadsheet program.

Other data may be available in mass user databases. These are commercial (and sometimes governmental) services that have stored vast quantities of information such as daily stock market transactions, news reports, statistical reports, biographies, and journal articles, that users can access for a fee by means of a telephone hookup. Specialized databases have become a basic research tool for many businesses and professions. Each relies on a particular data management program which, in turn, has its own characterisitics for information storage and retrieval. Once again, the negotiator's chore is to find out what data is available, how it was compiled and stored (so that reliability assessments can be made), who knows how to retrieve it, and in what forms it can be accessed.

The negotiator need not master the skills of retrieving data from a database. Generally it is more cost effective to rely on specialists and consultants to provide guidance on what is available and what must be done to retrieve desired information. Of course, the bargainer should take steps to be certain that the specialists and consultants have credentials commensurate to the tasks.

Some transactions are so complex that managing the information particular to that negotiation itself becomes a complex, difficult task. This is another opportunity for the skilled negotiator to gain efficiency by turning to computer data management techniques. Instead of using pads, file envelopes, contents sheets, index cards, and the like, the data can be fed into a data management program, categorized and coded as appropriate, and assorted and retrieved as needed. Computerized data management should greatly improve the speed and accuracy of information assortment and retrieval. However, unless a very substantial amount of data is involved, the benefits may be offset by the costs and time consumed in customizing the data management program to the unique needs of the particular transaction and in placing the information into computerized storage. In addition, as further discussed below, there is always danger of data being distorted or lost in the process of being transferred from a written or printed format to the computer's system of data storage.

D. Word Processing Programs

Word processing is the name given to the computer method by which a text is stored, revised, and corrected prior to being printed. Word processing has made marked improvements in the speed with which a final, accurate, attractive looking printed document can be produced. Devices such as laser and ink jet printers, combined with a computer word processor, make it possible to quickly, easily, and relatively inexpensively produce final work products that have the appearance of being prepared by more traditional, more expensive, typesetting methods. This can assist the negotiator in getting the other side to accept preferred contractual terms because, as previously noted, people tend to be more reluctant to modify language found in very formal looking documents than that found in less formal looking ones.

The procedures by which computer word processing programs facilitate text editing also offer some techniques that are especially handy for the negotiator who settles for more. One characteristic of a better quality word processing program is its ability to scan text to find designated words, phrases, numbers, or symbols. (Actually, this is a data management technique incorporated into a word processing program.) This ability can serve negotiators in at least two special ways.

First, many negotiated transactions involve the revision of prior written agreements. A danger in making such revisions is the possibility of overlooking relevant language that must be rephrased or deleted to achieve the intended modification. If the agreement is long and complex, finding all relevant clauses and phrases can be tedious and time consuming and poses a real danger that pertinent language will be overlooked because of human error. Where the text of the agreement has been loaded into a word processor, these dangers can be reduced by supplementing a visual search with a word processor scan for key words, phrases, numbers, and symbols. (A computer search alone is insufficient because some key words or phrases, or something else essential, may be overlooked by the person who conducts that search.)

The second special value of the word processing program's ability to scan the text for particular language or symbols is that it provides a means of ensuring consistency in the agreement's text. Although verbal variety is a stylistic virtue when writing works designed to hold a reader's attention, it is a frequent source of uncertainty and dispute when encountered in an agreement. Generally, those who have the responsibility of interpreting contracts assume that the same words mean the same things throughout the document and that similar but different words are intended to convey some distinction in meaning. If synonyms are intended to have identical meaning, the contract should state this explicitly.

Therefore, those who prepare the agreement, or its revisions, can benefit from a word processing scan of the key terminology to help ensure consistent use of language or to determine whether there is a need to expressly identify intended synonyms.

Those who must apply the terms of a lengthy agreement need to readily find the language that controls any particular problem. If the executed agreement is available in computer-stored text, the processor's word scanning ability can aid in contract administration. A more common means of doing this is to provide a table of contents and index. Preparation of these aids for searching the document are time consuming and, especially in the case of a thorough index, tedious. However, many word processing programs have the feature of automatically compiling a table of section, paragraph, and similar headings. In addition, many such programs will scan the provisions and compile, in an index format, all key words and phrases that are selected for the index.

E. Graphics Programs

It was discussed in Chapter 6 that concise, dramatic, or graphic presentations often have a more potent persuasive impact than those that are lengthy and detailed. Therefore, the negotiator who settles for more often substitutes graphs, charts, diagrams, and sketches for words, or supplements words with eye-catching devices.

In the past, designing and preparing such exhibits often took special talents and equipment and generally took more preparation time than verbal presentations of the same information. Computer graphics programs reduce the time and degree of special talent needed to produce such communication aids. Many computer graphics programs require little more than selecting the category of desired visual aid and providing the data that is to be illustrated. The program and graphics printer then take over and produce the end product. Although there is an initial investment in the special equipment to produce such graphics, generally it is no more than a few hundred dollars and, used often enough, the ultimate expense of such preparation becomes insignificant.

F. Statistical Packages

Computer programs that perform the more commonly used procedures of statistical analysis are often sold as packages, a group of programs having related uses. They can often be (or already are) integrated into data management or graphics programs. Previously we observed that bargaining choices often involve questions of statistical probability (risk) and that most people, even those with statistical training, tend to resort to invalid assumptions about probability when making personal choices. A safeguard against this common self-entrapment is to use appropriate statistical programs as an analytic backup before making probability-oriented decisions.

G. Computer Traps for the Unwary

Each technology comes with its list of hazards. The computer is no exception. We usually associate the word computer with the word efficiency, yet misuse of computers is inefficient. The computer was developed to deal with large amounts of information and complex tasks. Generally it is inefficent to use computer technology to perform simple tasks involving small amounts of data (except when using a statistical program to guard against false statistical methods in measuring risks). For example, it is probably more efficient to use pencil and pad or index cards to compile a section index for a one-page contract than to do the same thing using a word processing program. It is probably more efficient to flip a page of a pocket calendar to determine what day of the week a contract terminates than to turn on a computer, select the appropriate data management program, and input the question that will extract that information from the computer's stored data. Accordingly, the computer should be reserved for those tasks that it can perform at a cost savings or with significantly greater reliability than manual techniques or techniques that use less sophisticated equipment.

One of the first formulas taught to those who study computer technology is GIGO. This stands for Garbage-In, Garbage-Out. It is a reminder that the computer is but a device that follows human instructions and manipulates data. If the instructions are wrong or if the data is incorrect, the computer-generated result is unreliable.

There are many ways human error can transform computer technology from a blessing to a menace. The internal design of the computer equipment or computer program can be faulty, with the result that it will not perform tasks it was expected to perform or will appear to do so but will in fact do them incorrectly. Generally, once equipment has been in use for a year or so, such bugs have been discovered and solved. However, new products enter the market so frequently and rapidly that design deficiencies pose a hazard that victimizes most consumers of computer technology from time to time. Therefore, a negotiator should avoid relying on computer equipment or programs until they have withstood the tests of repetitive use or until its reliability for a specific use has been tested.

Unless data have been correctly entered into a computer, data errors will mar whatever information analysis and reporting it provides. One way of avoiding data entry errors is to avoid human intervention as much as possible. Thus, data often can be electronically transferred from the equipment that produces the information (e.g., a temperature sensor, product counter, etc.) or from one electronic storage device to another (e.g., from a floppy diskette to a hard disk). A handy device in this regard is the optical scanner that is capable of transforming typed or printed text into the electromagnetic storage codes used by computers to represent letters, numbers, and other symbols. Thus, it is possible for a negotiator to have a prior written agreement transformed into the computer's memory by means of an optical scanner rather than have it transformed by means of someone typing the contents at a computer terminal.

Another way to reduce the hazards of human error in providing data for a computer is to duplicate the effort and then use a specially designed program to determine whether there are any discrepancies between the two versions of that information. For example, computer terminal operator A types a text into computer file A and computer terminal operator B types the same text into computer file B. The computer program then compares the two files and reports any differences between them. Those differences, of course, should represent the places where at least one of the operators made an entry error.

All stored information is subject to the risk of loss. Most forms of information storage are subject, as well, to the risks of destruction from fire, explosion, wind storm, or flood. However, anyone who has worked for any period of time with computer-stored information knows that there are the additional hazards of loss or destruction resulting from equipment failure, power supply disruptions, and environmental pollution. Thus, vast quantities of data sometimes are lost when an operator mistakenly commands the computer to erase a file rather than copy it or save it or do some other task. (Depending on the program and equipment, erased files frequently remain stored in the computer or the computer's storage device and can be recovered by use of the correct series of commands.) Interferences with the computer's electrical supply or with the electromagnetic environment, and dust and smoke particles and chemical vapors, can alter the electrical charges that are used to store information in the computer. These hazards can be reduced by using special electronic filtering and power storage equipment, properly grounding equipment and furniture, storing electronic media in protective containers, keeping the air free of contaminants, and reducing temperature and humidity fluctuations. Nevertheless, there are no absolute safeguards. As a result, steps should always be taken to safeguard computer data by duplicating it in more than one form and storing those backups at separate locations.

For example, in a typical application of computer technology by a negotiator, a microcomputer (e.g., an IBM PC or an Apple Macintosh) may be used to design a spreadsheet for ascertaining the impact of various changes in the potential terms of the transaction. To protect against the loss of this work effort, the cautious negotiator will direct that a copy of the spreadsheet file be made on a storage disk and stored in a separate location and the file, including the programing instructions, be printed and that printout be separately stored.

Of course, the more copies and forms of storage that are used, the more danger there is that something will go astray and fall into the wrong hands. There are computer techniques to reduce such hazards as well. For example, some programs establish access codes for computer files. Failure to use codes not only prevents the unauthorized user from discovering the file information but also might, eventually, result in an instruction that directs the computer to shut down or sound an alarm.

Another source of the hazard of information falling into the wrong hands arises out of the communications techniques designed to make computers accessible from distant terminals. Any computer connected to such a network, usually by a telephone line or microwave transmitter, can potentially be tapped by unauthorized parties. Protecting computers from such espionage is a subbranch of computer science. Access codes provide some security, as do filtering devices that help prevent transmissions from straying from their intended destinations. Probably the best security approach, though, is to disconnect the negotiator's computer terminal from such tie-ins and to use separate terminals to obtain or transmit information, on those occasions when it is necessary to communicate with other computers.

Chapter 10

The Bargaining Team

A. Coping With the Group's Potential Intrusion on Sound Judgment

Bargaining is frequently conducted by a team of representatives. Occasionally the full team makes strategic and tactical decisions by some form of voting or consensus. More often, one person has the ultimate decisional responsibility but dilutes the burdens of that responsibility by seeking guidance or even consensus from the other team members.

The element of team representation, as contrasted with individual representation, is a significant variable in bargaining dynamics because, as noted in Chapter 7 in discussing risk responses, research indicates that judgments made by individuals alone are more extreme than judgments made by those individuals as the group members. In addition, at the end of group deliberations, especially face-to-face deliberation (as contrasted, for example, with exchanging memos), the judgments of individual members are modified and move further in the direction of the group's final decision.

Although it is possible that the change in individual judgments brought about by group deliberation reflects the benefits of the cumulative impact of the group's collective knowledge and reasoning, the fact is that group decisions often appear to go beyond the postdeliberation assessments of the individuals who form the group. Thus, the experimental evidence suggests that there is a psychological herd or crowd effect that becomes a force of its own. Accordingly, an apparent consensus may exaggerate the true collective judgment of group members. Hence, if team judgments are to benefit from the group's collective wisdom, an effort must be made to counteract this herd instinct.

218

Because behavioral scientists are just beginning to study the dynamics of group deliberations, it is not possible to draw any hard, fast rules. One consideration is that the experimental findings tell us more about the personalities of particular decisional groups than they do about particular individuals operating in a group. In other words, while many groups may be composed of people who are prone to go with the flow, clearly there are those representatives who are sufficiently independent, or arrogant, or ornery, to resist such a group dynamic. To overcome the dangers of judgments being distorted by the herd instinct, bargaining team leaders may want to recruit more of the latter type of decisional participants or encourage subordinates to develop greater independence by rewarding such traits.

In addition, there may be ways to organize and conduct group deliberations to significantly reduce the influence of this apparent herd instinct upon the end result. For example, as suggested in Chapter 7, one precaution a bargaining team leader can take is to have members record their positions in writing prior to beginning the group's discussions. This provides a benchmark for weighing whether the deliberated judgment is more a product of the tendency of groups to move toward the extreme or a product of the weight of the merits as revealed in the course of deliberations. It can also serve as a basis for challenging participants to reexamine their positions to test whether they have been swayed by wisdom or are merely bending in the wind.

B. Team Member Assignments

1. Divisions of Labor

Negotiating entails a number of simultaneous tasks. One must listen and observe, keep track of the information that has been conveyed and the proposals exchanged, analyze the costs and benefits of all proposals under consideration, detect the nature of the other side's strategy and tactics, assess the effectiveness of the strategic style being used, weigh the tactics to employ next, and decide what to say and do at the moment. When a negotiator has the luxury of working as part of a team, it is most efficient for each team member to have assigned areas of primary responsibility. This should involve such procedural and analytic tasks as (a) maintaining a record of the information and proposals that have been exchanged;

(b) doing a cost-benefit analysis of all proposals; (c) observing the other side's presentation in an effort to determine its true perceptions; (d) assessing the other side's strategy; (e) selecting a style of presentation and weighing what tactics to employ next; and (f) presenting information, arguments, and proposals. In addition, the division of tasks should include assigning the responsibility for mastering areas of specialized knowledge about the subject being negotiated if it is complex or technical.

Good team work requires coordination and communication. In a bargaining setting this means not only assigning specific tasks, but also being certain that every team member is aware of those assignments. In addition, each team member must understand what built-in opportunities are available for caucusing (e.g., meal and toilet breaks) and what suitable locations are available for such team huddles. Similarly, it is useful to establish signals to indicate when a team member thinks it is necessary to hold a caucus or to push ahead.

2. Status Assignments Versus Functional Assignments

In American culture we generally expect the person who is in charge of a team to be its spokesperson. An exception to this rule occurs when a team member is the party's legal counsel. The slang reference to a lawyer as a mouthpiece describes the negotiating norm almost as accurately as it describes the courtroom norm. Therefore, if the team has brought along a lawyer, usually that person is designated to carry on a major part of the talking with the other side. Similarly, in American culture record keeping is a relatively low prestige position. Hence, generally we assume that the person with the lowest rank in the group will handle that responsibility.

However, each task to be performed in bargaining requires special talents if it is to be performed well and the distribution of particular talents does not necessarily correspond to the roles indicated by the team's internal status hierarchy. Therefore, with two exceptions, the team leader who settles for more assigns team tasks by matching special talents to the appropriate functions regardless of the cultural status normally attributed to the particular task.

The rule that team assignments should follow function rather than status should not be followed in those situations in which the team leader's or some other member's status is a significant source for generating the perception of reliability—either to those represented by the bargainers, to the other side, or to important third parties whose good will is vital to the transaction's success. For example, in international negotiations, foreign ministry specialists normally do the substantive work of reaching agreements but call upon the heads of state to "close the deal." Occasionally this backfires because a head of state lacks negotiating skill or lacks full appreciation of the substance of the bargain. Nevertheless, that person's participation is essential to ensure the sought-for level of national commitment to the agreement.

The other exception to the rule of basing team assignments on functional talents rather than internal status applies where the other side's cultural norms or personal values are likely to be affronted if they are not addressed by the highest status person available. Thus, if the Prime Minister of India poses a question at the negotiating table, his anger or distrust (or likely both) may be aroused if the Pakistani Second Vice Deputy Minister of Commerce shoots back with an answer.

One explanation for the last example is that the Critical Parent side of personality pays a good deal of attention to status. People who reach very high status positions usually have sacrificed a great deal of time, effort, personal friendships, family pleasures, and the like, to achieve their status. It is understandable that having paid that price, such people will place a high value upon their status. Probably, status is a centerpiece of their Critical Parent. Moreover, the Critical Parent often is a strong dimension of the personality of people who hold high status positions because it is a side of their personality that is frequently addressed by their subordinates and constituents. If the Critical Parent plays a prominent role in the other side's personality, or in the cultural norms that shape the other side's behavior, a violation of the normal hierarchies is likely to result in diminished perceptions of dependability and provoke adverse emotional responses toward the party who violates those hierarchies. Hence, when such reaction can be anticipated, status must prevail over function in assigning bargaining team tasks.

3. Cognitive Style—A Model to Guide Team Assignments

Aside from those tasks that are dependent upon specialized background knowledge, negotiating tasks largely involve particular personal skills. Is the person an astute observer of body language? A careful listener? An accurate, thorough record keeper? A clear, controlled, cautious, persuasive speaker? A calm analyst? A creative thinker? These characteristics involve assessing special types of intelligence rather than general intelligence. It is rare to find individuals who excel in all of these skills, but not so rare to find people who excel in several of them. What is most interesting is that the pattern of skills in which one group of generally intelligent people have special strength frequently matches up to the pattern of skills in which another group of generally intelligent people are deficient. To understand this last statement, we must examine what psychologists call cognitive styles—that is, the patterns or processes by which people understand things and make decisions.

There are many competing theories among behavioral scientists respecting the models that best describe cognitive styles. Years from now, possibly centuries from now, the experts may arrive at a consensus to fully explain clinical and experimental observations concerning these matters. In the meantime the negotiator who wants to settle for more needs an understandable model that offers enough guidance to provide an edge over mere guessing. Such a model has emerged from studies that were initiated during World War II in an effort to understand why some otherwise excellent pilot trainees had far greater difficulty than others in the tasks of instrument flying and detecting camouflaged objects.

The initial experiments were performed in totally darkened rooms. In one, the subject faced a luminous rod within a luminous frame which were set at angles. The subject had to adjust the rod to the true vertical position (rod and frame test). In the other, the subject was placed in a chair within a room that was tilted and the subject had to adjust the room tilt to the perpendicular position (tilted chair test). It was discovered that some people are more adept than others in making such judgments. Later experiments sought to discover if there were any patterns between these traits and other personality characteristics and whether other kinds of visual judgments correlated with the abilities and inabilities measured in the darkened room.

This later research revealed that some people are quite adept at finding a defined simple geographic shape that is drawn within a more complex shape (embedded figure) while others of comparable general intelligence have considerable difficulty and that this skill closely correlates with performance on the rod and frame and tilted chair tests. More important, it was learned that a broad range of personality characteristics correlate with ability or inability to perform well on these tests. The terms most often used to differentiate these two groups is field dependent and field independent. (Field dependent people are not adept at the test tasks; field independents are.) However, for our purposes, it is less confusing to use the more descriptive terms interpersonal orientation and impersonal orientation that were selected to distinguish the personality traits that correlate with the test results. These latter terms are used by Professors Herman A. Witkin and Donald Goodenough, in their book *Cognitive Styles: Essence and Origins*,[1] to describe the social conduct characteristics that differentiate those who do poorly on tasks such as an embedded figures test (interpersonal orientation) from those who do well on such tests (impersonal orientation).

It is typical of behavioral science findings that test scores and correlations of characteristics do not fall into two clearly separated groupings. Rather, there are gradations of scores and related characteristics, but some clear patterns emerge. In the studies of cognitive style, research indicates that those who have great difficulty performing tasks such as finding the simple figure hidden in the more complex design (the embedded figures test), process information and reach conclusions largely by making comparisons. Such people appear to deal with information in more generalized ways and have greater confidence in their judgments but less ability to recall the specific reasons that led them to their judgments. They not only have separate characteristics in their cognitive style of dealing with physical relationships, their general cognitive behavior follows a similar pattern, including how they deal with social relationships. As a result, it is important for such people to have base lines for comparisons in their social interactions. Not surprisingly, such people tend to be more observant of faces and personal reactions, demonstrate greater ability to deal with detail work such as administrative tasks, and are more aware of behavioral protocols and of adherence to or violation of such protocols. They tend to prefer more humanitarian type vocations (social work, rehabilitation counseling, teaching). Therefore, it is appropriate to characterize them as having an interpersonal orientation, particularly since such people also are more likely to be judged as being in good touch with what others are thinking and as being warm, affectionate, tactful, accommodating. In addition, people who have an interpersonal orientation (field dependent in the more traditional terminology) have been found to be less judgmental and

---

[1]International Univs. Press (1981).

more accepting about others and are less likely to express felt hostility directly toward others.

Reviewing their pattern of characteristics in relation to the dynamics of group decision making, we would expect those with an interpersonal orientation to be among those whose personal assessments are most significantly altered in the direction of the group judgment. In relation to bargaining styles, we would expect them to be more comfortable with those that accentuate the plus side of the bargaining strength paradigm and very uncomfortable with the hard nosed, more confrontational styles.

In contrast are those who show greater skill at performing tasks such as finding embedded figures—those traditionally labeled as field independent but who for present purposes are defined as having an impersonal orientation. Such people show greater autonomy in the way they assimilate information and make judgments. As a result, they are more likely to ignore protocols, to discard prior evaluations, to develop their own perceptions. They have less confidence in their judgments, have better recall of the reasons that led to their judgments, and are better prepared to reassess their judgments if confronted with new arguments or information. They do not have as intense a human welfare orientation in their vocational preferences as do people whose cognitive style is an interpersonal orientation and are more likely to be judged by others as being rude, cold, inconsiderate, and manipulative. People who have an impersonal orientation are more successful at jobs requiring independent judgment and those involving the sort of creativity that does not rely on detailed observations about people. For example, it has been found that they do better as architects than as novelists. Most likely they are more comfortable than are those with an interpersonal orientation in resisting compromise and in pursuing bargaining strategies that give emphasis to the negative side of the bargaining strength paradigm.

There is evidence that the difference between interpersonal orientation and impersonal orientation is not immutable. Each type of person can acquire the social and analytical skills that characterize the opposite style. For example, training programs have been developed to improve skills such as remembering names and faces. Similarly, an unpublished study of embedded figure test performances of law students indicated that the cognitive style necessary to perform that task improves during the first year in law school. This result is not surprising inasmuch as the program of study largely emphasizes questioning results and exploring alternative analytical approaches to a given problem.

Successful negotiating requires many of the traits that are characteristic of the interpersonal cognitive orientation and some that characterize the impersonal orientation. For example, strategic analysis, objective assessment of needs and proposals, and innovation of new proposals to take advantage of integrative dimensions of a transaction, or to find previously untried ways to meet a party's needs, call for the cognitive skills that typify the impersonal orientation. On the other hand, tasks such as fact finding, record keeping, accurate observation of personal reactions, using rituals and pastimes, discerning and adhering to cultural protocols, and the like, call for the cognitive skills that typify the interpersonal orientation. As has been noted, through training it is possible to gain a mastery of all of these skills. But when working as a team, it makes sense to try to match the task assignments, as much as possible, with the team members' apparent cognitive styles.

Using cognitive style as a guide for making team assignments does not require the leader to administer evaluative exams, such as the embedded figures test. Rather, the team leader should be sufficiently familiar with the overall personality characteristics of each team member to make a sound judgment separating those at the extremes of the scale. Of course, it is difficult to differentiate interpersonal from impersonal orientations among those whose characteristics are less extreme. But, that is of less consequence since such people are less likely to create problems because they have been cast out of character.

Obviously, there is no guarantee that in any bargaining team a choice will be available from among those with impersonal and those with interpersonal cognitive orientations. (Studies indicate that interpersonal orientation is the dominant style among college students and especially among women.) However, it must be remembered that the purpose of using this model is as a tool for predicting strengths and weaknesses in general skill areas. In the absence of this more general guideline, the team leader can still try to make the more particular, and more difficult, assessments regarding which team members are most likely to excel at specific functional negotiating tasks.

The prospect of using training to offset the skill deficiencies that generally accompany one or the other type of cognitive orientation suggests that the bargainer who wants to settle for more can benefit from gaining a better understanding of his or her own cognitive orientation. Taking an embedded figures test is one way of doing this. However, just as a team leader's assessment of characteristics should provide an adequate basis for characterization, introspection regarding one's own traits should suffice as well. In either case, knowing whether you have a predominantly interpersonal or impersonal cognitive orientation provides a good benchmark for predicting whether, as a negotiator, you are likely to need special skills training, or must exercise an extra degree of self control, to maximize potential bargaining talent. The cognitive style model is especially valuable to the team leader who is attempting to resist the temptation of assigning his own team role on the basis of status rather than functional ability. In addition, the interpersonal-impersonal orientation model of cognitive style also provides a useful guide for the team leader who has the opportunity to provide skills training to improve the negotiating team's overall strength.

4. The Other Side's Bargaining Team

The person sitting across the negotiating table does not always reveal either the complete nature and composition of its bargaining team nor the true identity of the constituency being represented and its relationship with that constituency. The lack of such information poses the danger of misconstruing both the relative weight of the elements of the other side's bargaining strength and the appropriateness of various tactics for modifying the other side's perceptions. Sometimes the failure to offer such information is unintentional; often it is calculated and, indeed, sometimes deception is used to give misleading impressions regarding the true bargaining parties and participants.

Independent research, can, of course, help to remove some of the mystery or confirm or reject the information provided by the other side. Often insight can be gained, as well, by getting substantial background information respecting the other side's bargaining team—e.g., their job positions, amount of time with the entity they are representing, who they know or do not know in that organization, the job positions of close family members and relations inside and outside the organization, educational and work experience background, relationships with each other both in terms of hierarchy and compatibility, and their respective roles in the bargaining activities. Using the TA terminology, Rituals and Pastime transactions engaged in during the course of preliminary activities and breaks offer a good opportunity to do much of the needed intelligence gathering. Special attention should be given at such times to the most junior, least experienced members of the other side's bargaining team—preferably out of earshot of other team members. Often, their excitement over being involved in the relatively novel process and important undertakings will spill over in the form of verbal leakage displaying knowledge respecting teammates and constituents.

As noted, understanding the nature and structure of the other side's bargaining team, and its relationship with its constituency, improves the reliability of estimates made respecting the other side's perceptions. It also provides a better appreciation of how the other side operates and the speed with which it can be expected to respond to offers. This understanding of the other side's team can also assist in making sound strategic and tactical choices. For example, in negotiating with an engineering company to fabricate a large piece of machinery, reluctance to specify the acceptable method of settling differences over the price impact of blueprint modifications carries a different level of significance depending on who is heading the team. Different decisions may be made if the engineering company is negotiating through a team headed by its chief executive officer with the assistance of its general counsel (who probably know very little about the day-to-day production costs and problems) or through a team headed by its comptroller assisted by the plant manager (who should know whether, and at what cost, the changes can be made).

Another aspect of assessing the bargaining team is to discern whether it is characterized by a particular cognitive style—that is, does the team itself appear to have either an interpersonal orientation or an impersonal orientation. The way the other side's bargaining team communicates and interacts will sometimes indicate the cognitive styles of its dominant member or members. For example, frequent caucusing respecting less significant matters, heavy reliance on visual aids, special emphasis on past practices, copious note taking, a high level of adherence to the protocols of polite behavior, and the like, are a good indication of a dominant interpersonal orientation. Given the nature of that cognitive style, success in altering the team's perceptions is more likely to be achieved by providing the guidance of analogous conduct, precedent, and graphic illustration of the points being made, than by offering analysis based on conceptual principles or suggestions of the excitement of innovative breakthroughs or experimentation.

Conclusion

In varying degrees, Western cultures devote considerable time and energy to competitive recreation, to seeing who comes out on top. Because there are competitive dimensions in negotiations, it should not be surprising that most people in Western societies view the negotiating process not as a method of resolving conflict through mutual accommodation, but as a contest of wills, shrewdness, and power.

If this book has succeeded in its purpose, the reader will recognize that while bargaining has elements of a contest, participants who seek to gain the most from the process distinguish negotiating from the sort of contest involved in games and sports. Unlike other contests, bargaining success or failure is measured not in some standard scoring unit; it is measured by the individual perceptions of the participants and their constituents. Therefore, each side can walk away from the same settlement feeling like winners or like losers. As a result, settling for more is not concerned with outdoing the other side. Rather, it involves meeting your own needs with a minimum of short-term and long-term costs, a goal that often is best achieved by aiding the other side in similarly meeting its needs.

Mastery of negotiating skills undoubtedly requires developing certain basic characteristics such as patience, persistence, flexibility, thoughtfulness, cautiousness, and firmness. But it also involves understanding the nature of bargaining power and the goals and means of bargaining strategy and tactics. *Settling for More* has offered specific models and behavioral science findings and concepts to inform the negotiator's understanding and to guide the bargainer's decisions. Because negotiating is an art, not a science, the practitioner should approach these models, findings, and concepts as tools to be shaped and adapted until they have the right feel so that they can be wielded in comfort and with grace.

Finally, a few concluding observations about the use of models or paradigms as a guide for making bargaining decisions. The models offered in this book have what can be described as linear or geometric qualities. The elements of the models are interrelated, and although some elements may have particular effects on others, a change in any one has a seemingly immediate impact upon the total structure. The degree of that effect may be constant in relation to the other elements (linear) or may be magnified or reduced (geometric), but the impact is direct and immediate. Thus, as portrayed in the paradigms, a change in a party's perception of the other's Probability of Performance modifies relative bargaining strength. Similarly, a shift from a listener's Nurturing Parent ego state to her Adult ego state modifies the listener's response to what was said. While these models improve our understanding of the bargaining process, they will help us even more if we understand their limitations.

Those at the forefront of theoretical investigations of biological and physical processes have observed that patterns of change do not always follow predictable paths or fixed time sequences. Some changes move from a stable structure to a highly altered structure with only the briefest period of instability—as can happen when a liquid changes to a crystal. Others can be in an unstable state for extended periods and then quickly achieve stability—as when an ecologically imbalanced environment finally achieves balance. Moreover, often the change does not follow a specific pattern. For example, evolutionary adaptation to a change in atmospheric carbon dioxide can take and has taken numerous paths. The best models of biological processes may help determine whether an adaptation will have to be made and may help in understanding the nature of the adaptation but fail to predict whether in fact it will be made (if not made, the system dies) and, if so, precisely what it will be.

The models in this book, like the most successful models of biological and physical processes, inevitably leave room for speculation and uncertainty. To borrow a phrase from physicist Roger Penrose, we have offered tools for "intelligent groping." This is not said with apology because it is important that we understand that "intelligent groping" is the path to greater success as a negotiator.

Perhaps, this last point is best illustrated with still one more model. It is that of the person who is piecing together a jigsaw puzzle. Often a group of pieces appear to hold promise but nothing seems to quite fit together, and maybe nothing does. However, frequently if one additional piece is discovered or one piece is turned or shifted in a manner that was not previously tried, suddenly all the parts slip into place. The negotiator who settles for more often goes through the same sort of experience. Movement to the desired solution may not follow a linear or geometric progression. But with persistence, often the missing piece is found or the transaction is seen from yet one more perspective and suddenly all the parts slip into place.

Appendix

The diagrams identified in the text as the paradigms constituting the bargaining strength model can, alternatively, be stated in algebraic form. For some readers, the algebraic summary of the model may provide greater precision than the diagrams in portraying the interrelationships of the bargaining strength elements and in describing the impact of an element of bargaining strength having zero or negative value. Therefore, those negotiators who are equally or more comfortable with the mathematical form of symbolic presentation may want to work with the following formulas when engaged in strategic analysis.

Paradigm 1

$$BS_A = P_B[POP_A(OMON_A) + DA_B(AC_B) - PA_B(BAPA_B) - PA_B^1(COIN_B)]$$

Paradigm 2

$$BS_B = P_A[POP_B(OMON_B) + DA_A(AC_A) - PA_A(BAPA_A) - PA_A^1(COIN_A)]$$

Where:

$$
\begin{aligned}
BS_A &= \text{Side A's Bargaining Strength} \\
BS_B &= \text{Side B's Bargaining Strength} \\
P_A &= \text{Side A's Perception} \\
P_B &= \text{Side B's Perception} \\
POP_A &= \text{Side A's Probability Of Performance} \\
POP_B &= \text{Side B's Probability Of Performance} \\
OMON_A &= \text{Side A's Offer to Meet B's Needs} \\
OMON_B &= \text{Side B's Offer to Meet A's Needs}
\end{aligned}
$$

$BAPA_A$ = Side A's Best Alternative to Proposed Agreement

$BAPA_B$ = Side B's Best Alternative to Proposed Agreement

DA_A = Side A's Data Accuracy

DA_B = Side B's Data Accuracy

AC_A = Side A's Accrued Cost Of Bargaining with B

AC_B = Side B's Accrued Cost Of Bargaining with A

$COIN_A$ = Side A's Cost of Impending Negotiations with B

$COIN_B$ = Side B's Cost of Impending Negotiations with A

PA_A = Side A's Predictive Accuracy regarding BAPA

PA_B = Side B's Predictive Accuracy regarding BAPA

PA_A^1 = Side A's Predictive Accuracy for its COIN

PA_B^1 = Side B's Predictive Accuracy for its COIN

Paradigm 1 describes A's bargaining strength; Paradigm 2 describes B's bargaining strength. Separate notations are used to distinguish Predictive Accuracy respecting the Best Alternative to the Proposed Agreement from Predictive Accuracy respecting the Cost of Impending Negotiation because often one's ability to predict will not be the same for both elements.

The formula describing A's relative bargaining strength is set forth in Paradigm 3.

Paradigm 3

$$RBS_A =$$
$$P_B[POP_A(OMON_A) + DA_B(AC_B) - PA_B(BAPA_B) - PA_B^1(COIN_B)]$$
$$- P_A[POP_B(OMON_B) + DA_A(AC_A) - PA_A(BAPA_A) - PA_A^1(COIN_A)]$$

Where:

RBS = Relative Bargaining Strength of A

As we can see by looking back at Paradigms 1 and 2, the Relative Bargaining Strength of A is determined by taking the formula for A's Bargaining Strength and subtracting the formula for B's Bargaining Strength. B's Relative Bargaining Strength is, of course, determined by reversing the sequence—subtracting A's Bargaining Strength from B's.

Paradigm 4

$$NR = \begin{cases} (P_A \, [POP_B \, (OMON_B) + DA_A \, (AC_A)] \\ \quad > P_A \, [PA_A \, (BAPA_A) - PA_A^1 \, (COIN_A)] \\ \quad \text{and} \\ (P_B \, [POP_A \, (OMON_A) + DA_B \, (AC_B)] \\ \quad > P_B \, [PA_B \, (BAPA_B) - PA_B^1 (COIN_B)] \end{cases}$$

Where:

NR = Power conditions favoring a negotiated resolution.

Paradigm 4 shows us the conditions under which reasonable negotiators should be able to reach a settlement. That is, a settlement should be attainable as long as each side perceives that its current investment in negotiating with the other side (plus what it expects the other side to do to meet its needs) outweighs its perception of what it will cost to bargain to the point of settlement (plus what it thinks it probably could gain by pursuing an alternative to settling with the other side).

Acknowledgments

We share a common introduction to bargaining. As infants we have needs for food, cleanliness, and strokes. In exchange we offer strokes of our own in the form of smiles, coos and other soft sounds, or cries, screams, grimaces, and the like. As a result of the bargains we strike, we are fed, cleansed, and cuddled. Some psychoanalysts assert that that early bargaining experience shapes our personalities. Likely, therefore, my understanding of the negotiating process began over half a century ago.

My parents, Emma Berger Goldman and Joseph I. Goldman, had an additional impact upon my interest in the negotiating process. Although they were young children when they came to the United States, through their parents and their own experiences they had an intimate understanding of the European marketplace custom of haggling over retail purchases. Mother, particularly, was a master. As a child I often accompanied my parents on trips to the stalls in the municipal market and to shops in New York City's Lower East Side. It was a wonder to behold. It seemed as though for each one of the vast number of commodities being marketed, Mom knew a particular quality characteristic to look for and upon discovering its absence added the persuasive power of a reason to back her insistence upon a lower price. She also had her favorite vendors, the ones she knew would offer decent quality merchandise at competitive prices so that even on the rare occasion that she paid what was asked, she felt confident that she had not "been taken." But Mom was not about to let anyone take her for granted. So, periodically, just to keep them honest, she would do business in a nearby competitor's stall in hopes that the preferred vendor would notice and remember the next time she came around. Dad was similarly skilled but he had a vulnerable spot. He, too, was in business, with the result that he usually stopped short of pressing for the rock bottom price. As Dad explained it: "The other guy has to make a living, too."

There was another emotion mixed with the awe of watching my parents exercise their bargaining skills. It was embarassment.

237

Wealthy, well-educated people did not appear to do their shopping in this manner. People of high social status seldom did any business at such places. They seemed to prefer to pay what was asked. Indeed, the higher the price, the more willing they seemed to be to pay it. Nor did we do all of our shopping on the Lower East Side. Generally, those trips were confined to times when Dad's business was slow, or my folks wanted to buy items that were not available in neighborhood stores (we lived in as ethnically neutral a community as you could find in New York City), or the purchases were relatively high ticket for my parents' means.

It was not until many years later that I realized that there was at least equal dignity in bargaining at the shops or stalls of the Lower East Side as in doing business in the "priced as marked" stores on Fifth Avenue. In places like the city markets you had to be a smart shopper; you did not shop in ignorance of what you were getting or ignorance of what you might be able to get it for elsewhere. In contrast, on Fifth Avenue people typically shopped in ignorance. They were content to do so because the price of the purchase had less significance to them in relation to the time and effort to be expended in haggling and in relation to the size of the alternative transactions they could engage in during that time. Generally, those shopping in the city market did not have the resources to spend their time on the golf course, attending a Broadway show, watching the stock exchange ticker tape, or the like. Eventually, I learned that those who confined their shopping to Fifth Avenue type shops did their share of haggling too. But for them haggling over price was mainly confined to business transactions involving much larger amounts of money—amounts that exceeded a week's or a month's or a year's income for most who lived or worked on the Lower East Side.

In addition to introducing me to the epitome of an exchange bargaining environment, my father provided me with my first understanding of a key element of bargaining strength. One of his favorite phrases in doing business was: "My word is my bond!!!" And, he always said it as it was just written; it was a most emphatic exclamation. Moreover, he meant it despite the fact that he was in a business that had an unsavory reputation—the used car business. Perhaps because he adhered to that principle, Dad survived in the business at a time when many who had entered it when he did were failing, and he left the business when he felt he could no longer survive and do business on his terms. At any given time, Dad also generally had one or two real estate investments. There, too, he stuck to his motto, "my word is my bond." Most important to the development of my understanding of negotiating power, I learned that Dad never did business with someone he suspected of not living by that motto. He knew that he operated on too small a scale to be able to spend money seeking the aid of lawyers to enforce his agreements. Therefore, he placed a very high premium on his perception of the other side's Probability of Performance— an often neglected element of bargaining strength.

My brothers, William and Norman Goldman, also aided my early understanding of the negotiating process. Since they were older, stronger, and more athletic, they taught me some basic lessons in bargaining from weakness. One was the value of alliances, whether a usually futile two-on-one attempt to thwart Bill's dominance, or an "I'll tell Mom" type warning. Fortunately for my survival, enough of our parents' Nurturing Parent characteristics rubbed off on my brothers so that I was also able to negotiate with them by relying on the strength of appeals to conscience, love, and pity.

There have, of course, been numerous others who have aided me in refining my understanding of negotiating. I must confine my list to but a few. Negotiating was not taught when I went to law school, but while I was in the Arthur Garfield Hays Civil Liberties Program, its director, Professor Norman Dorsen, taught us the important lesson that several years later was capsulized in the title of Marshall McLuhan's book *The Medium is the Massage*.

John Jay and Alvin Stein of the then Parker, Chapin & Flattau law firm, provided me with my first professional experiences representing the interests of others in seeking settlements. Two other lawyers in that firm also made special impressions upon my understanding of this aspect of lawyering. They were Leo Pillar, who had so much more understanding of people than I was able to absorb in my three years at the firm, and Seymour Levine, a master of the skill of drafting a contract so that it resolves the transaction without creating new conflicts.

At the University of Kentucky, where I have taught since 1965, Professor John Batt's contributions to my work require special acknowledgment. Often he has shared with me his broad knowledge of behavioral science, guided me to fruitful resources, and encouraged me to develop models as tools for analysis and teaching. He was especially influential in prompting me to uncover the potential of the Transactional Analysis model as a tactical guide for the negotiator. I should also note in this last regard that the bulk of the research I have done respecting TA was sponsored by a grant from the University of Kentucky.

My work in teaching negotiations was indirectly encouraged by my friends and colleagues in the Labor Law Group who, early in my teaching career, entrusted to me the task of preparing a coursebook examining alternative methods of conflict resolution— including bargaining. About a decade later, my dear friend and overseas colleague, Professor Roger Blanpain of the Catholic University in Leuven, Belgium, persuaded me to prepare a chapter for a comparative labor law book that required me to take a still closer look at the differences among the various methods by which disputes are settled.

My understanding of settling for more has undoubtedly been influenced by the vast literature about bargaining that has been published in recent years. Some of the authors are mentioned in the text. Among those not cited, there are two that call for special acknowledgment—the course books that provided the framework for the many current law school courses on bargaining. Professor Cornelius Peck, another Labor Law Group colleague, was one of those able pioneers, and Professor James White and Professor (now Judge) Harry Edwards were the others.

More than anything else, this book is a product of over twenty years of helping law students become better negotiators. Accordingly, I want to acknowledge the contributions of those students. Several made very particular contributions. Edna Lowery, a computer programmer as well as lawyer, first called my attention to the spreadsheet's potential utility in negotiating; Fred Hensinger helped me refine my understanding of how to use spreadsheet programs; and Brian West aided me by suggesting the acronym COIN.

Much that is learned about negotiating relies on the clinical method. One learns by observing. Sometimes it is one's own experience, sometimes it is based upon the anecdotes of others. Here, too, students have been a source of my learning. Friends, such as Steve Caller, have also provided me with the opportunity to share lessons learned from doing.

In writing this book, I received special assistance from Doug Goldman and Paula Goldman, who prepared the computer graphics initially used to diagram the bargaining strength model and from Bruce Feist, who patiently guided me in finding ways to improve my symbolic notations.

Ann Merritt of the College of Law staff at the University of

Kentucky handled manuscript production tasks with her usual high level of efficiency, intelligence, and pleasantness.

I also owe very special thanks to Camille D. Christie of BNA Books for her congenial but incisive editorial guidance and to Professor Kathy Kelly of the McGeorge School of Law, University of the Pacific, whose thoughtful critique and suggestions helped remove many stumbling blocks from the text.

Finally, as in all my work, the burdens were shared by my life partner, Elisabeth Paris Goldman. The moment of gestalt that brought together my first vision of the bargaining strength model came while at the wheel driving to Colorado. It was Ellie who humored me by making the apparently nonsensical notations I requested. And, it was Ellie who tolerated my 4 a.m. departures to the word processor to modify some pages, and who pretended not to see when I stuffed chapters into the suitcase to be redrafted while on vacation.

Index

About the Author

Alvin L. Goldman, a professor of law and labor arbitrator, has been teaching negotiating to law students for almost two and one-half decades. He was born and raised in New York, where he received his A.B. from Columbia and his LL.B. from New York University. Before joining the faculty of the College of Law of the University of Kentucky, Alvin Goldman practiced law with the New York firm of Parker, Chapin and Flattau. He has served as Professor-in-Residence at the National Labor Relations Board; Visiting Scholar at the Institute for Labour Law, Leuven, Belgium; and Visiting Professor at the University of California-Davis.

Professor Goldman's other books are: *Legal Protection for the Individual Employee* (West, 1989) (with M. Finkin & C. Summers), *Labor Law and Industrial Relations in the U.S.A.*, 2nd ed. (BNA Books, 1983), *Legislation Protecting the Individual Employee* (BNA Books, 1982) (with R. Covington), *The Supreme Court and Labor-Management Relations Law* (Lexington Books, 1976), and *Processes for Conflict Resolution: Self-help, Voting, Negotiation, and Arbitration* (BNA Books, 1972). His other bargaining process related publications include: "Settlement of Disputes Over Interests," a chapter in *Comparative Labour Law and Industrial Relations*, 3rd ed. (R. Blanpain ed.) (1988); "Comparative Overview of the Role of Third Party Interventions in Resolving Interests Disputes," 10 *Comparative Labor Law Journal* 271 (1989); and "Collective Bargaining Without Work Stoppages," 57 *Kentucky Law Journal* 215 (1968).